W9-CBB-848

THINKING
STRATEGICALLY
PLANNING FOR YOUR COMPANY'S FUTURE

THINKING STRATEGICALLY
PLANNING FOR YOUR COMPANY'S FUTURE

William L. Shanklin
John K. Ryans, Jr.
Graduate School of Management   Kent State University

RANDOM HOUSE BUSINESS DIVISION
NEW YORK • TORONTO

First Edition
987654321
Copyright © 1985 by Random House, Inc.

All rights reserved under International and Pan-American Copyright Conventions.
No part of this book may be reproduced in any form or by any means, electronic or
mechanical, including photocopying, without permission in writing from the publisher. All inquiries should be addressed to Random House, Inc., 201 East 50th Street,
New York, N.Y. 10022. Published in the United States by Random House, Inc., and
simultaneously in Canada by Random House of Canada Limited, Toronto.

Library of Congress Cataloging in Publication Data

Shanklin, William L.
  Thinking strategically.

  Bibliography: p.
  1. Corporate planning.   I. Ryans, John K.
II. Title.
HD30.28.S4   1985   658.4'012   84-17964
ISBN 0-394-39500-X

Manufactured in the United States of America

To
Joan, Andrea, and Courtney Shanklin
and
Cinda Ryans

What we anticipate seldom occurs; what we least expect generally happens.

—Benjamin Disraeli

CONTENTS

ix

CONTENTS

OVERVIEW

Strategic management is a never-ending managerial process of keeping an organization constantly ready to seize the very best external opportunities that become available to it, meanwhile steering the organization away from threats to its continuation. Strategic management is expressed—and given formality and an action orientation—through strategic planning. Indeed, a company's strategic plan, or lack thereof, is the best a priori indicator of the depth and quality of top management's thinking about the future and the company's role in it.

Strategic planning and long-range planning are not synonymous terms. Although strategic planning is long-range, however that is defined in a particular industry or market, long-range planning is not always strategic. A long-term physical facilities plan, for example, may have minimal strategic consequences for a service firm. Another distinction: We see strategic planning as being broad, conceptual, long-term, and focusing on the organization's raison d'être, whereas an operational plan is far more specific, tactical, and short-term. Typically, the operational plan describes implementation during the first year covered by the strategic plan.

Why have strategic management and its byproduct, strategic planning, emerged as such crucial processes in organizations in diverse industries and of all sizes? Simply because the overall environment for doing business is now different and far less predictable than it was for most of the twentieth century. Heretofore, the climate for business in the developed countries of the world was relatively predictable, if not always stable. Even the catastrophic two world wars came as no great surprises; prior events provided plenty of warning. Things have changed. Today's environment for business is far less forecastable. The developed economies lately have seen oscillations between inflation/disinflation, employment/unemployment, and scarce/abundant resources like oil and gasoline. High-technology and service industries are revolutionizing and displacing basic industries. In this country, sunbelt states are fighting with frostbelt states for industry. And many formerly domestic-only companies are now involved in or at least impinged upon by international business. To complicate matters further, the vagaries of politics, cultures, and economics in third-world countries have frequently given multinational firms unwanted surprises.

With a variety of discontinuities, imponderables, and vicissitudes to contend with at home and abroad, it is little wonder that forecasters and the art and science of forecasting have fallen into disfavor in many quarters. Forecasting, because it is typically "past-oriented" and extrapolative, is unsuited to conditions of fluid and often seemingly random change. As the environment for business has become more volatile—and forecasting less reliable and less accurate as a consequence—the task of operating an organization of any size has become correspondingly more arduous, more risky.

Some thirty years ago, *Fortune* magazine began publishing its list of the 500 leading industrial companies in the United States, as measured by their sales revenues. Only about half the companies on the original list remain on it now. And as recently as the early 1970s, about one-third of the present *Fortune* 500 did not exist as independent companies. So even the corporate *crème de la crème*, with the wherewithal to attract the very best managers, are by no means assured of sustained success.

Thus, prosperity does often breed complacency and a dangerous sense of self-satisfaction (or possibly a sense of immortality) as an organization. Count the number of supposedly invulnerable businesses of a short yesteryear that are today in lamentable "titanic" shape because complacent managements saw little need to plan for anything other than an extrapolated status quo. With such history as a severe teacher, it comes as no shock that strategic planning has markedly moved to prominence within forward-thinking business and nonprofit institutions of today. The role of strategic planning is to get and keep organizations ready to exploit the many possible challenges of plausible tomorrows, rather than to prepare them for a single forecasted tomorrow.

We believe that strategic planning—the thinking behind it and the actual process that follows the conceptualization stage— is the most important single task of chief executives and their respective cadres of top managers. Results from an inquiry made among chief executive officers of major U.S. corporations (provided to us by Richard Hise and Stephen McDaniel, who conducted the research) indicate that the vast majority of these CEOs agree with us. The consensus was that the establishment of corporate objectives/goals and the development of facilitating corporate strategies are the most important sources of growth and profits for their companies. Understandably, then, these tasks were cited by the CEOs themselves as those requiring the most personal involvement on their part.

Recently, the whole area of strategic planning has come under fire from some quarters, particularly on the grounds that it is rigid and militates against entrepreneurial creativity. We believe much of this disenchantment is misplaced. In our judgment, strategic planning properly done can actually nourish and facilitate entrepreneurial innovativeness.

It is true that when strategic planning is confused with past-oriented extrapolative financial planning and forecasting, poor results often result. The future may very well be unlike the past, as many companies have, to their dismay, found out. Moreover, whenever strategic planning is complicated by overly complex processes or layers of bureaucracy, or glossed over by line management and delegated to staff, the output of such planning will almost certainly be disappointing. Complex planning processes confuse, guaranteeing that few managers have the same ideas in mind about what is to be achieved and how. Complex bureaucracies will assuredly impede the design and implementation of even the best of plans. And top management's lack of interest in or support for strategic planning is a sure ingredient to failure.

As we explore later in this book, in most instances strategic planning is not at fault when companies come up short in performance. What is at fault is management's *failure* to plan strategically in the real sense of the term. When done properly, strategic planning—far from restricting options and building in rigidity—actually opens up options, permits flexibility, and better readies a company for future contingencies. Of course, neither strategic planning nor any other management technique can produce entrepreneurial creativity. Entrepreneurship is more of a personal trait of individual managers or characteristic of a corporate culture. The climate for entrepreneurship in a company is set mostly by its CEO. If his or her policies reward risk aversion, then extreme caution will become standard operating procedure. But if entrepreneurial creativity is rewarded, or more accurately if failed entrepreneurial creativity is not punished, then managerial innovativeness will flourish.

Recently, a bank executive was asked to account for the continued innovativeness of Citibank of New York compared to its sister institutions in an industry generally known for extreme caution. He offered the thought that most bank CEOs adhere closely to the "ready-aim-fire" sequence as it applies to market opportunity. Citibank also does this to an extent, of course, but not nearly as rigidly. At Citibank, principally because of former chief executive officer Walter Wriston, a "ready-*fire-aim*" philosophy is encouraged and not penalized whenever a market opportunity looks good enough so that the potential returns are well worth the risks. And the type of person whom Wriston and his board chose to succeed him as CEO manifestly signaled an intent to continue such an entrepreneurial environment.

Our point is simply this: Strategic planning can point an organization toward commercial opportunities, but somewhere along the line a calculated-risk-taking CEO is needed to be willing occasionally to alter the company's more conventional "ready-aim-fire" caution in favor of the far more entrepreneurial "ready-fire-aim" stance. That is, the CEO must build the right culture—and accept the consequences, good or bad. Of course, entrepreneurship does not mean recklessness; the Citibank top executives of the business world are calculated-risk-takers, not fools. Entrepreneurship is far from synonymous with forms of gambling in which player skills have little effect on outcomes.

Neither success nor failure in the marketplace is a necessary end result of strategic planning. Too frequently, when the result has been success, management's "brilliance" and "savvy" have been given the credit. And when the consequences were mediocre or disastrous, strategic planning has often been blamed. It is our view that strategic planning has not received the credit it has deserved on the upside and has been a scapegoat of sorts on the downside.

Misconceptions also crop up concerning strategic planning's proper role and importance in an organization. In our experiences, we have encountered several recurring fallacies about strategic planning:

- "We really can't plan in our business because of uncertainty. We don't know what next Tuesday is going to bring about, let alone three, four, five years from now."

- "If you focus too much on planning, nothing ever gets done. Planning is for dreamers ... fancy MBA staff types ... not for doers."

- "We don't have time to plan. It takes too much attention away from the day-to-day operations—and day-to-day operations are what show up on the bottom line."

- "We don't concern ourselves with the long-term. As Keynes said, 'In the long-run, we're dead.'"

- "We are a small business and don't need to plan long-term. All we want to do is get this business going and bail out (sell it) in four or five years."

In this book, we endeavor to show why these kinds of comments are fallacious and result more from misconceptions about strategic planning than from fact. In particular, the foremost cause of such negativism stems from the continual confusion of forecasting with strategic planning, even sometimes by top managers who should know better.

One extremely successful CEO lamented to us that he has to sell middle managers on the need for their wholehearted participation in the company's strategic planning. When this CEO took over at his company, one of his first tasks was to disabuse many of the firm's managers of negativism and wrong-headed thinking about the process and value of strategic planning. In the CEO's view, good strategic planning is an organizational imperative.

As with any other topical subject, there is a plethora of information about strategic planning. Books, articles, seminars, and consultants abound. Some of the information proffered is valuable and some is not so valuable. In the latter case, the information is too often needlessly complex and streaked with jargon—and far more oriented to techniques than to implementation, results, and the strategic thinking which underlies all plans that ultimately bear fruit. Complexity in planning cannot be equated with planning sophistication.

What we have attempted to do in this book is convey the basics of strategic management, as embodied in strategic planning, in a very practical, readable way. In short, we wrote the material for managers. In keeping with this objective, we have supplemented our own thoughts with original chapter-length interviews with three executives experienced in strategic planning. In the appendix, we have also included a number of illustrations and articles that provide insights into both strategic concepts and analytical approaches to planning.

Strategic thinking—and the planning that gives it substance and brings it to life—can be exciting and challenging. Unlike many tasks, strategic planning need not be a chore. Those executives who are integrally involved in the formulation of long-term business strategy are permitted a degree of creativity not commonly found in most managerial positions. In their own way, strategic thinkers and planners are pioneers, who continually explore the unknown future and their organization's place in it. What better challenge than to be able to work daily on the frontier of change? And the degree and skill with which a firm's management is able to meet this kind of challenge are ultimately what determine the organization's destiny.

ACKNOWLEDGMENTS

We alone are responsible for whatever strengths and weaknesses this book has. However, we do wish to credit three executives who contributed much time from their demanding schedules to share their thoughts with us: Stanley Gault of Rubbermaid, William Shaw of Venture Capital, Inc., and Robert Spahr of American Motors. In addition, Janet Currey, our secretary, and Alison Husting of Random House deserve special commendation and thanks.

THINKING STRATEGICALLY
PLANNING FOR YOUR COMPANY'S FUTURE

ENVIRONMENTAL ANALYSIS AND CORPORATE GROWTH

1

Go as far as you can see and when you get there you will see farther.

To be effective, any organization's growth strategies must begin with systematic, ongoing scanning and analysis of the current and future external environments. Since the future is beyond the cognizance of mortals, several alternative scenarios are necessary. Higher management in a corporation might ask, for example, how the company would fare under a certain strategic plan if a worst-case scenario were to occur. "Crossing a strategic bridge when you get to it" is indeed hazardous. Strategic rehearsal now is far more prudent than a "worry about it later" philosophy.

Management needs also to decide which of the possible modes of corporate growth it intends to pursue within the time frame outlined by the strategic plan. To a large extent, this decision is dictated by the strategic-window process, whereby management works to align and time

external opportunities with what is feasible using internal capabilities and available resources. Growth avenues need to be evaluated for their strategic fit with the company's business definition (which should be tight and focused) and for synergies with the firm's existing offerings. In keeping with the need for strategic focus, management continually needs to assess whether it has the sustainable strategic competence that will give it differential competitive advantage and long-term marketplace success.

The milieu of any firm is the world in which it exists and competes. Changes in this world discipline the organization; the organization is either economically rewarded for adapting well or penalized for adapting poorly. The purpose of strategic planning is to steer the company toward tomorrow's opportunities and profits.

In strategic planning the ever-present danger is that management will devote so much attention to planning processes, organizational arrangements, and planning techniques that its focus becomes overly internal while opportunities and threats in the external corporate environment either go unnoticed or are discerned but inadequately assessed. In other words, an internal planning system can be managerially efficient without being terribly effective; such a system cannot save a firm in the throes of technological obsolescence. Although the managerial processes, organization, and techniques of strategic planning are eminently important, all are for naught if the world around the firm changes and the organization is not poised to adapt to the changes. As Peter Drucker and others have astutely observed, it is far more important to do the right things than to do things right.

Keeping a large organization adaptable to external changes requires the lead time that only creative strategic planning with a pervasive outward orientation can provide. Like battleships, most companies cannot be maneuvered much on short notice.

In our view, the single most important facet of strategic planning is external environmental analysis. That is why we chose to consider the subject up front. For management to maintain a strategic mentality about the company, its products, brands, and services, and the role each fulfills today and may or may not fulfill tomorrow, an external *bias* is imperative. It is commonly assumed that "someone" in authority in most all "successful" organizations has such an outward orientation, is astutely observing changes, and is shepherding the organization in response. But a cursory glance at the top 400 to 500 U.S. and multinational companies of thirty, twenty, and ten years ago, compared to those today, will show that many once premier companies are no longer dominant, while a number of today's legendary firms were not in existence a short time ago.

Sports coaches often post sayings in their locker rooms to teach and motivate their athletes. If organizational strategists and planners were to follow suit, we would suggest one adage for display on office walls: *Change is the only constant.* If this perspective is taken to heart, managerial satisfaction with past successes is set aside in favor of the resolve to take a hard look at external forces and what they augur for industries, markets, products, and services.

ENVIRONMENTAL MONITORING

An organization must have an early warning system—a business dew line—if its management is to have the lead time necessary to exploit potential opportunities in its external environment and to cope with potential perils. *Environmental scanning* is a systematic procedure for monitoring the world in which the organization receives its sustenance, for the purpose of identifying opportunities and threats.

As to timing, environmental scanning can be carried out continuously, regularly, or irregularly. Continuous scanning provides for a system of ongoing and structured data collection from the external environment. In contrast, regular scanning pertains to periodically (e.g., annually) updated environmental studies that are decision- and issue-oriented. Finally, irregular scanning refers to ad hoc environmental studies that are initiated in response to crises.[1] Reliance on irregular scanning indicates poor strategic management; it represents a corporate firefighting mentality in which management reacts to instead of prepares for contingencies.

In the prudent and strategically oriented organization, both continuous and regular scanning will be firmly entrenched activities that have top management support and involvement. A staff office (or maybe officer in a small business unit) will be assigned the formidable task of *continuous* environmental intelligence gathering and storage. Computerized management information systems, of course, can play an important facilitative role here. In a supplementary way, *regular* scanning provides detailed information on specific topics that is not otherwise available from the data collected by continuous scanning. Regular scanning is one place that such staff support functions as marketing research and economic analysis can contribute greatly to strategic planning.

Because of the need for close coordination among management information system (computer) personnel, marketing researchers, and economic analysts, it makes a great deal of sense to integrate these functions under a business research head. This organizational arrangement also assures that someone has specific responsibility for continuous and regular environmental scanning and, as important, has the commensurate authority and technical personnel to implement it.

The degree of importance of various types of external environmental information will differ across industries, companies, and markets. Consumer-products firms may be far more interested than industrial-products companies in cultural-social trends in society. Multinationals will be more focused on international political intrigue than firms that perhaps only tokenly export or do not conduct any business abroad at all. Regulatory and antitrust actions will intensely concern large firms involved in acquisitions of other firms, while many smaller companies will take much less note.

However, caution needs to be exercised. It is playing a game

---

[1]Liam Fahey and William R. King, "Environmental Scanning for Corporate Planning," *Business Horizons,* August 1977, pp. 61–71.

of strategic Russian roulette for any management virtually to ignore any major environmental category on the ground that it really is of no concern to its kind of business. Even a small firm, say an Acme, Inc., with no intention to acquire another company might have a far more than passing interest in antitrust developments. Suppose impending modifications in antitrust law or federal policy interpretations thereof are likely to improve the legal ability of a larger competitor to acquire Acme? Then an ostensibly remote environmental happening suddenly becomes entirely pertinent. Similarly, high-technology industrial-market companies are inclined to consider themselves largely insulated from some of the environmental vagaries that particularly affect consumer-products firms. Yet high-technology industrial producers and marketers *are* ultimately affected by broad social-cultural and demographic trends, albeit in a more circuitous manner than their consumer-products counterparts.

For purposes of environmental scanning and analysis, firms are wise to collect and classify data pertaining to diverse externalities. At the bare minimum, we suggest that environmental monitoring needs to cover these categories in some depth:

- Competitor analysis
- Cultural and social patterns
- Demographic trends (particularly population projections)
- Ecological considerations (especially availability of raw materials, notably energy)
- Economic situation
- Legal and regulatory climate
- Political situation
- Technological prospects and occurrences

There may well be other environmental categories that impinge on a particular industry. Moreover, truly useful environmental information must be collected and segregated for every nation in which a firm does business. Differences across countries regarding politics, culture, economics, and the other crucial externalities can be considerable.

Information pertaining to environmental categories will typically be obtained from a variety of sources both internal and external to the corporation. For example, many firms will conduct their own competitor analysis while purchasing economic or political information from commercial sources. Decisions about methods of data collection are complex, which provides yet another solid reason for organizationally placing all business research under the aegis of a single business research head. The resulting coordination of marketing research, economic analysis, technological assessment, and the like militates against redundancies in data collection and allows for more consultation and consensus on what data are best collected by the corporation and what data are best purchased from commercial sources.

A sample competitor analysis is shown in Figure 1.

ENVIRONMENTAL FORECASTING

Futurists, psychics, and other prognosticators aside, no mortal can see the future or conjecture about it with any degree of accuracy and consistency. Seeing around corners is not within human faculties—and certainly not what strategic planning is all about. As management philosopher Peter Drucker has said, strategic planning is essential because forecasting is so inexact. Or, in his words, "We must start out with the premise that forecasting is not a respectable human activity and not worthwhile beyond the shortest of periods. Strategic planning is necessary precisely because we cannot forecast."[2]

Consider, for instance, these "not-so-brilliant forecasts" that have been made by "experts" over the years:

- Twelve years before the U.S.S.R. fired the first ICBM in 1957, the chief of the U.S. government's Office of Scientific Research and Development confidently predicted that using rockets to deliver bombs was impossible and would remain so for many years to come.
- In the 1950s, most Japanese leaders were opposed to heavy investing in a domestic automobile industry; they urged reliance on importation of cars from the United States.
- In 1938, *Fortune* magazine said that few scientists foresaw any serious or practical use for atomic energy.

---

[2]Peter F. Drucker, *Management: Tasks, Responsibilities, Practices* (New York: Harper & Row, 1974), p. 124.

- Lee De Forest, inventor of the radio, in 1926 asserted: "While theoretically and technically television may be feasible, commercially and financially I consider it an impossibility, a development of which we need waste little time dreaming."
- The ideas for the movies *Star Wars* and *Jaws* were initially rejected—as were, repeatedly, the initial books by Dr. Seuss.
- Seven years before the introduction of anesthesia in 1846, a Dr. Alfred Velpeau stated: "The abolishment of pain in surgery is a chimera. It is absurd to go on seeking it today. Knife and pain are two words in surgery that must forever be associated in the consciousness of the patient."
- In the 1950s, the potential demand for computers was widely thought to be 50–100 units worldwide.
- *The Quarterly Review* of 1825 fulminated, "What can be more palpably absurd than the prospect held out of locomotives traveling twice as fast as stagecoaches?"
- As late as 1901, submarines were considered technologically infeasible because of the "suffocation" factor.
- *Popular Science Monthly* in 1895 boldly predicted that the twentieth century would bring on "the trolley age."
- In the mid-1980s, pundits are predicting great attrition in the middle class in the United States.
- Both Thomas Edison and Albert Einstein were in their formative years considered to be intellectually slow.
- Seattle Slew won the American Triple Crown of horse racing. One of the 40 breeding shares in him recently sold for $3 million—making him worth about $120 million. As a yearling, he sold at public auction for $17,500. Yet, several $1 million-plus yearling purchases have never won a race.
- In the 1930s, Chester Carlson, the inventor of xerography, could not find a mimeograph firm willing to buy his process or help him develop it.

J. Scott Armstrong of the Wharton School has proposed "The Seer-Sucker Theory."[3] It goes, "No matter how much evidence exists that seers do not exist, suckers will pay for seers." Armstrong points out that objective studies of the stock market and of predictions in psychology, economics, medicine, sports,

[3]J. Scott Armstrong, "How Expert Are the Experts?" *Inc.: The Magazine for Growing Companies,* Inc., December 1981, pp. 15–16.

WHO IS THE COMPETITION NOW? WHO WILL IT BE IN THE FUTURE?	CONTROL DATA CORPORATION ABOVE PLUS JAPANESE AND CHIP MANUFACTURERS (DIVERSIFICATION)	DIGITAL EQUIPMENT CORP.	EXXON OFFICE SYSTEMS
WHAT ARE THE KEY COMPETITOR'S STRATEGIES, OBJECTIVES, GOALS?	STRESS PERIPHERALS, AVOID DIRECT COMP. IN MAIN FRAME MARKET ESP IBM. 15% ROE BY 1985. MAINTAIN MARKET SHARE, WITH EMPHASIS ON BOTTOM LINE.	CONCENTRATE ON MINI/ MICRO EQUIP. WITH ORIENTATION TO SPECIALIZED END USE MARKETS. GAIN LARGE MARKET SHARE IN MINI AND OFFICE AUTO. MARKET GROWTH IN SERVICE AND PERIPHERAL BUSINESSES.	BUY UP SMALL ENTREPRENEURIAL COMPANIES WITH NEW TECHNOLOGY IN THE OFFICE AUTO. MARKET TO BECOME A MAJOR FORCE IN THE OFFICE AUTO. MARKET. DIVERSIFY USING OIL PROFITS IN FAST-GROWING NEW MARKETS.
HOW IMPORTANT IS A SPECIFIC MARKET TO THE COMPETITORS AND ARE THEY COMMITTED ENOUGH TO CONTINUE TO INVEST?	STRONG COMMITMENT TO CORE BUSINESSES: LARGE SYSTEMS, DP SERVICES AND PERIPHERALS HAVE DEMONSTRATED WILLINGNESS TO FOREGO PROFITS TO GAIN MARKET POSITION.	DEC'S EARNINGS ARE EXCELLENT. HOWEVER, THEY CONTINUE TO REINVEST 100%--HAVE NOT PAID ANY DIVIDENDS. STRONG COMMITMENT TO CORE BUSINESSES.	AT THE PRESENT TIME EXXON IS WILLING TO ABSORB LOSSES IN HOPES OF BUILDING A MAJOR NEW BUSINESS. HOWEVER, THEIR REAL COMMITMENT IS TO ENERGY-RELATED BUSINESSES.
WHAT UNIQUE STRENGTHS DO THE COMPETITORS HAVE?	LARGEST IN PERIPHERAL MARKET. SELLING TO MOST OEMS: VERY STRONG IN EDUCATIONAL SYSTEMS PLATO.	DEVELOPED MODULAR PRODUCTS TO ADD ON TO THEIR EXISTING EQUIP.--THIS PROVIDES A READY-MADE MARKET ENTRY POSITION.	THE ONLY UNIQUE STRENGTH OF EXXON IS THEIR SEEMINGLY BOTTOMLESS POCKETS AND TOLERANCE OF RISK AND FAILURE.
DO THEY HAVE ANY WEAKNESSES THAT MAKE THEM VULNERABLE?	MAY NOT BE ABLE TO MEET NEED FOR SMALLER SYSTEMS IN OFFICE AUTOMATION MARKET. STRONG SOCIAL AGENDA.	HEAVILY DEPENDENT ON UNIQUE SOFTWARE-- POOR COMPATIBILITY WITH COMPETITIVE SYSTEMS.	BIGGEST WEAKNESS IS NO REAL TECHNOLOGY BASE. THEY ARE TOO SLOW TO BRING ON NEW PRODUCTS. ALMOST NONEXISTENT HUMAN RES.
WHAT CHANGES ARE LIKELY IN THE COMPETITORS' FUTURE STRATEGIES?	NO SURPRISES, MAINTAIN SHARE IN CORE BUSINESSES, CONTINUE TO STRESS BIG SYSTEMS, WHILE LOWERING COSTS.	MORE EMPHASIS ON TURN KEY SYSTEMS AVAILABLE FROM RETAIL DISTRIBUTORS. EXPECT MORE ACTIVITY IN PROCESS CONTROL COMPUTERS.	CAN BE EXPECTED TO BAIL OUT AFTER A RESPECTABLE PERIOD. FUTURE CONSOLIDATION WILL PROBABLY NOT SUCCEED!
WHAT ARE THE IMPLICATIONS OF COMPETITORS' STRATEGIES FOR THE MARKET, THE INDUSTRY, AND ONE'S OWN COMPANY?	ECON. OF SCALE WILL PROVIDE CDC WITH LOWEST COST POSITION IN PERIPHERALS AND DP SERVICES. NO REAL THREAT TO THE OFFICE AUTOMATION MARKET-- THEY'LL GET THEIR SHARE FROM OTHER OEMS.	STRONG COMPETITION IN OFFICE AUTOMATION MARKET. LIKELY TO DOMINATE SPECIALTY MARKET SEGMENTS DUE TO STRONG ORIENTATION TO END USER NEEDS.	NO ONE WILL MISS EXXON ■ THEIR PRODUCTS ARE ALREADY SEVERAL GENERATIONS OLD. IMPACT ON THE MARKET WILL BE NIL.
REFERENCES	BUSINESS WEEK, NOV 30, 1981 MOODY'S FACT SHEETS, 10/26/81 MIS WEEK, OCT 21, 1981 FORBES, JAN 5, 1981	FORBES, JAN 5, 1981 IBM COMM. ANALYSIS SUPPORT HANDBOOK, MAY 1980 MOODY'S FACT SHEETS, 8/27/81 MIS WEEK, OCT 21, 1981	FORBES, FEB 16, 1981 BUSINESS WEEK, AUG 24, 1981 BUSINESS WEEK, NOV 14, 1981 MOODY'S FACT SHEETS, 8/6/81

FIGURE 1
Competitor Analysis Computer Industry, December 1981

IBM	WANG LABORATORIES	XEROX
SET PACE FOR THE INDUSTRY; BE A FULL LINE SUPPLIER; MAINTAIN STRONG PEOPLE RESOURCE. BE THE INDUSTRY LEADER IN SALES AND PROFITS. FOSTER INNOVATION TO RETAIN THEIR MARKET LEADERSHIP.	STRATEGY CONSISTS OF 6 FACTORS WHICH ARE THE BASIS OF OFFICE AUTOMATION: DATA, WORD, IMAGE, AND AUDIO PROCESSING, NETWORKING AND HUMAN FACTORS. DOMINATE SMALL COMPUTER SYSTEMS-STATE OF THE ART TECH.	DEVELOP NEW COPIER LINES TO MEET COMPETITION, ESTABLISH POSITION IN COMPUTERS FOR OFFICE AUTOMATION. REVAMP SALES AND MANAGEMENT--MORE RESPONSIVE. GROW WITH TREND TO OFFICE AUTO. FEND OFF JAPANESE THREAT.
IBM IS COMMITTED TO INVEST IN ALL THEIR BUSINESSES AND WILL NOT BE INTIMIDATED BY ANY COMPETITOR--ANNUAL R&D BUDGET APP. $1.5 BILLION.	STRONGEST COMMITMENT TO OFFICE AUTOMATION--CONCENTRATION ON SYSTEMS DESIGNED FOR SPECIFIC END USE MARKETS. WILL CONTINUE TO INVEST BIG IN R&D.	STRONG POSITION IN BUSINESS MARKETS. WILL INVEST TO DEFEND POSITION AT ALL COSTS.
BEST R&D IN THE INDUSTRY; BEST SALES FORCE (MOST LOYAL & BEST TRAINED); EXTENSIVE WORLDWIDE FACILITIES.	NEW AUDIO-ACTIVATED SYSTEMS ARE TYPICAL OF THEIR OUT FRONT ATTITUDE TO TECHNOLOGY.	STRONG SERVICE NETWORK, EXTENSIVE CHANNELS OF DIST. ETHERNET, ALTHOUGH NOT AS HOT AS TOUTED, IS WELL KNOWN.
TOO BIG--ANTITRUST A CONSTANT THREAT.	RELATIVE SIZE CAN BE A PROBLEM FOR WANG WHEN OFFICE AUTOMATION TAKES OFF-MAY BE SHORT OF PRODUCTIVE CAPACITY.	SLOW TO RESPOND TO LOW END THREAT FROM JAPANESE. FAT, DUMB, AND HAPPY FOR TOO LONG-- MANAGEMENT STAGNATION.
LIKELY TO CONTINUE CONSOLIDATION OF SALES ACTIVITIES AS MORE CUSTOMERS REQUIRE MULTIPLE SYSTEMS-- OTHERWISE MORE-OF-THE-SAME SUCCESS FORMULA.	CONTINUED EMPHASIS ON NET-WORK SYSTEMS, MAY STAY OUT OF LOW END SYSTEMS WHICH WILL TEND TO BECOME COMMODITY ITEMS.	BIG MOVES INTO INTEGRATED OFFICE SYSTEMS. NEW LEAN, MEAN MANAGEMENT. NEXT GENERATION OFFICE COPIERS.
IBM WILL CONTINUE TO BE THE INDUSTRY LEADER--BEST STRATEGY FOR COMPETITION IS TO MAKE AS MANY IBM-COMPATIBLE SYSTEMS AS POSSIBLE.	WANG HAS ESTABLISHED THE HIGH-TECH IMAGE IN OFFICE AUTOMATION. THEY WILL BE TOUGH COMPETITORS--THE MARKET SHOULD LOOK TO THEM FOR INNOVATIONS IN THIS SEGMENT.	NEED TO MEET XEROX HEAD ON. ATTEMPT TO BE MORE FLEXIBLE AND RESPONSIVE TO USERS' NEEDS. USE SOFTWARE CAPABILITIES TO CUSTOMIZE SYSTEMS.
IBM COMM. ANALYSIS SUPPORT HANDBOOK, MAY 1980 NEW YORK TIMES, OCT 1, 1981 FORBES, JAN 5, 1981 MOODY'S FACT SHEETS, 10/26/81 BUSINESS WEEK, SEPT 28, 1981	MIS WEEK, NOV 11, 1981 TIME MAGAZINE, NOV 23, 1981 WANG ANNUAL REPORT, 1980 MOODY'S FACT SHEETS, 10/14/81	BUSINESS WEEK, OCT 12, 1981 MIS WEEK, JUNE 17, 1981 INDUSTRY WEEK, NOV 16, 1981 MOODY'S FACT SHEETS, 10/12/81

Source: We are grateful to L. R. Carapellotti for contributing this competitor analysis.

and sociology show that expertise does not promote better forecasts. Indeed, expertise beyond a minimal level is of insignificant value in forecasting change. According to Armstrong, and we heartily concur, the "implications are clear: Avoid hiring expert forecasters. And if you must hire an expert forecaster, don't hire the best, hire the cheapest."

Constructing Scenarios

A scenario in a literary or theatrical context is a script, a plot, or a screenplay. In a business context, a scenario is a possible future environment in which the business might find itself competing— a script. Because forecasting a single "most likely" future environment is so problematic, alternative scenarios are often used to formulate strategic plans. Thus the firm is prepared for several contingencies instead of just one forecasted environment. The scenarios are based largely on the data gathered by environmental scanning.

We suggest that at least three scenarios be constructed, but, for the sake of manageability, no more than four or five. The most prevalent practice is for firms to designate three scenarios and label them to denote disparate views of the futures—optimistic (if things really go well), most likely to occur, and pessimistic (often a quasi-disaster plot). However, some scenario users prefer to provide multiple scenarios without assigning (or implying through descriptors) probabilities for each scenario. The intent is to lessen the chances that planners will consciously or unwittingly devote inordinate attention to a most likely forecast and too little attention to scripts projected as less likely to occur. We personally see much logic to recommend this latter viewpoint, although some strategic planners report satisfactory results with either approach.

At the end of this chapter, we have included two five-year sample scenarios. Both are "most likely" scenarios. One pertains to U.S. commercial banking and the other scenario is for a company competing in the long-distance phone business.

Scenarios typically need to be reexamined and rewritten on an annual basis. The actual scenario writing should be the work of an interdisciplinary group to reflect the diverse nature of the information collected in environmental scanning—cultural and social, economic, technological, legal, and so forth. The group could be composed of corporate line executives and staff specialists and, as needed, could be augmented with individuals from outside the corporation—such as sociologists, economists, and demographers. Each member of the group need not be a renowned expert in some specialized field. Some firms, notables like Sears, Arco, and Monsanto, are using full-time *issues managers* for the purpose of alerting top executives "to emerging political, social, and economic trends and controversies and to mobilize the company's resources to deal with them." Sears sees the system as a "precrisis approach." Arco installed its issues-manager system in part because it felt its planning was too "numbers-oriented." Consequently, a more qualitative trend-spotting approach was established. Issues managers come from diverse backgrounds. Arco's staff encompasses people trained as engineers, lawyers, marketing managers, and congressional consultants/legislative analysts. It even includes one former journalist and one erstwhile English professor.[4]

What is crucial is that group members be conceptually and analytically adept at assimilating and synthesizing the plethora of information that is provided by staff in charge of environmental scanning. As a rule of thumb, individual scenarios in the range of 1,500 to 2,000 words are suggested. The goal of the writers is to provide enough scope and detail to make the scenario meaningful to the individuals who will actually be doing the planning, but not so much information that it will obfuscate and overwhelm.

Crossing a Strategic Bridge When You Get to It Is Hazardous

During the American military action in Grenada in 1983, several U.S. soldiers were separated from the main fighting force and were pinned down in a building by firing from Cuban soldiers. To exacerbate matters, the Americans evidently had no two-way field radio or had one that malfunctioned. As hopeless as the situation seemed, one of the men alertly called his home military

---

[4]Earl C. Gottschalk, Jr., "Firms Hiring New Type of Manager to Study Issues, Emerging Troubles," *The Wall Street Journal,* June 10, 1982, p. 21.

base in the United States by using the regular telephone in the building and his own AT&T credit card. Fortunately, the Cubans had not put the phone out of order by cutting the lines. The home base promptly notified other American forces on Grenada, and the men in distress were rescued.

This example cogently illustrates the potential value of alternative scenarios in any type of planning, including strategic planning. Although the military planning for Grenada could not have accurately forecast the men's being pinned down exactly as they were by enemy fire, it could nonetheless have required rehearsals of a variety of plausible emergency contingencies. Through such contingency planning, the troops would be able to react more coolly and effectively to actual battlefield situations that eventuated than would be possible if they had not been exposed to alternative (in this case, disaster) scenarios at all. Importantly, which men were most and least able to cope with contingencies would also have become apparent during the contingency training.

Strategic planning employing alternative scenarios is nothing more than simulation. Just as astronauts rehearsed on flight simulators for the contingencies of the first lunar landing, so can strategically minded managers devise anticipated responses to simulated tomorrows. And just as the astronauts were prepared for a plethora of landing possibilities, so can top management in an organization be ready for a multitude of broad-based future events.

Strategic planning within the framework of alternative scenarios takes much of the luck out of management's decisions about the future and the organization's role in it. Such an approach is antithetical to the adage, "Let's cross that bridge when we get to it." Rehearsing now how to cross a strategic bridge takes much of the trial, error, and luck out of actually having to cross it later.

CORPORATE GROWTH

The raison d'être of environmental scanning and scenario writing is to facilitate management's attempt to identify opportunities and threats facing the company under different assumptions

14

about the future. Then management tries to design strategies to seize the opportunities and cope with the threats, so that the company can grow and prosper financially. And, in our view, strong growth and profit objectives are mandatory; once management decides that the status quo is satisfactory, the company is in peril. Managerial complacency is a sure prelude to diminished corporate performance.

The technical nomenclature used by planners and management to identify various growth strategies, and the meaning attached to each, are too vital to gloss over. Technical terminology provides a common language that reduces the chances of misunderstanding by those involved in the process and implementation of strategic planning. It is crucial for line executives and staff planners to be talking about the same concepts when reference is made, for example, to market development or vertical integration. Otherwise, what is planned one way may be implemented another.

Fortunately, an almost generic vocabulary has evolved pertaining to the modes of growth available to a company; there are not a vast number of confusing differences in jargon to contend with. The more or less universal descriptors and meanings for the possible modes of corporate growth are as follows:

Market Penetration
This strategy is practiced by the majority of firms. Strategically, the company endeavors to grow by selling more of its present products/services to its present markets or customers. For most companies, this is a realistic growth strategy. Exceptions could be found in dying or saturated markets, in which costly market-share battles work to depress profitability, or when raw materials shortages within an industry preclude aggressive marketing or possibly require demarketing—for example, electric utilities in certain U.S. cities.

Market Development
Like market penetration, this growth mode is almost universally employed in practice. It refers to seeking additional geographic markets and new segments of customers for the company's present products and services. Geographically, market development can run the gamut from a very local business extending itself to a nearby city to a multinational entering another country. How-

15

ever, market development does not always indicate geographical expansion. It can be achieved also by a firm targeting additional market segments—for instance, IBM entering the market for in-home personal computers.

Product Development
This strategic growth mode involves developing new or significantly modified products for sale to the firm's present markets and customers. Still, these new or changed offerings are in some way closely related to the company's present products and product lines.

Concentric Diversification
In this strategy, as the word "diversification" connotes, the company makes a marked departure from what it knows best—that is, from its present products and markets. The firm simultaneously enters markets new to the company with products also new to the company. Yet it is not a total departure from the old. As the word "concentric" implies—that is, emanating from a common center—there is an exploitable technological and/or marketing relationship between the old and the new. For instance, the company might be able to apply its engineering expertise and manufacturing facilities to the production of the new product. Or it may be feasible and cost-efficient to distribute the new product through the firm's existing logistical system.

Conglomerate Diversification
In this growth strategy, the firm also departs significantly from its present products and markets. The company enters markets new to it with products new to it. Unlike concentric diversification, however, in conglomerate diversification there is no exploitable technological and/or marketing relationship between the old and new products and markets. An example is Mobil Oil's acquisition of Montgomery Ward.

The concepts of market penetration, market development, product development, and diversification are depicted in Figure 2.

Vertical Integration
This commonplace growth strategy is the process whereby a company begins either to move forward to its markets or to move

16

	Existing Markets	New Markets
Existing Products	Market Penetration	Market Development
New Products	Product Development	Diver- sification

FIGURE 2
Product/Market Strategies for Business Growth
Source: Adapted from H. Igor Ansoff, "Strategies for Diversification," *Harvard Business Review,* September–October 1957, pp. 113–124.

backward toward its sources of supply, through the establishment or acquisition of raw materials suppliers or sources, manufacturing facilities, wholesale operations, or retailing outlets, as the case may be. A totally vertically integrated firm is one that owns all the institutions within its channel of distribution—from supply to market. The strategy is often used to increase a company's competitiveness—for example, a manufacturer might decide to do its own wholesaling with the dual goals of achieving cost savings and gaining control over the selling effort to end users or middlemen. The strategy is also used for defensive reasons, as when a company integrates in a backward fashion to assure itself of the availability of raw materials. The Du Pont acquisition of Conoco is an example.

Horizontal Integration
Whenever a firm begins acquiring other firms at the same level of competition, it is engaging in horizontal integration. For example, a retailer may acquire another retailer. Horizontal integration is a prevalent growth strategy in the retail department store business, although it is also used at the manufacturing and wholesaling levels of competition.

In addition to selecting several of the foregoing modes of growth, management must also determine whether the selected strategies are to be achieved by external or internal growth. External growth is implemented via merger and acquisition, whereas internal growth is accomplished by means such as corporate research and development and the establishment of new businesses and facilities from scratch. Take these examples, which contrast the two: a firm could pursue the growth strategy of product development by creating its own new products (R&D), or it could acquire new products or manufacturing rights from another firm. Similarly, in pursuit of forward vertical integration, a manufacturer could establish industrial distributors where none existed before (internal growth), or acquire distributors already in operation (external growth), or use a combination of the two.

The importance of using a common language in strategic planning is so great that we suggest a glossary of terms and their meanings be agreed upon, put in writing, and discussed among all line and staff officers concerned. Nowhere are such definitions more critical than with respect to the foregoing modes of corporate growth. If a strategic plan designates market development, or concentric diversification, or whatever growth strategy is intended to be implemented, everyone involved in the design and execution of the plan had best be on the same wavelength.

SEEKING A STRATEGIC FIT

In the CEO's never-ending quest for corporate growth, his or her overriding strategic objective should be to accomplish a synergistic, exploitable fit between, on the one hand, the company's existing operations and management/technological expertise and, on the other hand, the proposed new lines of business. Even a company in a slow-growth or moribund industry is best advised to look initially for new opportunities in ventures where its know-how and facilities can be used to strategic advantage.

Consider an extreme case in which an industry was for all practical purposes dying—buggy-whip manufacturing in the early 1900s. In order to survive and perhaps prosper, a buggy-whip manufacturer would not necessarily have had to seek growth opportunities that were radical departures from its core skills. Surely, the company would have concluded that it must diversify, but just as surely it would not have wanted to go too far afield from its basic skills. Its chances for success in, say, fashion retailing or subway construction would have been minimal, whereas its manufacturing know-how might well have been successfully transferable to such leather-goods products as purses, briefcases, or even shoes.

Sometimes a company tries to diversify into an area where it has no skills or previous background by relying on its current good will and reputation. For example, when Exxon departed considerably from its core business by entering the office automation industry, it displayed the Exxon tiger in its office automation advertisements, thereby telling many would-be customers of Exxon's reputation for financial stability, power, and resources. Even so, Exxon is not a force in office systems. Over many years, the performance track records for conglomerate diversifications have simply not been good when compared to the other modes of corporate growth that build on a company's existing competencies. In most instances, companies have been better off pursuing growth strategies that exploit their extant know-how.

Achieving a strategic fit is often easier said than done. Perhaps this one aspect of strategic planning subjects management to what we call "strategic fallacies" more than any other. In looking for strategic fits, management may be tempted to define its business too broadly and thus lose strategic focus when evaluating growth opportunities. Again, take our hypothetical buggy-whip manufacturer. A disaster scenario would have the buggy-whip executives thinking that the company is in a transportation-related industry and therefore should stay in transportation by going "high tech" and serving in some way the infant, but booming, horseless carriage industry. No doubt the less than successful Sohio acquisition of Kennecott Copper was based on the tempting reasoning that there was an ideal strategic fit because both companies were in the energy business. Similarly, General Foods obtained Burger Chef on the grounds that General Foods knew the food business. As GF soon found out to its dismay, the manufacture and distribution of food products are a world apart from the retailing of fast food.

In order to mitigate possible strategic miscalculations of this kind, the CEO must have a well-publicized, integrative theme for the company against which all growth opportunities are judged. If the company departs from this theme—and many companies have special entrepreneurial units that do so—then the depar-

19

ture should be by design. We suggest that to evaluate growth opportunities the CEO needs a *tight and focused business definition* that is based on answers to the following questions:

- Who are (or should be) our customers?
- What customer needs and wants do we (or should we) fulfill?
- What technologies do we (or should we) use to serve our customers?
- What is (or should be) the geographic scope of our operations?

In addition, the CEO will make these queries time and again:

- What are the potential technological (R&D and manufacturing) synergies between our existing operations and the proposed growth opportunity?
- What are the potential marketing synergies between the old and the new?

STRATEGIC WINDOWS

At the outset, we looked at environmental scanning and multiple scenario writing as means for identifying potential opportunities and possible threats to the company in the years ahead. Afterwards, we focused on the ways—which we called the modes of corporate growth—available to the company to exploit the opportunities and cope with the threats identified. What is missing thus far is linkage between the identification of external opportunities and threats, on the one hand, and the selection of growth modes on the other. We think that this linkage is provided by an idea called the strategic window.

The term *strategic window* was popularized by Derek Abell of Harvard. His idea is that "there are often only limited periods when the 'fit' between the 'key requirements' of a market and the particular competencies of a firm competing in that market are at an optimum. Investment in a product line or market area has to be timed to coincide with periods in which a strategic window is open, i.e., where a close fit exists. Disinvestment should be considered if, during the course of the market's evolution, changes in market requirements outstrip the firm's capability to adapt itself to the new circumstances."[5]

Through a strategic-window perspective or analysis, management can relate potential market opportunities to company capabilities—capabilities in terms of capital requirements, technical expertise, management personnel, and so on. It is not enough for management merely to identify opportunities in the external environment. It is also not enough to go a step further and determine what growth strategies are needed to take advantage of the potential opportunities. This additional question must be addressed: Will the opportunity be there at the same time that the company has the competence and resources to seize upon it? In other words, will the growth strategy needed to capitalize on the opportunity be within the company's capability at the *right time?* For instance, three years hence, will the firm be positioned to afford the acquisition of the firm that it will need to enter a new high-tech market? If so, the strategic window will be open; if not, the strategic window will be shut and the growth strategy will not be feasible. Likewise, with regard to possible environmental threats, the overriding question is: If the potential threats become realities, will the company have the competence and resources to cope with them? If not, disinvestment may be indicated. For example, if a small personal computer manufacturer cannot ultimately survive IBM's entry into the market, it had better get out sooner rather than later.

Successful application of the strategic-window idea requires top management to address three critical planning concerns and how they affect one another. First, during the period of time covered by the strategic plan, what general and specific external events may represent exploitable opportunities and threats to be avoided or dealt with? Second, what specific strategies for corporate growth—concentric diversification, vertical integration, or whatever—would be needed to do so? Third, will corporate competencies and resources be adequate to execute the desig-

---

[5]Derek F. Abell, "Strategic Windows," *Journal of Marketing,* July 1978, pp. 21–26; Derek F. Abell and John S. Hammond, *Strategic Market Planning* (Englewood Cliffs, N.J.: Prentice-Hall, 1979), p. 63.

nated strategies at the *time* when the opportunities or threats may eventuate? Considerable background information from staff and long, hard thought and analysis by planners and top-line management are needed to answer these questions.

A strategic-window view is integrative. It requires a thorough analysis of (1) current and projected *external* environments, (2) current and projected *internal* corporate capabilities, and (3) how, whether, and when it will be feasible to reconcile the two by implementing one or more growth strategies.

We have observed that frequently the biggest inhibitor to developing implementable strategic plans is management's failure to reconcile prospective opportunities with corporate capabilities. Particularly, there is a tendency to identify "brilliant" opportunities that realistically are well beyond the company's reach in terms of money, human resources, and expertise.

An opposite problem of this kind is created when a company is cash-rich but has no idea where to put its money. We are acquainted with a large company that has recently disinvested itself of a number of "unsatisfactory" divisions and operations. Although the chief executive officer has undoubtedly done an effective job of putting the company on a sounder financial footing, he has, nonetheless, never "grown a company" and is apparently having a difficult time reconciling his sizable pool of cash with market opportunity. Ironically, while he is searching for opportunities, the company's cash-richness makes it an attractive acquisition target for some other "opportunistic" firm.

STRATEGIC COMPETENCE

Irrespective of the opportunities presented by its external market environment, a firm will flounder and maybe eventually founder if it does not have something of sustainable value to offer. That something might be the lowest price, the best value, the most prestige, or a host of other possibilities and combinations. Consequently, an absolute prerequisite for sustainable marketplace success is for the company to have a clear definition and understanding of just what it intends to offer prospective buyers, in a specified market segment, to fulfill their needs and wants better than competitors. If management has a hard time articulating its company's *strategic competence,* there is lack of strategic focus.

In strategy formulation, we suggest that managers use the word "market" sparingly. It is too impersonal, too dispassionate, and tempts managers to view buyers as automatons. Instead, we advise strategists to speak in terms of actual and prospective consumers and their needs. After all, "market" is nothing more than a catchall term for would-be human buyers with a generic class of needs and desires that can be met by companies' goods and services.

Corporate strategists continually need to ask themselves whether they would select their firm's offerings over those of competitors were they buying. This type of assessment is difficult, given management's predilection toward its own products, but the assessment does need to be undertaken—and in as objective a manner as possible. A successful residential real estate developer told one of us of a deceptively simple rule that had served him well in evaluating possible development sites and lots: Were he in the market for a home, would he personally want to live in the location?

A corporate competence that translates into value for buyers is fundamental to strategic management. As the aphorism goes, "Nothing happens until someone makes a sale." In other words, in the blur of internal operational activities in a corporation, it is easy for management to lose sight of the company's raison d'être—buyers.

Providing value to buyers is essential but not enough. The value proffered must be communicated in a persuasive manner. In fact, what is perceived is far more important to commercial success than what may be objective reality. Many U.S. manufacturers, for instance, may have better products than their Japanese competitors, but it does them little good if buyers believe otherwise. Have not the Japanese been masters in getting themselves seen as masters of product quality?

Moreover, what represents value in today's market may not constitute value in tomorrow's, as customer needs and wants can be ephemeral. So the query, "What is our strategic competence?" is one that must be raised again and again. The question never changes, but the answers do.

A hard look ("let the chips fall where they may") and objective answers to several potentially telling questions can go a long way toward enabling the CEO and his or her top managers to determine whether their company has an exploitable strategic competence in its existing and coveted markets:

1. What are the primary benefits sought by the kinds of customers we seek to serve?
2. Do we have a competence in providing the benefits that customers want? Or does our competence involve factors that make little difference to customers or that are not decisive in the buying process?
3. Do customers and prospective customers perceive us and our products/services the way we perceive ourselves? If not, what can we and should we do about it?
4. Based on our answers to these queries, what is our differential competitive advantage?
5. Do we really know our markets or just think we do? Have we been inner-directed, perhaps even myopic, in our strategic thinking? Are we really sure of our answers to the preceding questions? Have we asked customers about what benefits they want and what benefits we and our competitors are seen as providing? Or are we (dangerously) relying mainly on our own intuition?

The thoughtfulness and candor with which top management addresses these questions can determine—in fact, are likely to determine—the long-term future of the company. In addition, we think it critical to make the very same kinds of inquiries about the competition. Only by knowing the strategic competencies of our competitors, what benefits they offer to prospective buyers, and how they are viewed by consumers can we make valid conclusions about our own strategic strengths and weaknesses.

SAMPLE SCENARIOS
ILLUSTRATIVE "MOST PROBABLE" FIVE-YEAR SCENARIO FOR MCI COMMUNICATIONS CORPORATION[6]

The future is dominated by growth and opportunities for the long-distance networks as they find their niche in a communications society.

All long-distance phone companies will be on equal competitive footing in 1988. Phone users will inform the local phone company as to which long-distance network they intend to use regularly, and the calls will be automatically routed over the chosen network. Long-distance users will be able to employ rotary dialing methods to make their long-distance calls. (Presently only push-button phones may be used to place calls, which is a great disadvantage since push-button phones make up only 40 percent of the market.)

The reason that all long-distance phone companies will be on equal footing in 1988 is that, beginning in 1984, AT&T was divided into seven independent regional companies handling local service, leaving a leaner, more flexible AT&T in the long-distance business. Because of this divestiture, the seven new

---

[6]Researched and prepared in 1983 by Theresa Maskulka of Kent State University.

local phone companies will have to offer the same interconnections to MCI and other long-distance networks that are now offered only to AT&T.

The only limit on growth of the long-distance phone companies will be their ability to build their networks. Thus, it is expected that long-distance networks will continue to expand their systems at a rapid rate until the late 1980s, when growth will be slow. At that time, MCI will enjoy a 5 percent market share but will find it increasingly difficult to continue expanding its system at the present rate.

AT&T's long-distance phone rates are higher at this time because approximately 35 percent of its revenues are used to subsidize local phone service. This accounts for MCI's current ability to undercut AT&T. Recently, the FCC decided it will phase out AT&T's heavy local subsidy over the next five years.

Economic growth will aid in the expansion of the networks in many ways. More people will be entering the middle-income, 35–49 age bracket, and their demands for goods and services will increase. At the same time, consumers will be looking for more ways to save and invest, as excessive government regulations are removed. In addition, people comfortable with computers will be more receptive to new ideas in data transmission.

In order for the long-distance networks to maintain market share in the late 1980s, new telecommunications services will evolve, such as paging services, cellular radio systems, mergers with cable TV, and banking services. Digital capacity, including projected fiber-optic lines for voice and data, will be prevalent west as well as east of the Mississippi. The long-distance networks will continue to explore the market for new opportunities as the age of high technology unfolds.

Long-distance companies will be involved in *more* court battles, but *smaller* court battles. Predatory pricing, which occurs when a financially strong company temporarily cuts prices below its costs to cripple or wipe out a competitor, will continue to be one of the major issues. More courts will throw out antitrust complaints on the basis of the cost test (a comparison of the prices charged and the cost of production).

Long-distance companies will continue to enjoy successful operations while watching out for potential threats to their market. All their activities will be directed toward increasing the usage and thus the profitability of their networks.

ILLUSTRATIVE "MOST PROBABLE" FIVE-YEAR SCENARIO FOR U.S. COMMERCIAL BANKING[7]

Events in the commercial banking industry continue to be the result of numerous dynamic influences. Because of the pervasiveness of the banking industry in the lives of businesses and individuals, changes in one area not only affect the commercial banking industry directly, but set off multiple chain reactions in other areas which, in turn, have their own effects on the banks. This situation results in a heightened rate of evolution in the banking industry. Consequently, bankers are forced to take an increasingly "marketing" approach to the way in which business is done.

The new marketing orientation leads to a heightened level of competition in the commercial banking industry. Competitive pricing of loans and deposits, combined with increased advertising, promotion, and consumer education, brings about an increase in consumer awareness of bank services, attributes, and particularly prices. Price wars for large deposits and important loan customers exacerbate the deteriorating financial condition of many banks, causing the number of bank failures to remain relatively high. The acquisition of weak banks by stronger and larger ones, as well as mergers that result from other market influences, further the trend of bank consolidation that blossomed in the late 1970s and early 1980s.

In an effort to reduce their exposure to losses in any given segment of the financial services market, commercial banks (and particularly bank holding companies) continue to diversify into virtually every aspect of financial services. As the end of the decade approaches, the commercial banking industry becomes more

---

[7]Researched and prepared in 1984 by William T. Hoover of Huntington Banks.

fully recognized for its roles in providing financial and economic services. As a result, attitudes toward banks tend to polarize, and publicity becomes both more and less favorable.

The Political Situation

Attitudes and ideals continue to be a controlling influence at the federal level. This has consequences in many areas that affect the commercial banking industry. Legislation results in many laws aimed at increasing the abilities of businesses to compete domestically and internationally.

Antitrust regulations are relaxed, particularly as more legal interpretations are made in favor of large business interests. Similarly, regulatory agencies relax their hold over the various industries that they supervise and/or control. Consequently, many businesses become more profitable, particularly the larger companies with resources to develop and expand into new markets. By the end of the decade, however, increased freedom for business leads to a renewed interest in consumer advocacy.

The political stalemate in Washington results in continued large budget deficits for the federal government. Conservatives continue to hold the line against significant tax increases, while liberals retain sufficient power to prevent any kind of sizable cuts in social welfare programs. With the problem exacerbated by increased defense spending, the Treasury is forced to continue financing the deficits in the debt market.

The Economic Situation

Unemployment stabilizes, but, due to structural unemployment, fails to go below the 8 percent level. This lack of improvement is primarily the result of continued layoffs and shutdowns in the smokestack and automotive industries, as part of a structural change in the labor market. Unemployment also contributes to Congress's difficulty in cutting the budgets of social programs.

Increased net investment by business reduces the ratio of labor to capital employed by producers. Inasmuch as this increase must be funded from somewhere, and entails a wide variety of financial transactions, the commercial banks find themselves competing more directly with firms that had not previously been in competition with the banks. This situation intensifies both in markets that were previously the exclusive property of the banks, and in markets from which the banks were previously excluded.

Continued unemployment prevents income from increasing fast enough to cause a return to the inflation rates of the 1970s. Consequently, wages and prices remain at a relatively low growth rate.

Government deficits, combined with increased net investment demand, cause a slight bidding up of interest rates. However, foreign investment in the United States increases, offsetting the trade deficits caused by a strong dollar.

The Legal and Regulatory Situation

The U.S. government moves to permit interstate banking. And all of the states find themselves forced to sanction statewide banking. These actions are denouements of the trend to deregulate banking, which allows commercial banks to enter all financial markets. Although only a few states authorize full-blown interstate banking within their confines, most allow for some type of affiliations or holding company organizations on an interstate basis. This deregulation results in an increased rate of bank consolidations as small, one-community banks virtually disappear, either through merger or through failure.

The increased size of banks, however, leads to a heightened public interest in their regulation. This prevents any significant reduction in the degree of monitoring and supervision done by federal agencies. Consolidations and mergers, however, cause a number of states to require that all banks be nationally chartered. In the process, banking and credit regulations become more uniform.

Technology

The central consideration in this regard is the continued proliferation of personal computers and communications technology.
Personal computers increase the ability of the consumer to carry
out financial transactions from the home or office. Consumers
can now make stock trades almost instantaneously, on their own,
through automated stock exchanges that are run by major bro-
kerage houses, banks, and other financial institutions. By the
end of the decade, about two-thirds of the financial transactions
in the United States are paperless.

Cultural and Social Patterns

Cultural and social changes are closely tied to technological
developments and to the United States' transition from predominantly heavy industry to predominantly service and information
industries. Continued national debt and international financial
problems help to keep public awareness of the financial services
industry at a high level. Plastic and paperless transactions
become the norm rather than the exception.

A widening of the gap between rich and poor begins to
increase the popularity of radical ideals and solutions, and continues to generate hostility from developing nations and cultures. It remains a popular third-world (and in some instances
second-world) game to play at defying the superpowers, and
even the Soviet Union experiences significant problems in places
such as Poland. Many third-world countries teeter on the brink
of bankruptcy—and U.S. money-centered banks have a large
loan portfolio outstanding to such countries. Demographically,
one important factor is increased mobility of individuals. This
contributes to the development of intra- and interstate banking,
as a more nomadic population demands more uniform access to
financial services. The overall increasing age of the population,
combined with greater longevity, results in a plethora of special
banking services for the elderly.

A wide variety of circumstances leads to the further sophistication of the banking public and, accordingly, to a wider range

of financial services, many of which are themselves more sophisticated.

Cost Containment

Efforts at cost containment in the commercial banking industry are tied to technological developments as banks attain a higher degree of automation. In doing so, the banks substitute capital for labor, and pursue the goals of identifying and reducing the costs of each kind of financial transaction. To augment cost controls, commercial banks expand fee-based services.

PLAN FOR STRATEGIC PLANNING

2

Prior to the full-fledged launch or significant modification of a strategic planning system, a well-thought-out and carefully implemented preplanning phase is prudent. Otherwise, the company is likely to expend needless time, energy, and dollars, plus it more likely than not will end up with a strategic planning apparatus that is not as effective as it could be with better forethought and groundwork. The issues that need to be addressed in the preplanning phase are these:

- *Who is in charge of preplanning?*
- *How much planning bureaucracy is needed initially?*
- *What qualifications do the planners need to ensure a well-balanced and creative strategic planning team?*
- *What planning horizon is appropriate, in terms of years, for the corporation as a whole and its components — that is, divisions, strategic business units, functional areas, or other organizational setups?*

- *Does the company need an investment banker and, if so, with what qualifications and specific expertise?*

A competent board of directors should be integrally involved in considering, debating, and ratifying strategic policy. When properly selected and used, a board of directors can provide a CEO with invaluable strategic assistance. Also, small-to-medium-size companies without the wherewithal to maintain a full-time strategic planning organization (or consultants) have other options, in particular the use of quasi-boards of directors. Such boards provide companies with expertise not affordable on a day-to-day basis, objective and fresh opinions from knowledgeable individuals outside the company, and a place for the CEO to discuss new or sensitive matters confidentially.

There is no doubt that the intensely competitive and rapidly changing environment for most businesses in the United States and elsewhere has greatly increased the need for strategic planning. In a few high-technology industries, change and obsolescence are so rapid that "long-range" now means at most three to five years—for example, in telecommunications and personal computers. Certainly, current "high-flying" companies in these and a multitude of other industries could readily become "low-flyers" if they slight preparations for the changes that a not-too-distant tomorrow will surely bring.

Consequently, it is not at all surprising that strategic planning is in vogue in the modern business organization. This emphasis is but a logical, survival-driven corporate response to the forces of change that can either make or break companies.

Yet a managerial "rush" toward strategic planning is ill-advised. The process of instituting an effective corporate strategic planning system itself requires careful forethought and planning. A counterproductive result of management's hurrying into strategic planning can be a ponderous planning bureaucracy that fails to steer the company toward opportunities and away from pitfalls and stagnation. For this reason, consider the major preliminary determinations that need to be made before a strategic planning function is implemented or reorganized.

WHO IS IN CHARGE OF PREPLANNING?

Initiating a strategic planning function is an enormously complicated task. Well before a vice president (or director or manager) of strategic planning is hired, a multitude of decisions are necessary. The CEO does not have the time to undertake the preplanning job but must be involved in key decisions. So another corporate official needs to be put in charge considerably in advance of the time when a chief strategic planning executive is actually selected and brought aboard. This person needs to be a member of top management who has clout and has the confidence and ear of the CEO.

The CEO's preplanning designate must develop at least a skeletal concept of the planning function and establish a tentative budget. In addition, the yet-to-be-hired chief planner's place in the organizational hierarchy—especially his or her relationship to the CEO—must be stipulated and a job description provided. Otherwise, it would be impossible for corporate recruiters to know what kinds of qualifications to look for, nor would they be able to converse with prospective planning executives regarding the scope, responsibility, and authority associated with the position.

Proper preplanning serves to mitigate personnel, budgetary, and related misunderstandings that are likely to occur later without it. It also involves the CEO in the planning system from the ground up and thus helps to gain top management support.

HOW MANY ORGANIZATIONAL LEVELS?

The organizational imperative of a streamlined and lean bureaucracy applies to strategic planning, just as it does to other corporate functions. The fewer the organizational levels and the smaller the planning staffs that can effectively accomplish the objectives set by top management, the better.

Approximations of these optimum amounts of bureaucracy and personnel are best achieved through an incremental or *ratchet approach* to developing the planning organization. Incrementalism enables management to add organizational levels and staff gradually and only after a clear need is demonstrated. The alternative is a "sudden planning" approach, whereby an organizationally pervasive system is imposed virtually all at once. But this approach is almost sure to result in redundancies in both organizational levels and staff—redundancies that will then have to be pared.

For simplicity, this discussion assumes the normal situation of a complex company organized around divisions (or some similar profit center arrangement). The corporate level concerns itself with portfolio planning—that is, investing in and divesting broad lines of business through mergers and acquisitions and through allocation of resources to the divisions. Divisions focus on strategic business plans, with each division emphasizing and deemphasizing products in its general line of business. Again, this is achieved through internal resource-allocation decisions and at times through divisional acquisitions and divestments. Functional areas within divisions concern themselves with strategic programs such as financial and marketing planning and strategy.

In our judgment, the all-important first step in a ratchet approach to establishing strategic planning is the development of a full-time planning function at the corporate level. It is corporate's job to map the company's overall direction in the three, five, ten, or maybe twenty years hence. It does so by identifying, studying, and recommending to top-line management the portfolio of infant, growing, and mature lines of business that will attain long-term performance goals. The corporate group also coordinates and monitors divisional planning activities.

In general, the more a corporation's operating divisions are in dissimilar lines of business, and thus do not complement one another in production skills, marketing expertise, or whatever, the larger the planning staff required at corporate. Whenever corporate is engaged in a smorgasbord of unrelated businesses, a broad range of industry expertise is necessary, and accordingly the planning staff should be larger. Economies of scale and favorable effects of experience tend to accrue to companies that grow through related lines of business.

Whether full-time planning staff is needed at the divisional level—and, if so, how much staff—depends on a division's size and diversity and the scope of its activities. Notably, when a division makes acquisitions on its own, some full-time staff is essential. Similarly, at the functional level within divisions, diverse product lines often necessitate additional strategic program planners and analysts.

As a company grows, of course, it may become critical to keep the planning task manageable by adding organizational levels. Between corporate and its divisions, for example, it might be justifiable to institute *strategic business units* (SBUs) to handle the planning task for divisions in related businesses.

Strategic business units are self-contained businesses that meet three standards:

- They have a set of clearly defined external competitors.
- Their managers are responsible for developing and implementing their own strategies.
- Their profitability can be measured in real income, rather than in artificial dollars as transfer payments between divisions.[1]

Experience has taught both U.S. firms and the Japanese that, when initially setting up SBUs, companies often err by creating so many SBUs that each tends to be too small and, therefore, largely meaningless from a marketing and planning viewpoint. For instance, Toshiba Corporation began with 104 separate SBUs, but over a five- to six-year period pared down to 43 SBUs. The larger number simply made resource allocation unwieldy.[2] Again, it is worth repeating that the gradual or incremental approach to expanding the planning bureaucracy is a sound one.

Even if there is a full-time planning staff, it is axiomatic that appropriate line officers should be involved in strategic planning;

---

[1] "A U.S. Concept Revives Oki," *Business Week,* March 1, 1982, pp. 112–113.
[2] Ibid., p. 112.

after all is said and done, they are accountable for performance results. This maxim applies to the CEO at corporate, to the divisional chief executive, and to appropriate functional officers.

WHAT QUALIFICATIONS DO THE PLANNERS NEED?

A cursory reading of want ads for strategic planning executives readily shows lack of consensus as to what skills and backgrounds are thought most desirable. Some ads stipulate financial backgrounds, others stress marketing experience, a few specify general managers, and the list goes on. Realistically, what is needed for strategic planning is an appreciation for an interfunctional perspective—regardless of the specialty of the executive who is selected—because so many different congruencies between the company's strengths and growth options must be evaluated.

At the corporate level, a wide range of opinions and expertise is required, such as production and engineering, marketing, finance, research and development, legal, and personnel. Executives with backgrounds in these areas may all be made full-time planners, temporary members of a project team, or more likely a mixture of full-time and part-time planners. As pointed out in Chapter 1, some notable firms are using issues managers to improve strategic planning.

We have come to conclude, however, that the best place for top management to at least begin looking for an executive to head the corporate strategic planning function is among successful marketing managers. Individuals from marketing management are—by training, experience, and inclination—oriented toward the external environment. Seasoned marketing executives have been on the corporate "front line" and are therefore used to identifying external opportunities or threats and dealing with environmental change. Indeed, success in their jobs depends on their abilities to do so. Moreover, because of their eye for competitive advantage, marketing executives tend to look at growth opportunities in terms of how well they mesh with existing corporate operations and expertise and whether the opportunities are capable of producing synergies.

On the divisional level, an interfunctional planning group is also best. What proportion of the team is full-time or part-time depends on divisional size and whether the team makes its own acquisitions.

At all organizational levels—corporate, divisional, and functional—conceptually creative and integrative thinkers are needed for strategic planning, in addition to the technical personnel in finance, marketing, and other business activities. Because people with these creative gifts and analytical skills can come from most anywhere, it is essential that the search for members of a strategic planning team not be limited exclusively to top management.

HOW LONG THE PLANNING HORIZON?

Strategic planning horizons can run the gamut from the short-range—one to three years in the future—to extremely long-range—twenty to thirty years hence. The attention that management devotes to detail in strategic planning naturally corresponds to the planning horizon, with increasing exactitude becoming necessary as the horizon shortens. For the very long run, rough strategic sketches of corporate responses to alternative scenarios are all that are appropriate.

These relationships between planning horizons and attention to detail need to be spelled out and agreed upon at each organizational planning level. For example, in Figure 3, for a typical corporation, the ideal strategic orientations of its three organizational levels—corporate, divisional, and functional—have been depicted in order to show the approximate strategic focus at each level.

At corporate, the task is to pose and answer questions about corporate missions and directions in the, say, three to five to ten to twenty years ahead. Accordingly, these strategic plans, ipso facto, will often be broad in orientation and will extend far beyond the present-day operational specialties in which the company does business through its various divisions.

Ordinarily, divisions must strike a fine balance between general and detailed strategic planning, all the while shading their orientations just slightly to the right of the line demarcating the

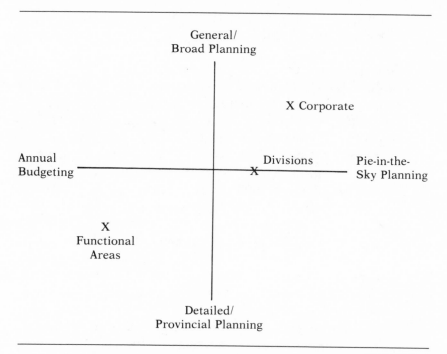

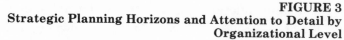

FIGURE 3
Strategic Planning Horizons and Attention to Detail by
Organizational Level

annual budgeting/pie-in-the-sky quadrants in Figure 3. This perspective promotes expansive thinking yet does not force a division so far away from its current operational expertise and the practical aspects of strategic planning that its plans lack reality.

Strategic planning in the various functional areas within divisions gravitates more toward the present (one to three years) and toward the precision required to implement the programs decided upon. The functional areas are necessarily operations-oriented, because they are basically developing implementation plans that fit within the context of the strategic goals set down by top divisional management.

Problems with the installation or reorganization of strategic planning in a complex company can be mitigated with careful preplanning. To summarize, in this crucial preliminary phase, several key questions need answering:

- What executive from top management will be assigned to shepherd the strategic planning system into existence during the preplanning phase, including the skeletal design of the system, the establishment of a budget, and the hiring of a chief corporate planning manager?
- What steps will be taken to assure that top-line managers at every organizational level—corporate, divisional, and functional—are integrally involved in creating and later participating in the strategic planning system?
- How many organizational planning levels are needed initially? What proportion of the planners at each level will be full-time or part-time?
- Does the proposed planning system make provisions for an interfunctional team with diverse organizational and environmental viewpoints?
- Are conceptual, expansive thinkers represented adequately?
- Are the proposed strategic horizons at the corporate, division, and functional organizational levels established? Do all agree that these horizons are appropriate?

THE STRATEGIC ROLE OF INVESTMENT BANKERS

One or more of the strategies that a firm selects to achieve its growth objectives often necessitate the services of an investment banker. This need usually reflects success because the company is expanding and wants help in raising capital to finance the growth or to acquire another company with internally generated resources.

The choice of an investment banker is itself of strategic importance. Investment banking firms differ considerably in their specialties, competencies, and the size of firm they cater to. A few investment bankers are large by going standards. They employ a hundred or more people in their merger and acquisition section alone and serve the giants of industry. At the other extreme are investment bankers who specialize in far smaller clients and deals.

Investment bankers can be useful in assisting a company in implementing a spectrum of strategic-related activities—for example, mergers and acquisitions, corporate divestitures and partial divestitures in the guise of joint ventures, and issuance of corporate securities to raise capital for growth. These institutions can also assist a firm defensively. For instance, hostile takeover attempts of Conoco by Mobil Oil and Seagram were circumvented by an "arranged" corporate marriage between Conoco and its white knight—Du Pont. And SOCAL saved Gulf from the clutches of several groups that were led by Boone Pickens of Mesa Petroleum.

Top corporate management and its planning staff should not wait until the services and advice of an investment banker are imminently needed to consider which bankers to use. That could be too late in the event of a hostile takeover attempt by another company. Or an acquisition opportunity might arise unexpectedly and management would need to move with alacrity to seize it.

A good example of the strategic importance of having a capable investment banker on line is the case of Bendix and RCA. Within only several days of a Bendix purchase of a large bloc of RCA stock, in the open market, and a purported impending takeover attempt, RCA's CEO had met personally with his counterpart at Bendix, in the company of RCA's investment bankers and representatives of a law firm that specializes in thwarting hostile acquisition attempts. (Bendix was itself later acquired by Allied Corporation after a bitter battle with Martin Marietta.)

Accordingly, as part of organizing for strategic planning, a responsible executive within the firm needs to be put in charge of finding out about and evaluating investment banking houses that the firm conceivably might use. Questions to ask about each investment banker are:

- With what size firms and in what size transactions do they typically deal?
- Who are and have been their clients?
- What services do they offer?

41

- What are their specialties, if any?
- How much do they charge for their services?
- What is their reputation for competence and ethics?

Answers to most of these questions can be obtained from the individual investment banker. However, the best indicator of competence and ethics is the investment banker's track record. Ask for a list of present and past clients and for permission to contact them. Then follow up.

THE ROLE OF THE BOARD OF DIRECTORS

One main purpose of a board of directors in a large corporation is to frame and approve overall organizational policy. Most boards in premier companies are eminently qualified to do so. In a company of this kind, the inside directors are drawn from the company's top management and the outside directors typically come from upper-echelon executive positions in other major but noncompeting firms. Thus, on the board there is a plethora of experience in corporate policymaking that can be brought to bear. Moreover, these successful companies are careful to balance their boards between inside and outside directors; they are well aware of the objective and creative perspectives that outside directors can provide.

The very essence of corporate policymaking is long-range strategic planning. Accordingly, we see the board of director's role (indeed, other than selecting a CEO, its chief function) to be that of conceiving, debating, and ratifying the company's strategic plan. Naturally, a board is best not involved in the nitty-gritty of such activities as capital budgeting and acquisitions; these are more in the domain of implementation, a management function. But the board initially needs to conceptualize and debate the company's strategic goals/objectives and the grand designs for achieving them. It is not enough for a board of directors to be retained simply to rubber-stamp top management's preconceived objectives and strategies. This is an ineffective way to make decisions that will be affecting the corporation in a significant way for years to come, and is an underutilization of the talents of the directors, particularly those who come from outside.

Based on our research, we have concluded that the chief responsibility of the board is to formulate specific answers to two key questions:

- Where does the company intend to proceed in the next (more or less) five years?
- How are these objectives and goals (mission) to be achieved?

What is more, the board should be thoroughly familiarized with—and should have the authority to approve—at least the basics of the strategic plans of the company's primary operating units (that is, sectors, divisions, SBUs, or whatever the appropriate organizational designation).

The ideal composition of a board of directors is in itself a critical strategic decision that the CEO makes or at least influences greatly. In addition to an ample number of outside members to promote "hybrid vigor" and freshness of viewpoint, the perceptive CEO wants knowledgeable and highly capable board members who seem able to contribute substantially to the development of corporate strategy. In our experience, we have found that an effective CEO seeks to elect board members whom he or she is comfortable with and trusts, yet vigorously resists installing an "old boy" rubber-stamp board. The confident CEO knows the value of a well-meant "devil's advocacy" approach in board deliberations. Such a climate facilitates a productive type of debate whereby strategic assumptions and plans are put to the test of challenge and sometimes argumentation. In the process, sounder corporate plans surely result. So, as in other staffing matters, the keen CEO wants to elect a board of directors who are bright, participatory, and constructively independent thinkers.

To recap, we believe that the choice of board members is in itself a strategic decision of the highest order. Top-flight corporate performers who have sustained their success year after year historically have recruited and maintained first-rate strategic thinkers for their boards. And, of course, the CEO is the driving force behind the selection process.

STRATEGIC PLANNING HELP FOR SMALLER COMPANIES

As desirable as it may be for large, multidivisional companies to install a full-time planning organization, the hard monetary realities often preclude the small or medium-sized corporation from doing so. It might not be financially feasible, for example, to have specialized staff performing environmental scanning and assessment regarding a variety of externalities—for example, the economic situation, technological advances, demographics, and competitor analysis. Even if money were not a constraint, a company might well be too small to need a full-time strategic planning function and staff.

Similarly, hiring consultants to perform the needed groundwork and tasks connected with strategic planning may also not be the best choice. It could cost too much. What's more, the consultants, unless retained, will not be around when the plans are implemented. Thus, strategic mid-course corrections would be left solely to management.

A pragmatic way around these problems is through the use of what Harold Fox has labeled *quasi-boards of directors*.[3] A quasi-board is a group that performs much like a full-fledged board of directors, with the distinction that the quasi-board is advisory and lacks official power. Fox suggests that membership for a quasi-board can come from a number of places, including:

- Staff work in a giant corporation
- Top-level responsibility in a bank or a small, noncompeting concern
- Technical knowledge (e.g., chemical engineering) of the company's business

---

[3]Harold W. Fox, "Quasi-Boards: Useful Small Business Confidants," *Harvard Business Review*, January–February 1982, pp. 158–165.

- Consulting experience or professorial status in business administration
- Contacts with regulators, vendors, or large buyers
- Professional specialty such as practicing attorney or practicing psychologist
- Broadly diversified business experience with a record of success[4]

One of us serves on a printing company's quasi-board, which meets quarterly. The major benefits that accrue to this company and to other effective users of such advisory groups are compelling. Notably, a quasi-board can, in our observation:

- Provide diverse expertise that the company cannot afford to hire on either a full-time basis or from consultants.
- Provide the CEO with access to knowledgeable individuals who do not have the economic and political interests in the company that employees do; thereby, more objective decision making regarding corporate policies and operations is promoted.
- Provide the CEO with fresh and maybe innovative viewpoints about the company and the direction in which it is heading.
- Provide the CEO and other managers with the chance to periodically get away from day-to-day operations and spend time thinking strategically. (Always hold meetings away from the company offices; interruptions are less likely to occur.)
- Provide the CEO with a group of confidants with whom to discuss particularly sensitive company matters.
- Provide the multidisciplinary knowledge and views needed to construct alternative future scenarios and to develop the company's best strategies for meeting the contingencies projected. By keeping current in their areas of expertise, board members are, in effect, engaged in a continuous process of environmental scanning; thus they can supply a font of relevant specialized and general information about such exter-

---

[4]Ibid., p. 162.

nalities as economic developments, legal and regulatory trends, and technological progress.

Quasi-boards can be useful as well to those small divisions and subsidiaries of major corporations that cannot justify the maintenance of a full-time strategic planning function. Additionally, we are acquainted with a *Fortune* 500 company that is considering the formation of an advisory group—at corporate headquarters and composed of a few corporate executives and a few outsiders—for the purpose of identifying and evaluating growth opportunities in general and acquisition candidates in particular.

STRATEGIC PLANNING IN ACTION

3

Strategic planning is too vital to the future of any organization for higher management to delegate it largely to staff planners. The latter can provide groundwork, data, and analyses, as well as make valuable recommendations, but it is not the job of staff planners to make strategic decisions. So only through active involvement can top-line management (corporate or division) be aware of and evaluate critically the strategic options available to the organization. In particular, top management needs to make sure that the corporation as a whole and each division (or other such organizational subdivision) have appropriate and tightly focused business definitions encompassing customers, needs, technologies, and geographic scope.

The planning process — which, in farsighted companies, is a never-ending cyclical function — is inestimably more important than the actual planning documents that are produced. Through a dialectic process of debate and argumentation, planning can reveal strengths and weaknesses regarding proposed corporate strategies and can move line management toward consensus.

A strategic plan — at any organizational level — need not and indeed should not be any more complex than is absolutely necessary. Needlessly complex plans serve only to obfuscate, to make managers unsure of selected objectives/goals and strategies, and to turn executives off on planning per se. A process does not have to be complicated and jargon-filled to be effective; quite the contrary.

There is no such thing as the "right" strategic planning horizon for all organizations. In a mature industry, long-term might be five to ten years, whereas in an incipient high-technology market, long-term may very well be one to two years. Planning horizons also vary across organizational levels, with the planning spectrum lengthening as one moves up in a company from the functional areas to divisions to corporate headquarters. Whatever the horizon, management needs to ensure tight linkage between the strategic plan and the annual operating plan. In practice, year 1 of the strategic plan is the same as the annual operating plan. This close correspondence is necessary — and must be budgeted for in a highly exact way — if intended strategies are to be well executed.

The word "process" means "something going on." It conjures up an image of action. The term "dynamic process" aptly describes what goes on in *effective* strategic planning.

As one master planner, Dwight D. Eisenhower, purportedly remarked, "Plans are nothing, planning is everything." While the General obviously overstated to make the point more striking, his intent and meaning are clear. Once prepared, a *plan* is static—written today with only conjecture about what many tomorrows hold in store. For this reason, a plan is bound to some extent to be wrong. Therefore, a plan is never truly complete, and the all-important revisional process (strategic *planning*) must be ongoing. Strategic planning as a dynamic process is "everything" because it requires top management to be on top of the actual and projected opportunities and threats facing the organization. The process forces management to continually evaluate and choose among the range of strategic options available, in order to meet the future in an opportunistic and advantageous manner.

In all organizations that use strategic planning effectively, the process is never-ending. Most typically, a strategic plan in business is written to encompass a five-year period. However, the plan is "rolled over" or revised every year. A five-year planning period is only a guide at best.

As discussed in Chapter 2, a planning horizon that is considered to be long-range in one industry may well not be in another. In volatile infant industries and markets, strategic planning might be feasible for, say, three years hence. By contrast, in very mature industries or product markets, the planning period might be extended to cover eight, nine, ten, or more years.

A caution: Oftentimes, too much attention is devoted to the long-run boundary of the strategic plan and not enough to the short-term. It is our observation and experience that inadequate *linkage* between the strategic plan and the annual operating budget is frequently where plan implementation falls short. A *workable* strategic plan must provide for close linkage with the annual operating budget. Hazy correspondence between year 1 of the strategic plan and the forecasted annual operating budget for the same year indicates inadequate coordination between the planning staff and the financial and accounting budget personnel. It also indicates trouble ahead.

In year 1 of the strategic plan, detailed budgeting of the strategic moves delineated in the plan is imperative. Otherwise, implementation of the strategic maneuvers—as planned with regard to timing—may very well be impractical. Financial commitments to planned-for projects take time to firm up. In any size business, the process of raising debt or equity dollars itself necessitates careful planning if the money is to be raised at relatively propitious times. Even internal reallocations of existing resources take considerable time. Especially in larger businesses, there is also normally a considerable bureaucracy to contend with in obtaining approvals for a major expenditure. In sum, adequate lead time is essential.

A STRATEGIC PLANNING PROCESS

Far too often, strategic planning is made needlessly complex. When this occurs, management soon abandons strategic planning (de facto if not de jure) on the ground that it is ineffectual in the firm's "kind of business." The KIS principle (Keep It Simple) could not be more germane than when applied to strategic planning. The fact is, irrespective of a firm's size—be it a *Fortune* 500 company or a small business—there is a virtuously simple, clear-cut, and universally applicable step-by-step process that can be followed. And this simple process is useful regardless of whether the plan is a corporate, divisional, or functional one. This step-by-step process needs to be the readily discernible skeleton upon which the verbiage and illustrations in the planning document are built. If this is not the case, beware—the plan lacks clarity or omits key considerations, or both. A "good" strategic plan should basically follow the process depicted in Figure 4. Here are the steps in the recommended planning sequence.

Undertake Situation Analysis and Momentum Assessment

This phase is analogous to a medical examination of a patient by a physician, only in this case the patient is the business under scrutiny and the doctor's role falls to top management and its planning staff. Initially, the business is *diagnosed* as to its present overall well-being: where the company is today in terms of return on investment, cash flow, market share, growth, liquidity, and so forth. Diagnosis also entails a solid, comprehensive review of internal company capabilities—human resources, plant and equipment, specific competencies—and of the external environment in which the firm does business, with an eye toward identifying existing opportunities and threats. External concerns can derive from any number of factors, notably those identified in Chapter 1—competitor strategies and tactics, cultural and social patterns, demographic trends, ecological considerations, the economic situation, the legal and regulatory climate, the political situation, and technological progress.

Once the company's general vitality has been adjudged, a *prognosis* is in order. Where is the firm's momentum taking it,

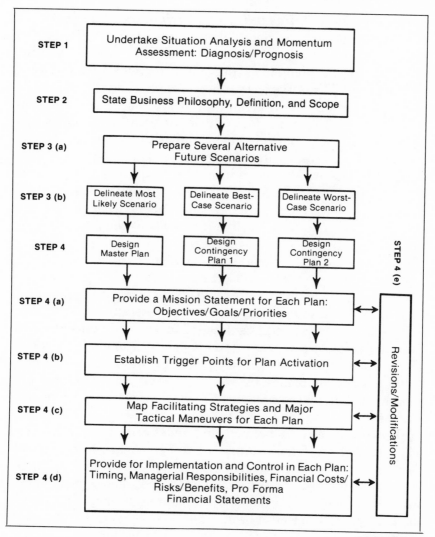

FIGURE 4
A Strategic Planning Process

assuming more of the status quo—that is, assuming no significant internal and external changes? What will the company's
financial statements look like three to five years from now if its
recent performance is merely extrapolated into the future?

51

State Business Philosophy, Definition, and Scope

Depending on what is revealed by the situation analysis and momentum assessment, top management may reaffirm, modify, or abandon the company's prevailing definition, philosophy, and/or scope. The question that needs to be asked is whether the firm's current definition is appropriate to the future. The proverbial buggy-whip manufacturer of America in the 1900s certainly should have concluded not. Similarly, what about the cigarette manufacturers of today? Or the oil companies with their depletable resources? Or traditional colleges and universities? All organizations in decaying markets or industries are candidates for business redefinition. Survival demands as much.

How much detail management devotes to the business definition stage in the planning process, and how frequently the stage is gone through, should hinge largely on the stability of the relevant industry or market. Certainly, firms in new and volatile markets require annual strategic assessment regarding business definition. Firms in more stable markets generally would need to devote less frequent and less detailed attention to business definition. Every third year is often enough for companies in *slow-growth* markets. However, as with fledgling firms in volatile markets, mature companies in *no-growth* and *decaying* markets need to reevaluate their business definitions often and in depth. Disintegration can take place quickly.

Businesses can be defined and redefined in several major ways. A firm could look to new customer groups, to additional customer needs, to new technologies, or to a combination of these. A company, for instance, could broaden its geographic scope (new customer groups) by expanding to more regions of the United States or even to international markets.

The really essential point pertaining to business philosophy and definition is: in order to achieve a complete and instructive definition, both products and markets must be considered. Neither suffices by itself. What is more, it may additionally be necessary to include technology in the definition. For instance, a president of a printing company always considered his business to be printing. After much thought he realized the inadequacy and vagueness of his definition. Now he defines his business to be certain kinds of printing (the products or services), for identified segments of end users (the markets), using various printing processes (the technologies). In this redefinition process, he has sharpened his strategic focus, particularly regarding opportunities and threats facing what he formerly thought of as his "printing" business.

Indeed, it is difficult to overstate the importance of business definitions in strategic management. Without a lucid definition of an organization's purpose, top management cannot consistently formulate effective strategies for the future.

Too frequently, executives say vaguely that their business is "a consumer-products company" or sometimes simply "any endeavor that makes a profit." Try this experiment on two or three executives you know: ask them for a concise, one-paragraph business definition of the company they work for. Be prepared for hesitancy and stumbling ("we uh, uh, . . .") or for glib answers that are strategically all but useless ("we are a broad-based consumer-products company") or for definitions that are myopically product-oriented ("we are into chemical manufacturing").

Certainly, upper-echelon management needs to have a well-thought-out definition that is broad enough to be strategic yet narrow enough to be useful. It might take months to write a one-paragraph definition. As Woodrow Wilson observed about speeches, it takes far more time to write a short one than a long one. Moreover, the definition agreed upon needs to be well known to all managers within the company, regardless of their levels in the organization. Given these difficulties, it is not wholly surprising that the vast majority of corporate executives cannot spontaneously provide a strategically focused business definition of their respective companies.

A good business definition should be committed to writing and, as already indicated, should identify the following:

1. What customers (market segments) the company intends to compete for
2. Which customer needs and desires the company intends to fulfill
3. What technologies the company intends to use to fulfill these needs and wants
4. What is the intended geographic scope of the company's efforts—regional, national, or international

A skeptic might say: "You are asking too much. We are a conglomerate involved in so many product lines that our company defies such a specific definition." Our answer would be that, if the skeptic is correct, the company has great cause for concern. It has no unifying theme, and consequently no strategic beacon to guide and sustain it.

Prepare Several Alternative Future Scenarios

A CEO remarked that he and his organization cannot engage in strategic planning because the future is too uncertain. Unfortunately for his organization, he confuses forecasting with planning. Forecasting is indeed uncertain in that it attempts to predict what the future will be like. Planning is necessary for just this reason—because forecasts are subject to considerable error.

The only safe bet in planning is that there is a future. It may be disastrous, it may be run-of-the-mill, it may be glorious, but it will occur. Because predicting what is to come is so inexact, the prudent planner conjectures about several plausible futures and prepares contingency plans for each. As discussed in Chapter 1, we suggest that three alternative future scenarios be used—an optimistic scenario (if things really go well), a pessimistic scenario (if things really go badly), and a most likely scenario. We also suggest that these be assigned probabilities of occurrence. Such estimates about the future can be based on various well-researched assumptions about competitor strategies, cultural and social patterns, demographic trends, ecological considerations, the economic situation, the legal and regulatory climate, the political situation, and technological prospects and events. Each factor will have a different relative emphasis, depending on the particular company and industry. The regulatory climate might be of great import to a public utility, yet be of little consequence to a small business in a competitive industry. Recessions tend to have far more impact on heavy manufacturing companies than they do on high-technology businesses.

In nondiversified companies, such as General Motors, alternative scenarios could be conceived at the corporate level and provided to divisions engaged in identical or very similar businesses. By contrast, in diversified companies, the task of coming up with the scenarios is likely to be best performed at the divisional level. In the first place, a huge corporate staff would be required to prepare scenarios for numerous and diversified divisions in a large conglomerate. More compelling, however, is the fact that divisional personnel are likely to be far more familiar with the "futures" they may face than are the executives at corporate headquarters.

Design Master and Contingency Plans

Once committed to writing, the alternative future scenarios become the contexts for constructing the actual long-range plans. Note that the word *plans* is plural. Under this system, there is not *one* strategic plan, but rather a number of strategic plans—one corresponding to each scenario. This characteristic, more than any other, truly distinguishes strategic planning from forecasting. In the latter, the company gets ready for a future; in strategic planning, it prepares for *futures*.

We do not mean to imply that a company using scenarios lacks a master plan. It certainly has one—namely, the plan corresponding to the most likely scenario. But in addition to this master plan, the firm develops contingency plans for best-case, worst-case, and any other plausible scenarios it may wish to consider.

An executive with whom we talked believes that contingency planning is too often given only token attention. In his view, good contingency plans are usually more challenging and time-consuming to prepare than the master plan because executives are less familiar with the unusual issues raised by pessimistic and optimistic alternative scenarios. It is the worst-case and best-case scenarios that require the most creative long-range thinking.

The primary advantage to preparing a master plan and contingency plans is that the process enables management to rehearse possible strategic actions and reactions to potential future events. In this manner, the firm becomes more poised to be proactive. The forethought that goes into these kinds of "what if" rehearsals can be invaluable later when events inevitably occur that force the company away from its master plan.

Provide a Mission Statement for Each Plan

Mission is used here in the military sense—which is where it originated. A mission is the set of objectives and goals that the organization wants to achieve within the specified time period covered by the plan. Moreover, the mission statement sets down management's *priorities*—that is, which objectives and goals should be attained before others are pursued. Obviously, priorities imply much about management's preferences and desires regarding how it intends resources to be allocated. For example, when General Electric's marketing-oriented CEO, John F. Welch, Jr., assumed the leadership mantle from his more finance-oriented predecessor, Reginald H. Jones, Welch reportedly set down the policy objective that GE be first or second in market share in every market it competes in. Presumably, this mission statement implies that GE would withdraw from those markets where reaching the number 1 or 2 position is seen as unfeasible and therefore not worth GE's resources and efforts.

Some managers and planners make no distinction between objectives and goals—a practice supported by dictionary definitions of the words. We prefer to do otherwise. An *objective* should be a written statement about where the company wants to go, whereas a *goal* should quantify the written statement of objective; in other words, a goal should provide an operational measure. For example:

Objective: To increase sales of new wood lathes to U.S. furniture manufacturers in the upcoming fiscal year.

Corresponding goal: To increase sales of our wood lathes to U.S. furniture manufacturers, Standard Industrial Code 2511, by 17 percent in the upcoming fiscal year.

Our preference for quantifying objectives via quantitative goals derives from our experience that, where quantification is absent, the objectives turn out to be too nebulous to provide strategic direction or to enable anyone to later determine whether they have in fact been attained.

Objectives and goals need to be tailored to the particular scenario under consideration. Some objectives and goals, of course, are scenario-neutral; that is, they are the same across scenarios. For example, the objective of "divesting [dog] Division XYZ in 19——" may be applicable regardless of which scenario eventuates. However, most objectives and goals are affected by assumptions made about the future and should reflect such.

One CEO follows the old "bow and arrow" idea about objective/goal setting. In his mind, if one wishes to shoot an arrow at a distant target, one purposely aims high. Then the arrow's natural descent will propel it downward toward the target. Consequently, his view is that business objectives and goals should be optimistic, so that if they are not reached, an adequate performance will still result. In principle, we concur. Yet we quickly add the proviso that, while objectives and goals regarding performance should be optimistic, they need also to be realistically attainable under the scenario to which they pertain. If not, the objective-setting step becomes but an exercise in futility and counterproductive to management morale. A firm, for instance, that sets goals for itself that are far above industry norms for ROI, net profits/sales, and similar performance measures may very well be deluding itself. Whether it is or not is a question that must be asked for the sake of keeping the company attuned to realistically obtainable missions.

Establish Trigger Points for Plan Activation

Perhaps the question most asked by managers not used to dealing with contingency plans in addition to a master plan is this: "How will I know whether to go by the objectives/goals and strategies/tactics in the master plan or to turn to one of the contingency plans?"

In practice, of course, none of the plans will be followed precisely. In most cases, the future events that result will be some blend of the alternative scenarios outlined. Consequently, a combination of the master and contingency plan aims and actions will evolve and be the course actually pursued by the company.

Even so, in planning it is best to formalize *trigger points* to alert management that it is off the course blueprinted in the master plan, and that the company needs to consider switching to a contingency course of action.

Employing trigger points in planning is basically a management-by-exception approach. Look at these two hypothetical trigger points:

- If sales revenues decline in our SBU in two successive quarters during 1986, consider switching to the strategic course delineated in the worst-case contingency plan.

- If the U.S. Consumer Price Index reaches double-digits, reevaluate all capital expenditure plans above $100,000.

So, if management's master plan had assumed continual sales revenue increases and single-digit inflation, the occurrence of either of these contingencies would represent an exception in need of immediate attention. Moreover, these kinds of preestablished (i.e., in the original planning phase) exceptions provide early warning signals (trigger points) that the master plan may well no longer be appropriate in regard to objectives and strategies. In essence, trigger points are nothing more than control mechanisms.

Trigger points are attempts to quantify decisions as part of a management-by-exception approach to strategic planning; however, they are no substitute for qualitative executive judgments. As the former CEO of Westinghouse, Robert E. Kirby, has said, the skill required of the chief executive officer is sensing when to jump from one strategic plan to another as changes in the business scenario dictate. Kirby remarked that a prudent, well-managed company will have multiple strategic plans, and it is up to the CEO to know which one to pursue as environmental conditions evolve. Again, we see that visionary CEOs are cognizant of the important differences between forecasting the future and planning for alternative futures.

Map Facilitating Strategies and Major Tactical Maneuvers

A strategy is a grand or broad design for achieving objectives and goals. A tactic is more specific and more operational in nature. For example:

Strategy: Undertake a major media campaign to increase awareness of our Brand X so that we can attain the objective/ goal of a 15 percent sales increase during each of the next two years.

Tactic(s): Retain the Smith Advertising Agency, spend $1 million on television promotion, hire the Jones PR firm, etc.

In practice, it is sometimes difficult to distinguish between strategies and major tactical maneuvers. However, semantic arguments over whether a move is strategic or tactical are not very useful. The crux of the matter is whether a strategic plan provides a lucid map of how the organization intends to achieve the objectives and goals that have been set. Strategies should be sweeping enough to give a lasting sense of direction for the company over the time frame of the plan, yet specific enough to supply real operational guidance. To say, for example, that the company wants to grow by 10 percent during the upcoming five years (the objective/goal) via diversification (a strategy) is not specific enough by itself. How the company wants to diversify should be addressed; will diversification be achieved through starting a new business from scratch or by acquisition? What kinds of industries is management contemplating entering and, if growth is to be achieved through acquisition, what companies in these targeted industries might be acquired?

During this strategy-mapping phase, to foster understanding by everyone involved in designing *and* implementing the plan, management must be quite specific in identifying the modes of growth that have been selected to reach the stated objectives and goals. As discussed in Chapter 1, corporate growth must necessarily come from one or more of these modes: market penetration, market or product development, concentric or conglomerate diversification, and vertical or horizontal integration.

Provide for Implementation and Control

The aim in this step of strategic planning is threefold: (1) to test the plan for feasibility and wisdom from a cost/risk/benefit standpoint; (2) to approximate the desired timing of the proposed strategic moves; and (3) to assign managerial purview, so that there is no question as to who—what executive officer(s)— is responsible for shepherding through specific elements of the plan.

Cost/risk/benefit analyses of strategies that have been developed usually require pro forma financial statements and financial ratio evaluations. This procedure enables management to assess whether the strategies are feasible and advisable. What ramifications, for instance, will a contemplated new product venture have on the firm's competitive position, as well as its liquidity position and near-term profitability? Responding to tentative answers to questions like these, the planning group will almost certainly have to retreat and revise parts of the plan completed already—that is, objectives/goals and facilitating contingency strategies. After financial evaluation, a goal might now be thought to be unattainable or not worth the risk of the strategy needed to achieve it. Thus, strategic planning is both a sequential, step-by-step process *and* an iterative process.

Implementation and control precautions also dictate that close attention be devoted to when management wants its designated strategies carried out and by whom. Many military experts have concluded that Robert E. Lee's history-shaping defeat at Gettysburg was due far more to faulty implementation by his generals, particularly regarding timing, than to a faulty strategic battle plan. Execution of strategies at the planned-on time is crucial. Accordingly, strategic plans need to be quite clear in establishing executive responsibilities by task and time horizons. Otherwise, what everyone is responsible for, no one is responsible for. In capsule, business strategies need designated executive patrons to shepherd and monitor their progress and to push them through to achievement on time.

A Caveat

We strongly recommend that companies which are neophytes in strategic planning *do not* attempt to adopt the full-blown use of master and contingency planning too quickly. At first, the formulation and implementation complexities of multiple scenarios and plans can be confusing. As a consequence, management may sour on the whole idea and write it off as being unworkable. A *Fortune* 500 energy-based company abandoned multiple scenario planning for just this reason. The problem was attributable to too much haste in adopting the method and a resulting misunderstanding, particularly among middle-level managers, of strategic planning within the framework of alternative scenarios.

In the early years of the installation of a corporate-wide strategic planning system incorporating the use of multiple scenarios, management is well advised to keep the system elementary. Initially, best-case and worst-case scenario assumptions can be introduced and discussed in terms of what they might mean to the objectives and strategies in the master plan. No effort is made at this point to design elaborate contingency plans. Then, over time, contingency planning can gradually become more formalized and more detailed as the company's managers gain experience with and confidence in alternative scenarios and trigger points.

Also, when strategic decisions are made, they are made with assumptions in mind. These assumptions should be documented and periodically referred to in order to see if they are still valid.

TOP-DOWN OR BOTTOM-UP PLANNING?

Primarily, planning should be the task of the managers who will actually implement the resulting plans. Long experience confirms that executives are more receptive to implementing plans that they have had a large hand in formulating—which argues for decentralization or bottom-up planning. Thus, divisional plans are best delegated mostly to top divisional managers, and, similarly, functional plans in marketing, finance, or production are best left to the appropriate functional executives. Yet for anyone to urge decentralization without a healthy dose of qualification is decidedly poor advice. Particularly, the role of top corporate management needs to be carefully defined and understood. And this role should vary depending on whether planning is taking place at the corporate, divisional, or functional organizational level.

At the corporate level, top management needs to be integrally involved in the *entire* strategic planning process. Plans left mostly to a corporate planning staff cannot possibly adequately reflect top management's thinking on important strategic issues. It is at corporate that the direction of the company is determined for years to come. And determining where the corporation should go (objectives/goals) and how it should get there (strategies) is one of the very, very fundamental tasks of top management. In addition, top corporate management needs to approve the business definitions and missions of its SBUs. Even more basic is the task of evolving the company's overall business definition, philosophy, and scope.

While strategic planning at the divisional level is best handled by divisions management, corporate management nonetheless has an important part to play. Corporate management needs to work closely with each division in formulating the division's

61

mission statement—that is, in determining its objectives, goals, and priorities. For instance, if corporate management has decided to treat a division as a net provider of cash to the corporation (a "cash cow"), this decision impinges greatly on the facilitating strategies that are appropriate for divisional management to pursue. Thus, a division's role within the overall corporation needs to be decided in collaboration by corporate and divisional management and then spelled out clearly. The fact is, all of a company's divisions will want to be treated as "stars" when resource allocations are made by corporate top management. Since this is not possible, or even wise, corporate management must make hard and reasoned choices concerning divisional missions. It is in this respect, especially, that "top-down," centralized planning is essential. Only top corporate management is in a position to view all the divisions with respect to one another and make commensurate judgments about how resources should be allocated among them in order to promote overall corporate profitability.

Likewise, within divisions, a decentralized planning system is recommended. Functional planning in marketing, finance, production, and so on is best left to functional executives. However, again, top divisional management has a vital collaborative role to fulfill in negotiating and approving missions for products, markets, and perhaps technologies.

So strategic planning is ideally both top-down and bottom-up. This two-way flow results from a cyclical approach to planning. In the initial cycle, SBU managers propose alternative business definitions and missions and negotiate with top management concerning these important matters. For example, a divisional general manager might deal with top corporate management concerning the business definition and mission of his or her division. Once a business definition and mission are settled upon for each SBU, then in the second cycle, it is left largely or entirely to SBU management to come up with facilitating strategies. Ultimately, in cycle 3, the first year of the strategic plan is made operational through specific budgeting for the intended strategies. This last cycle is especially critical because it is here that linkage between the long run (e.g., years 2 through 5 of the plan) and the short run (year 1 of the plan) is achieved. The chances for effective implementation improve accordingly.

ANALYTICAL AIDS TO STRATEGIC PLANNING

4

The purpose of the various analytical aids to strategic planning is just what the word aids *denotes: to assist management in making better strategic planning decisions but not actually to* make *the decisions for management. Analytical aids help management cut through complex relationships and visualize the likely long-term effects of possible strategic maneuvers.*

There are at least four published techniques of portfolio analysis available for analyzing a company's mix of businesses and products/services. Which technique is best is arguable. Moreover, debates over this are often counterproductive; attention is diverted from weightier matters. Planners need to focus mainly on questions of strategic missions and strategies. They should not get bogged down in technical questions of methodology. This is not to say that analytical methods are unimportant, only that the overriding issue for management to address is how the organization intends to compete and prosper in the years ahead.

Importantly, in multidivisional companies, portfolio

analysis needs to be a multilevel operation. If only one analysis is done, and at too high a level, a product that is a star performer in a poor-performance division of an SBU may be obscured from top management's view.

A portfolio of businesses or products is not something that can be designed and then left alone until it is time to plan again. A portfolio has to be managed to be effective, with particular attention given to the way corporate headquarters treats its SBUs with respect to degree of autonomy, shared line of responsibility, and incentive compensation.

Of all the major portfolio models, the General Electric version is the one most applicable irrespective of the size of the business entity. It can be used by a Fortune *500 company or by a medium-sized or small firm. The Boston Consulting Group model pertains to those large companies in which market share is an important consideration.*

PIMS is the most quantitative of the analytical aids. Because PIMS is based on the mathematical technique of multiple regression, it is useful in evaluating specific "what if" kinds of questions pertaining to corporate strategies and tactics.

Analytical aids to strategic planning should not be viewed as mutually exclusive. That is, the use of one does not preclude the use of another. In fact, the company that employs several of the techniques is prudent; it provides itself with different and maybe strategically revealing perspectives of the same problems or issues. For example, in a Fortune *500–sized company, it is perfectly compatible for management to look at its businesses and products via both the GE and BCG portfolio models. And it should be remembered that some analytical aids take considerable time to integrate into the strategic planning process. As many as five years may go by before a company becomes a sophisticated user of portfolio analysis, with top management explicitly negotiating strategic missions with its SBU managers.*

Because of the enormous number of external and internal realities and contingencies to consider, strategic planning can easily present planners with a severe case of information overload. How to cut through and discard the irrelevant to get at what information is "really" important is a question that must be addressed time and again. Otherwise, the entire strategic planning process will stall or focus on the wrong issues—and often trivial ones at that.

For purposes of sorting through, simplifying, and making sense of the complexities associated with strategic planning, several analytical tools or approaches are available. Two popular techniques of note are those discussed here—portfolio planning and PIMS (Profit Impact of Marketing Strategy). A study by Philippe Haspeslagh has confirmed the rapid acceptance of portfolio theory by major companies.[1] And PIMS also has its users in leading corporations—for example, General Electric, where it originated, and numerous others.

We feel that portfolio analysis, PIMS, and kindred strategic planning techniques are helpful as long as their *proper* role is recognized. They are merely aids to strategic decision making— not strategic decision makers. Oftentimes, advocates of a particular analytical or quantitative method confuse ends and means. One should look for a technique to solve the problem at hand, not look for a problem on which to apply the technique. Any problem-solving tool is properly a servant of the decision maker, not the master.

Concern for the pros and cons of various analytical methods is certainly appropriate. However, when carried too far—that is, made the primary concern in strategic planning—a debate over methods becomes counterproductive. Argumentation gone overboard focuses management's attention on the wrong place, which is anywhere away from the strategic issues facing the business. In reporting his study, Haspeslagh got at the same point:

> . . . it is not surprising that [portfolio planning theory] has stirred up much debate. Most of it has been ill focused, however, for proponents and critics alike are more interested in a dialogue about analytic techniques than in solving the practical problems inherent in implementation. So they argue about which "portfolio grid" technology a company should choose between . . . that discussion is

---

[1] Philippe Haspeslagh, "Portfolio Planning: Uses and Limits," *Harvard Business Review*, January–February 1982, pp. 58–73.

sterile; the question of which grid to use and where to place a business on it is least important. The real issue is how a company can best define an SBU [strategic business unit] and assign a strategic mission to it. In short, what is a company to do with each of its businesses?[2]

PORTFOLIO ANALYSIS

This idea has been around for a long time. It originally was developed as a method for personal and institutional investing in securities. The basic concept is to hold a "balanced" portfolio of investments so as to reduce risk and promote a steady and even stream of earnings in prosperous, average, and down economic times. Balance can be sought by diversifying investments: (1) across industries that are not subject to economic vagaries at precisely the same time in business cycles, (2) across security types (e.g., capital-appreciating stocks versus fixed-income bonds), and (3) across companies ranging from mature (General Motors, for example) to high-growth (a high-technology, entrepreneurial endeavor).

The same general thinking and approach have been widely adapted to the strategic planning and management tasks within companies. In a multidivisional company, the aim at the corporate level is to hold a balanced portfolio of mature, high-growth, and high-potential divisions, so as to ensure present earnings and future growth and profits. Within the divisions themselves, the goal is to have a balanced portfolio of (a) mature, (b) high-growth, and (c) incipient, but high-potential, products. However, in multidivisional companies, portfolio analysis should be a multilevel operation. In relatively small companies without divisions, the sole level of analysis is products or product lines. If it is not, the wrong conclusions can easily be drawn, as the data are too aggregated. For instance, if portfolio analysis is used only at the corporate level, it is likely that some ostensible "poor performance" divisions or SBUs will be dismissed as such by top man-

---

[2]Ibid., p. 61.

agement, even though the units may have "star" product/service performers that go undetected in the very broad corporate analysis. As a first pass, corporate portfolio analysis and the "big picture" it provides are fine, as long as the analysis is repeated in more revealing detail for divisions of SBUs and their offerings.

Two portfolio models for evaluating and managing both divisional lines of business (or SBUs) and products have been prominently publicized. They are the models associated with the General Electric Company and the Boston Consulting Group. Two other similar approaches—the Arthur D. Little and Shell International Portfolio Models—have also received attention. To avoid redundancy we will discuss the first two better-known models.[3]

The General Electric Model

Here is the essence of the GE Portfolio Model, as explained verbatim in *Business Week:*

> General Electric Co. thinks it has found at least a partial solution to an age-old corporate planning problem: how to put a value on those critical elements in planning it is impossible to attach a number to. In a decision on whether a product will live or die, for example, the value of a patent or the impact of social change cannot be quantified. By using its Strategic Business Grid, or "stoplight strategy," GE can at least evaluate such factors with something more than just a gut reaction.
>
> "It's the best way we've found to sort disparate businesses," says GE planner Reuben Gutoff. "You eventually have to make a subjective decision, but you put into it all the hard information you can. It's one way to compare apples and oranges."
>
> GE, with 43 distinct businesses, has a lot of apples and oranges. In every annual planning review, each individual business is rated not only on numerical projections of sales, profit, and return on investment, but also on such hard-to-quantify factors as volatility of market share, technology needs, employee loyalty in the indus-

---

[3]For a technical discussion of all four portfolio models, see Yoram Wind and Vijay Mahajan, "Designing Product and Business Portfolios," *Harvard Business Review*, January–February 1981, pp. 155–165.

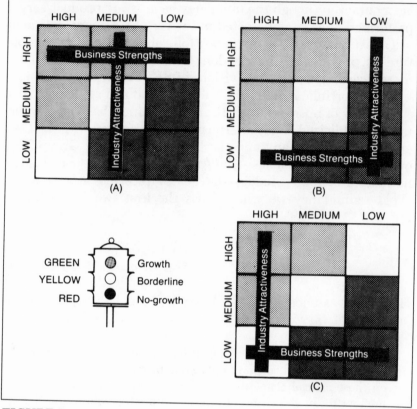

FIGURE 5
GE's Stoplight Strategy

try, competitive stance, and social need. The result is a high, medium, or low rating on both attractiveness of an industry and GE's strengths in the field.

How it works. If industry attractiveness is seen as medium and GE's strengths as high (Chart A), an "invest and grow"—or green light—decision would result, because the evaluation bars cross in a green square. Both industry attractiveness and business strength are low in Chart B, indicating a red light strategy, or a business which will continue to generate earnings but no longer warrants much additional investment by GE. Chart C represents a business with high industry attractiveness but low GE strength—a "yellow" business that might go either way.

A green business is expected to grow. A red operation's strategy, on the other hand, may involve consolidation of plants, limited technology infusion, reduced investment, and strong cash flow. A yellow business could be borderline, or the business—say, electronic components—could be diverse enough to have both red and green units.

"We don't give definitive weights to the non-numerical factors," says Gutoff, "but they do have weights. At the end of our discussion there is a good consensus on what's green, red, or yellow." The result, he says, is "semiquantitative." After three or four critiques at various levels, the final grids—and decisions—are made by the corporate policy committee—the chairman, three vice-chairmen, five senior vice-presidents, and the vice-president for finance.

The process is not just window dressing. It may prevent costly mistakes. "Interestingly," says one GE planner, "the financial projections are often best on businesses that turn up worst [in the red] on the grid."[4]

Considerations that might be weighed in determining industry attractiveness and business strengths are numerous. According to General Electric, key considerations could include the following:

Industry Attractiveness

- Size
- Market growth
- Pricing
- Market diversity
- Competitive structure change
- Industry profitability
- Inflation vulnerability
- Technical role
- Social
- Environment
- Legal
- Human

Business Strengths

- Size
- Growth
- Share
- Position
- Margins
- Technology position
- Strengths/weaknesses
- Image
- Pollution
- People

---

[4]Reprinted from the April 28, 1975, issue of *Business Week* by special permission © 1975 by McGraw-Hill, Inc., New York, NY 10020. All rights reserved.

The relative importance of each of these will vary from industry to industry and quite possibly from market to market within industries. For example, technology may be essential for success in one industry and unimportant in another. Likewise, market share may or may not be particularly important to profitability. Management experience and staff research must be used to identify and weight the factors that comprise industry attractiveness and business strengths. This very process is in and of itself valuable because it forces management to ponder the strategic considerations that underlie success or failure in given industries. The strategic-window idea from Chapter 1 is pertinent in this regard. The General Electric Portfolio Model requires management first to evaluate the degree of industry attractiveness, then to evaluate corporate competencies pertaining to the industry, and finally to evaluate the extent of fit between the two.

At the corporate level in a multidivisional company, portfolio analysis should be done individually for each division. Once this process has been completed, what General Electric calls Multidimensional Portfolio Assessment is feasible. That is, all the divisions are located on the same portfolio planning grid and viewed in relation to one another, as, for instance:

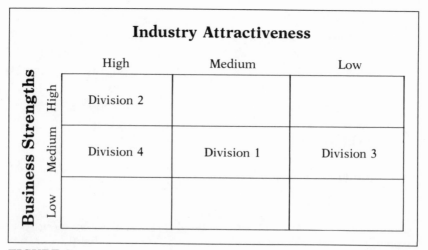

Industry Attractiveness		
High	Medium	Low
Division 2		
Division 4	Division 1	Division 3

Business Strengths — High / Medium / Low

FIGURE 6

In this example, the corporation has two "green-light" divisions (2 and 4), one "yellow-light" division (1), and a single "red-light" division (3). An important aim of Multidimensional Portfolio Assessment is to indicate to management the degree to which the company has balance among its divisions (or products). Does it have mature divisions, with good returns on investment, generating the wherewithal to finance future growth? If so, does it have divisions in high-growth industries to receive the investment? If the company does not have a balance among divisions in mature and growth industries, then it is a matter of considerable gravity. If the portfolio is out of balance with a preponderance of mature-industry divisions, management will need to enter high-growth industries, either from scratch or, more likely, through acquisition of existing companies in growth industries. By contrast, if the portfolio is heavy on high-growth divisions and light on cash-flow-generating mature divisions, management needs to determine how future growth is to be supported financially. In the absence of enough mature divisions to finance the growth from internal cash flow, management must look outward—for example, to a new stock offering. In addition, management may well need to establish priorities and divest the company of some high-potential divisions, while keeping others, in order not to spread management and cash resources too thin.

The use of portfolio analysis by management sets priorities and provides a basis for resource allocation. In fact, implied resource allocation *needs* are central to all portfolio models. "Red-light" or no-growth divisions *need* to be harvested or divested; "yellow-light" divisions *need* to be monitored closely and selectively cultivated (invested in); "green-light" divisions *need* to be invested in and "grown." Indeed, whether top management really understands and believes in portfolio analysis is readily discernible by the way resources are allocated in the organization. An even-handed, across-the-board top management approach to investing in divisions, or to cutting their budgets in economic crunches, is counter to the portfolio concept. Even-handedness of this sort is unsound strategic management and inevitably leads to across-the-board organizational mediocrity—in any type of organization, profit or nonprofit.

Precisely the same portfolio approach can be used within divisions to evaluate products or product lines. Initially, each product is considered individually within the general framework of industry (or market) attractiveness and business strengths. Thereafter, Multidimensional Portfolio Assessment is used to determine portfolio balance among all divisional products, from mature to incipient. Again, this analysis provides the basis for divisional resource allocation among products. It also pinpoints strategic product deficiencies in terms of growth; for example, a division might have all mature-market products in its portfolio. If this were the case, management might be able to rectify the situation via internal R&D efforts or through acquisition of high-potential products. However, in a slow- or no-growth industry, such as cigarettes, this achievement might be extremely difficult if not impossible. Whatever is the case, the portfolio analysis would serve the valuable function of directing management's attention to the problem at hand.

We recommend that portfolio analysis of industry attractive-ness/business strength be a group effort of an executive policy committee, as it is at General Electric. At headquarters, the policy committee would be composed of top corporate management, whereas at the division level it would be made up of upper-echelon divisional management. With staff help in gathering and analyzing data, the policy committee identifies and weights the factors that underlie industry attractiveness and business strengths in various industries (or markets). Once this step is completed, the policy group evaluates the company's divisions (or products) against the decided-upon industry attractiveness/business strength criteria and, accordingly, determines each division's proper place (red, yellow, or green light) on the portfolio grid. The harvest/divest ("red-light") and selectivity/earnings ("yellow-light") businesses are expected to generate the short-term earnings and cash necessary to promote the growth of the invest/grow ("green-light") businesses. The policy group then has a solid foundation for making internal resource-allocation decisions and determining external financing needs, thereby setting a strategic course for the organization.

For reference, at the end of this chapter, we have included a sample GE portfolio analysis of Walt Disney Productions. It offers an incisive look at a company that has been much in the news concerning dissonant stockholders and rumored takeover attempts.

The Boston Consulting Group Model[5]

Actually, the GE Model is more complex than it seems at first glance, since both the industry attractiveness and business strength dimensions of the grid are composites of a number of underlying factors or variables. However, with the BCG model, this is not the case. It consists of only two dimensions—inflation-adjusted market growth rate during a specified period of time (say, during the previous five years) and relative market share:

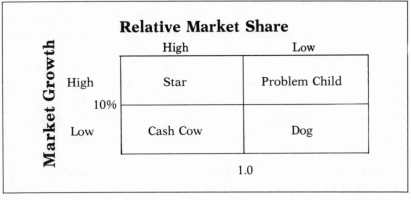

FIGURE 7

The horizontal line between high and low market growth typically depicts a 10 percent annual growth rate in total inflation-adjusted revenues for the market. Anything above 10 percent is considered to be high growth, although some companies prefer to set the cut-line at a more ambitious 15 percent. Our belief is that under no circumstances should an annual market growth rate of less than 10 percent be considered to be high growth. One of us was present at a corporate strategic planning

---

[5]For additional details, see Bruce D. Henderson, *Henderson on Corporate Strategy* (Cambridge, Mass.: Abt Books, 1979).

session where a member of management wanted to call 5 percent high growth and, in so doing, look better. Obviously, such game playing can negate the benefits of strategic planning.

Relative market share refers to a company's share of a market compared to the share held by its largest competitor. Suppose that during the past year Company A had sales of $30 million and the market leader's revenues were $100 million. Company A's relative market share is .30, which places it in either the "dog" or "problem child" cell of the BCG Portfolio Model, depending on the market growth rate. A relative market share of 1.0 would indicate that two or more companies are tied for market-share leadership. By definition, only a single company can have a share greater than 1.0 in any given market. Thus, in the BCG Model, there can be but one "cash cow" or one "star" per market.

As with the GE Portfolio Model, the BCG Model is applicable at both the corporate and divisional levels in a multilevel company. The appropriate focus of analysis at corporate is divisions. Within divisions, the usual focus of analysis is products. (Our discussion continues by using product analysis as an example.)

According to the BCG Model, a "star" is a product holding the leading share of a high-growth market. A "cash cow" has the leading share in a low-growth market. "Problem children" are question marks—products that do not have market-share leadership but do have much potential because they are in high-growth markets. "Dogs" are market-share laggards in low-growth markets.

The BCG Model implies resource-allocation rules regarding cash usage. Cash cows are to be "milked" of excess cash to support and grow stars and to move selected problem-children products toward the star category. Cash cows require only maintenance investment in order to hold their leading market shares. Dogs are to be harvested and/or divested, also for the purpose of supporting stars and problem children with cash. So, in principle, cash cows and dogs are net providers of cash while stars and problem children are often net users of cash.

The BCG Model enables management to view its portfolio of divisions and products for balance. It points out areas for concern—for instance, too many problem children or not enough cash cows to support growth, or too many cash cows and too few stars to ensure future growth. This perspective aids management in making resource-allocation decisions that maximize *overall* corporate or divisional financial performance, rather than the performance of a few divisions or a few products to the detriment of others. The BCG Model provides the "big picture" if all the company's divisions (or all of a division's products) are juxtaposed in the four-cell grid:

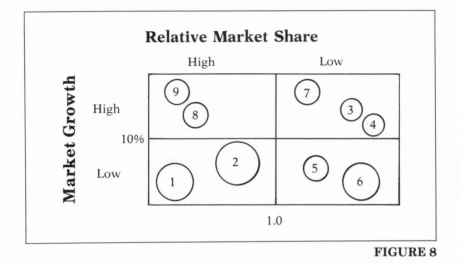

FIGURE 8

In this presentation, products 1 and 2 are cash cows; products 8 and 9 are stars; products 3, 4, and 7 are problem children; and products 5 and 6 are dogs. The relative sizes of the circles (bubbles) in each cell depict the relative revenues generated by each product. The revenues from product 4, for example, are only a fraction of the sales accounted for by product 2.

Several limitations of the BCG Model hinder its usefulness, especially for medium-to-small companies. First, there is the problem of data procurement and interpretation. In some markets, data on market share are not easy to come by. Moreover, what constitutes a market is not always clear. Markets are often defined differently across companies. For instance, a company operating exclusively in the Midwest might have a strong 20 percent market share in the "served" market of Illinois, Indiana, and Ohio, but a meager 1 percent share in the "total" market— the U. S. A. Which share is revelant for purposes of analysis is arguable.

The size of a firm's market share compared to its competitors' is an important issue because market share determines the extent to which a firm receives the cost advantages of both economies of scale and the experience effect. Savings due to size or scale of operations accrue to high-market-share companies— notably, savings attributable to spreading manufacturing and marketing overhead over more units of product and thereby lowering per-unit costs. Similarly, as a company becomes more experienced (measured in cumulative units of output, not in time) at manufacturing and marketing a product, it becomes more proficient. The company's *real* costs (nominal costs adjusted for inflation) associated with the product decrease. Take a firm operating on a 90 percent experience curve for a specific product. What this means is that whenever the firm's cumulative production of the product doubles, its per-unit costs decrease by 10 percent in real terms. These twin phenomena of economies of scale and the experience effect make a compelling case that the total market is more appropriate for strategic analysis than the served market, since the concern is with competitors' relative cost advantages and disadvantages.

Yet, a high-market-share strategy is not always the best one. A company with a small relative market share can be extremely profitable if it has a distinctive competence in filling a specialized market niche. As the successes of Mercedes-Benz, Michelob, Hewlett-Packard, and others of this ilk have shown, a low-cost, high-share strategy is not for everyone. Thus, for Mercedes-Benz, the served market concept is likely to be more meaningful for analysis than is the total market concept. Alan J. Zakon, himself the chief executive of the Boston Consulting Group, is quoted in *Business Week* as saying, "The relationship between relative market share and profitability doesn't hold as much significance anymore. . . . You can live well as a small company or as a big company. And you can be successful with a low-cost product or a high-value-added product. [But] It's getting tougher and tougher to live anywhere in between."[6]

Michael Porter of the Harvard Business School has suggested three generic competitive strategies that a company conceivably might pursue,[7] and which clearly illustrate what Zakon has said. Porter's analysis is worthy of special attention here because it suggests under what market conditions the BCG model might give management the right strategic signals or, conversely, lead it to the wrong conclusions. First, there is *overall cost leadership,* which requires a company to seek extreme "efficiency" in operations and hence the volume sales that make for economies of scale and allow the firm to garner the cost benefits of experience. In this strategy, large relative market share is critically important. Most commodity producers have no choice but to follow this tack, since product differentiation is difficult for them and the market turns mainly on lowest prices.

Second, there is *differentiation,* whereby a company attempts to position itself so that buyers view its offerings as being in some way economically or psychologically unique (i.e., as having benefits) and as representing a variety of products from which to choose. The approaches of Anheuser-Busch and General Motors are archetypes of this strategy. Importantly, differentiation is not usually a low-market-share strategy. In fact, as in the case of Anheuser-Busch and General Motors, it is likely to be used by market-share pacesetters.

Porter's third generic strategy is *focus marketing,* or "niche" marketing. Here the company endeavors to concentrate on the needs and preferences of a lucrative segment or niche within the total market. High value added is crucial. Examples of firms that have successfully implemented this strategy are Nieman-Marcus and Curtis-Mathes.

These three strategies are not mutually exclusive: the use of one does not preclude the use of another. Take General Motors. As a company overall, it follows a differentiated approach to the

---

[6]Alan J. Zakon, "For Executives of the 1980s, A Stress on Return," *Business Week,* June 1, 1981, pp. 88–91.

[7]Michael E. Porter, *Competitive Strategy: Techniques for Analyzing Industries and Competitors* (New York: The Free Press, 1980), pp. 35–39.

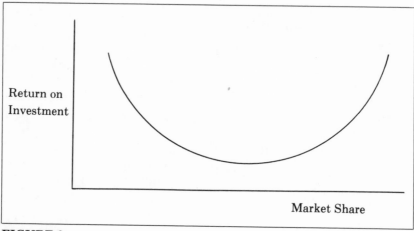

FIGURE 9
The Porter Curve
Source: Reprinted with permission of Macmillan, Inc., from *Competitive Strategy: Techniques for Analyzing Industries and Competitors* by Michael E. Porter, Copyright © 1980 by The Free Press, a Division of Macmillan Publishing Company, Inc.

automobile market by offering cars and a variety of benefits to all segments. Yet, across its various divisions (Chevrolet, Oldsmobile, etc.), as well as within each division, it also focuses on very specific buyer wants and thereby caters to targeted niches. What is more, GM emphasizes cost efficiencies (the approach of overall cost leadership) by sharing parts, components, and even bodies among its various divisions and by using marketing and advertising techniques that benefit all its offerings. In a proposed reorganization, GM is to pursue efficiencies even more by essentially dichotomizing its divisions into small-car and big-car. Such a reorganization should also give a boost to GM's marketing effectiveness by clearing up much of the confusion among potential buyers that stems from model proliferation.

The importance of a company having a well-defined competitive strategy is illustrated by Figure 9. According to the U-shaped curve depicted, a company can attain a relatively high return on investment (ROI) either by going after the leading market share in its industry or by focusing on a specialized but profitable niche within the industry. Naturally, a pure commodity producer, with little it can do to differentiate its products, has no reasonable choice but to go after large volume and share and thereby spread fixed costs over more units. But in most cases, there is room for both high-share and low-share approaches to the market.

In 1981, the consulting firm of McKinsey & Company was asked by the American Business Conference to study the characteristics, performances, and management practices of mid-sized (sales between $25 million and $1 billion) companies that have increased their sales or profits by more than 15 percent per year over a five-year period. Significantly, we think, the completed study showed that these companies generally concentrate on perpetually creating and developing small market niches and competing on value rather than going the experience-curve route and competing on lower prices. As might be expected from proven niche marketers, they are finely tuned to customer needs.[8]

On the one hand, a corporation can seek to obtain a leading market share and commensurate ROI through one of two generic competitive strategies—overall cost leadership (e.g., Georgia-Pacific in plywood) or differentiation (Brown-Forman in liquor). On the other hand, a low-share strategy can also yield a relatively large ROI for the niche marketers of the world. The companies that are neither market-share leaders nor firmly ensconced in a lucrative niche are the companies that lag when it comes to ROI. Most always, these firms are not as profitable in terms of ROI because they have (1) no recognizable distinction in fulfilling customer needs; (2) no outstanding economies of scale or experience effects to exploit through lower prices to would-be customers; and (3) no obvious or promotable differentiation from competitive offerings.

In brief, ROI exemplars adhere to an all-important strategic competence, whether it be low cost, high value added, or some combination. The market also-rans may be profitable, but not as profitable as they could be with a better idea (and action plan) to guide them concerning what they are all about—that is, what

---

[8]Richard E. Cavanagh and Donald K. Clifford, Jr., "Lessons from America's Midsized Growth Companies," *McKinsey Quarterly,* Autumn 1983, pp. 2–23.

their strategic competence is and needs to be. But what a company thinks its strategic competence is, or intends it to be, may be quite different from how the company is actually perceived in the marketplace. And, as we have noted, perception can be a far greater factor in purchase decisions than reality.

A second limitation of the BCG Model is that it employs only two dimensions—market growth rate and relative market share—in attempting to explain cash flow. Yet "statistical analysis shows that only about 6 percent of the variability in cash flow among businesses . . . can be explained by relative shares and growth alone."[9]

Another limitation is that BCG portfolio analysis can lead management to a kind of "throwaway" or "castaway" mentality in determining whether to keep or divest businesses and products—and how to treat them if they are kept. The portfolio classification of a division or product as a dog, or even as a cash cow, can tempt management to deemphasize or divest it prematurely. As William J. Abernathy and his collaborators have so rightly pointed out: "Thrown into a competitive turmoil, a mature industry can go through a rejuvenation."[10] This rejuvenation is normally technology-driven. For instance, U.S. automobile manufacturers might well convert what has often been for them a drab domestic industry into something much better. Technological innovation could achieve for General Motors and the other domestic firms the higher fuel economy, improved product quality, and increased productivity that would put them into a far stronger competitive posture vis-à-vis the imports. In particular, it would be strategically questionable for the domestic market-share followers—Ford and Chrysler—to largely recommit their resources from automobiles to other businesses just because they happen to have numerous models/brands that are dogs today. With significant technological advances on their part—for example, a wholesale move toward robotics—the dog classification may be laughable five years hence.

---

[9]Derek F. Abell and John S. Hammond, *Strategic Market Planning* (Englewood Cliffs, N.J.: Prentice-Hall, 1979), p. 284.
[10]William J. Abernathy, Kim B. Clark, and Alan M. Kantrow, "The New Industrial Competition," *Harvard Business Review*, September–October 1981, pp. 68–81.

Consider how Goodyear Tire and Rubber Company has resisted the temptation to seek greener pastures. Although Goodyear is diversified into aerospace, oil, and gas, management in this already dominant tire company has also decided to go after more and more market share in the slow-growth tire industry, rather than switch corporate resources drastically to promising non-tire lines of business. In addition, Goodyear is trying to rejuvenate the tire industry by making heavy monetary commitments to research and development and to productivity improvements. Thus, instead of milking a cash cow, as the BCG Model would indicate, Goodyear is actually infusing the cash cow with capital. In our view, market-share-gain strategies by market-share leaders like Goodyear will be safe from antitrust forces so long as the leader can point to the threat to jobs from vigorous foreign competition. Since the domestic onslaught by Toyota, Datsun, and the rest, how often anymore are there calls for divesting General Motors of its Chevrolet Division?

Unless a company is in a business or industry that, after thoughtful analysis, appears hopelessly on the decline—that is, there is no fighting chance to rejuvenate it—any decision to divest or deemphasize should be weighed with utmost care. It may be less risky and more profitable long-range for management to stay with and improve a business it knows well than to rechannel resources to "greener pasture" businesses that it has had little or no experience with.

A final limitation is that the planner using the BCG Model must be extremely cautious in evaluating the market growth rate. If, for example, the planner looks at the market growth rate, say, for building products during a past three-year recessionary period, he or she would possibly see negative growth (depicted in the BCG Model in a negative quadrant). This picture would be misleading, to say the least. A housing boom could vault a building products firm to "star" status quickly.

Do these limitations mean that we feel the BCG Model is of little value in strategic planning? Not at all, as long as its limitations are recognized. In our opinion, the BCG Model is applicable mostly in *Fortune* 1,000 kinds of firms that seek volume and rely on scale and experience effects. In such companies, the BCG Model can be useful in analyzing overall balance among corporate divisions and divisional products. The BCG portfolio

81

concept is helpful to management in evaluating the firm's *current* balance among stars, cash cows, problem children, and dogs. But the analysis should not stop there. Pro forma portfolio analysis enables management to project, evaluate, and target *future* portfolios of divisions and products. And that is how managers earn their keep.

Selecting a Portfolio Model

Our judgment is that across the wide spectrum of companies—running the gamut from the very large to the very small—the GE Portfolio Model has much to recommend it. It is universally applicable and useful. And it focuses management's attention on a variety of strategic considerations. Through discussion and debate among management, consensus can be attained as to just which considerations are thought important to success in various industries and markets—and in which industries/markets the company has the internal capabilities and resources to compete effectively. Such determinations provide bases for management to decide upon and prepare for contingent future courses of action—which is what strategic planning is really all about.

Using Portfolio Analysis in Planning

Earlier, we referred to a study of portfolio planning by Philippe Haspeslagh. According to his estimate, by 1979 about 45 percent of the *Fortune* 500 companies and 36 percent of the *Fortune* 1,000 organizations had, to varying degrees of sophistication, implemented portfolio analysis, and the number grows by 25 to 30 of these companies a year.[11] So, by now, well over half the largest companies in the United States employ portfolio planning in mapping strategy. Haspeslagh classified the portfolio users into two groups:

- Analytic portfolio planning. Use confined to a planning tool at the corporate level, no intention to negotiate explicit stra-

---

[11]Haspeslagh, "Portfolio Planning," p. 59.

tegic missions with managers, and business strategies influenced by traditional administrative tools and profit pressures.

- Process portfolio planning. Portfolio planning as a central part of the ongoing management process, as evidenced by the explicit negotiation of strategic missions with SBU managers.[12]

As Haspeslagh observed, "Getting to process planning is a long road," with the time to reach the process stage being about five years. In addition, Haspeslagh points out several potential pitfalls of portfolio analysis that need to be kept in mind and avoided or compensated for:

- If a company looks on portfolio planning as merely an analytic planning tool, it will not realize its benefits.
- In implementing portfolio planning, companies often write in biases that block its usefulness, including the tendency to focus on capital investment rather than resource allocation—or cost efficiency at the expense of organizational responsiveness.
- Portfolio planning seems unable to successfully address the issue of new business generation.[13]

PIMS[14]

History

The Profit Impact of Marketing Strategy (PIMS) program was originated by Sidney Schoeffler, then of the General Electric Company and later of The Strategic Planning Institute in Cambridge, Massachusetts. Under the name of PROM, Schoeffler in 1960 began developing computer models for use by GE as tools of strategic planning.

---

[12]Ibid., pp. 62–63.
[13]Ibid., p. 60.
[14]This section has been written drawing largely upon various publications of The Strategic Planning Institute and provided to the authors by Sidney Schoeffler. All materials are used with permission.

Between 1972 and 1974, PIMS was established as a development project within the Marketing Science Institute. In this two-year phase, the PIMS work:

- Was applied on a multicompany basis, instead of just at General Electric
- Corroborated the GE findings on a broader cross-section of businesses and explored additional areas of strategy
- Improved the computer software package used in the computer modeling
- Promoted interest (in both companies and business schools) in the comparative, quantitative analysis of the consequences of business strategy

In 1975, PIMS was organized as The Strategic Planning Institute, an autonomous and nonprofit corporation. Over 200 companies are now active in PIMS, including some 125 *Fortune* 500-sized firms, numerous medium-sized corporations in manufacturing and services, and an increasing number of large European companies.

The PIMS Program

PIMS is intended to provide each of its participant corporations with a quantitative basis for improving the company's strategic planning results. Each participant supplies data about its experiences in several different business areas to a combined data base. Using the statistical technique of multiple regression, the PIMS staff analyzes the information in the combined data base to ascertain the "general laws" that operate in the marketplace and determine what business strategy, in what kind of competitive environment, produces what results.

The meaning of the word "regress" is to go back, which is exactly what statistical regression does. Using data from the past and the appropriate computer program, regression analysis attempts to discover historical relationships between one or more independent or predictor variables (e.g., percentage of market share and R&D expenditures as a percentage of sales) and a dependent or criterion variable (e.g., return on investment).

PIMS is meant to provide strategic managers and planners with insights for answering questions like these:

- What profit is standard or normal for a specific business, given its particular market, competitive position, technology, cost structure, and so on?
- If the business proceeds on its current path, what will be its future operating results?
- What strategic changes in the business hold promise of improving these results?
- Given a specific contemplated future strategy for the business, how will profitability or cash flow change in the short- and long-term?

PIMS Membership

All members of PIMS accept certain conditions. They agree to contribute data from their own businesses to the PIMS data base; to observe the data-security measures used by The Strategic Planning Institute; to confine PIMS findings, reports, and other services exclusively to internal company use; to specify a liaison officer and an alternate to represent the company in dealings with the Institute; and to assume a pro rata share of the Institute's operating costs. In return, with a few agreed-upon exceptions, PIMS makes its resources, research findings, and reports available exclusively to its member companies.

The Data Base

PIMS uses standardized forms to collect data on businesses that member companies want analyzed. (These forms take one person two or three workdays to complete.) A "business" as defined by PIMS is essentially a strategic business unit (SBU)—that is, a division, product line, or other profit center within a company, marketing a distinct set of products and/or services to an identifiable segment of customers, in competition with a well-defined set of competitors, and for which meaningful segregation can be made of revenues, operating costs, investments, and strategic plans. So, although over 200 companies participate in PIMS, they have contributed the strategic experiences (data) of about 1,700 of their SBUs, covering five-year periods.

PIMS holds approximately one hundred items of information on each of the SBUs in its data base. An illustrative list is:

Characteristics of the SBU Environment

- Long-run growth rate of the market
- Short-run growth rate of the market
- Rate of inflation of selling-price levels
- Number and size of customers
- Purchase frequency and magnitude

Competitive Position of the SBU

- Share of the served market
- Share relative to largest competitors
- Product quality relative to competitors
- Prices relative to competitors
- Pay scales relative to competitors
- Marketing efforts relative to competitors
- Pattern of market segmentation
- Rate of new product introductions

Structure of the Production Process

- Capital intensity (degree of automation, etc.)
- Degree of vertical integration
- Capacity utilization
- Productivity of capital equipment
- Productivity of people
- Inventory levels

Discretionary Budget Allocations

- R&D budgets
- Advertising and promotion budgets
- Sales force expenditures

Strategic Moves

- Patterns of change in the controllable elements above

Operating Results

- Profitability results
- Cash-flow results
- Growth results

For purposes of security and confidentiality, all dollar data are rescaled by the corporation contributing them. Code numbers are used to identify SBUs. Further, the identity of the corporation owning the SBU is also coded.

What Member Companies Receive

A participating company receives reports on the general principles of business strategy—laws of the marketplace—that are disclosed by the analysis of the PIMS data base. A member company also is provided with specific reports on each SBU that it has contributed to the data base. There are several major specific PIMS reports.

The *PAR Report* indicates the return on investment and cash flow that are standard or normal (par) for the SBU (i.e., the division, product line, or other profit center meeting PIMS's strategic business unit requirements), given the nature of its market, competition, position, technology, and cost structure. Thus, management in the member company has a feel for how well its SBU is performing vis-à-vis similar SBUs. Importantly, the PAR Report also specifically identifies the major strengths and weaknesses of the SBU that account for its variation from average or par.

The *Strategy Analysis Report* answers "what if" kinds of questions. It enables management to pretest possible strategic moves for its SBU. This report indicates the normal short- and long-term consequences of each move tested, based on track records of other SBUs making a similar move, from a similar starting point, in a similar business environment. The profit or loss likely to result from such projected changes is specified, as well as the associated investment and cash flow.

Upper-echelon management can use the Strategy Analysis Report to experiment with potential effects of broad moves in market share, margin, capital intensity, and vertical integration.

Middle management can look for evidence of the possible effects of less sweeping actions, like increases in the ratio of marketing expenses to sales, changes in R&D outlays, and improvements in capacity utilization.

The *Optimum Strategy Report* identifies the package of strategic moves that promise to yield optimal results for the SBU, as determined by the experiences of other SBUs under similar circumstances. This report suggests optimal strategies for any of several different measures of profit performance—such as ROI for the next five years and discounted cash flow for the upcoming ten years.

The *Report on "Look-Alikes" (ROLA)* retrieves from the entire PIMS data base SBUs that are strategically similar to the SBU being analyzed (its look-alikes) and identifies a sizable number of the strategic and operating characteristics that assisted them in attaining specified objectives—for example, to augment net cash flow or to increase return on investment.

In addition to these reports, related services are provided. For instance, concerning an individual strategic business unit analysis, member companies are entitled to a one-day information synthesis session, a diagnosis of current position, an overview of major strategic options, and a strategy analysis and recommendation. And PIMS publishes newsletters and perspectives covering diverse general topics, as indicated by these titles: *Nine Basic Findings on Business Strategy, Strategic Determinants of Cash Flow, Productivity Benchmarks, Good Productivity vs. Bad Productivity, The Unprofitability of "Modern" Technology and What to Do About It, Coping with Double-Digit Inflation, Product Quality,* and *Marketing Position: Build, Hold, or Harvest.*

Does PIMS Help?

From a technical standpoint, PIMS has done extremely well. With a high probability of being right (95 percent or better), PIMS has identified 37 strategic considerations or variables that statistically account for approximately 80 percent of the variation in return on investment across a broad range of large companies. Or, put the other way, only 20 percent of the variation in

ROI among the strategic business units in the PIMS data base cannot be accounted for statistically by the 37 strategic variables used in the regression equation.

Moreover, The Strategic Planning Institute has adduced considerable "real-world" evidence to answer what it calls the "acid test": Are those SBUs that do what the PIMS findings say better off than those that do otherwise? According to The Strategic Planning Institute, about 90 percent of the time SBUs do better if they heed PIMS's signals than if they disregard them. And this finding is based on numerous comparisons between profit trends of SBUs that follow PIMS's signals and profit trends of SBUs that disregard them.

This is not to say that PIMS is without its problems. A thoughtful critique of PIMS by Carl Anderson and the late Frank Paine points out several concerns.[15] But, of course, any quantitative tool of analysis has its strengths and limitations. We feel that as an aid to strategic planning, PIMS's strengths far outweigh its weaknesses. It systematically contends with numerous and complex strategic variables and relationships in a way that is beyond the capabilities of the human mind. Although these relationships should not be thought of as exact, they do assist strategic planners and executives in seeing connections among variables, in testing possible courses of action, and in providing if not exactness, at least general direction.

How managers view quantitative tools for decision making is subject to error in one of two distinct ways. On the one hand is the manager who treats the tool as the decision *maker,* rather than as an aid to decision making. In this case, the tool's output is taken much too literally and is not sufficiently tempered with plenty of managerial judgment. On the other hand is the manager who avoids tools entirely; he or she does not trust them and prefers to "fly by the seat of the pants." For example, an executive might claim that his or her SBU is somehow "different" and therefore not subject to the general "laws of the marketplace" revealed by PIMS analysis. Recognition of these tendencies to err is an important step in not falling prey to them.

---

[15]Carl R. Anderson and Frank T. Paine, "PIMS: A Reexamination," *Academy of Management Review,* July 1978, pp. 602–612.

What PIMS Data Say About Portfolio Management

Writing in a thought-provoking and myth-bursting article in the *Harvard Business Review,* Richard Hamermesh and Roderick White asserted, " ... We found that corporate managers can have as much impact on a business unit's performance by attending to its administrative ties to headquarters as they can by managing according to detailed strategic portfolio analyses."[16] We could not agree more. Too frequently, in practice portfolio analysis fails to live up to expectations because of faulty implementation. In brief, the analysis is fine, but the "doing" is weak.

Using the PIMS data base, Hamermesh and White looked at the effects of three aspects of organizational relationships between a corporate headquarters and its operating business units that influence an SBU's performance:

- Autonomy, or the degree to which business unit managers can make decisions independent of other parts of the company, especially the corporate head office
- Line responsibility, or the degree to which business unit managers have direct and complete responsibility for key functions (sales, marketing, manufacturing, engineering, and so forth) or share responsibility for some of these with other unit managers
- Incentive compensation, or the percentage of the business unit general manager's total cash compensation attributable to the unit's performance[17]

Interestingly, and importantly, the study tended to dispel the so-called conventional wisdom about how corporate headquarters treats (or should treat) various kinds of operating units. Most notably, take these findings: the analysis of PIMS data revealed that, contrary to popular opinion about how to foster corporate entrepreneurship, rapid-growth businesses do better in terms of ROI if they have considerable overseeing and control

---

[16]Richard G. Hamermesh and Roderick E. White, "Manage Beyond Portfolio Analysis," *Harvard Business Review,* January–February 1984, p. 105.
[17]Ibid., p. 104.

from corporate headquarters (in other words, low autonomy), whereas mature businesses in stable environments are best given a much freer rein to operate. With too much latitude, managers in high-growth situations are prone to disregard the need to balance their sales growth with profitability. This, as we will see shortly, is but a natural reaction to the way headquarters executives tend to compensate their managers in accordance with sales increases rather than ROI results. Similarly, shared line responsibility between headquarters and an operating unit was found to be superior (as measured by ROI) in dynamic growth markets, whereas nonsharing was better for business units in stable, mature environments. Finally, and extremely salient: managers often give lip service to the need for an appropriate reward system tailored to the strategic mission of each business unit. Yet, the PIMS analysis showed that executives of SBUs with *low sales growth, but high ROI* averaged lower levels of incentive compensation than executives in high-sales-growth units, regardless of the ROI generated by the rapid sales growth. Hamermesh and White concluded, "Clearly, the connection between incentive compensation and business unit performance is not easily explained and we suspect often mismanaged, especially for units facing stable environments."[18]

These findings have plenty of significant ramifications. Unless headquarters compensates managers according to the negotiated strategic missions of their SBUs, portfolio analysis has little chance to work well in practice. If headquarters rewards sales growth over ROI, how many managers will want to take on the phasing out of a dog, or even manage a cash cow, if a fast-growing SBU is available? Moreover, the use of portfolio analysis does not necessarily warrant a "hands-off" approach by headquarters once strategic missions are in place. As we saw, an entrepreneurial unit needs considerable overseeing and counsel from headquarters. For instance, as Hamermesh and White point out, corporate managers at General Electric oversee high-growth businesses and spotlight the performances of venture managers.

We ourselves are aware of a company that went along seem-

---

[18]Ibid., p. 107.

ingly in a fabulous manner for several years by acquiring highly entrepreneurial growth firms in electronics and related fields. Corporate headquarters wisely retained incumbent managers in the acquired businesses whenever possible, but, as it turned out, not so wisely gave them virtually free rein. This arrangement worked well for a while and profits piled up. But later, many of the top managers in the acquired businesses lost sight of their strategic missions within the overall corporate portfolio, and their units developed severe cash-flow problems. As a result, quick corrective actions were necessary from corporate head-quarters. The erstwhile independent businesses had become so growth-oriented and free from headquarters profit constraints that they became involved in too many ventures beyond their competencies. They became, so to speak, jacks of all trades and masters of none. Because of too much of a "hands-off" approach from headquarters, a supposedly complementary portfolio of business units quickly proved otherwise.

A PORTFOLIO PICTURE OF
WALT DISNEY PRODUCTIONS[19]

Walt Disney went to Hollywood in the early 1920s and with his creativity, philosophy of life, and a vision, built a unique and highly successful family-oriented entertainment and recreation business. Walt Disney Productions has a worldwide scope and employs about 25,000 people.

Total revenues have topped $1 billion for several years. Even during the serious recession of the early 1980s, Disney maintained well over a decade of consecutive years of record revenues. During that period there was a drop in net income, which was attributed to "disappointing results of several live-action motion pictures ... and planned expenditures for Epcot Center." (Epcot, the dream of Walt Disney for an experimental prototype Community of Tomorrow, is now a reality in central Florida.)

Walt Disney Productions is organized into three general lines of business: (1) entertainment and recreation, (2) motion pictures, and (3) consumer products and other.

Entertainment and recreation. This segment contributes about 70 percent of revenues and approximately 66 percent of net income. Under this heading are Walt Disney World, Disneyland, Epcot, and Tokyo Disneyland. (The latter was opened in spring 1983 with no financial investment by Disney—the risk is to the Disney reputation. Disney receives 10 percent of admissions and this venture may add 15 cents a share to near-future profits.)

---

[19]Researched and developed in 1983 by Suzanne Desai of Kent State University.

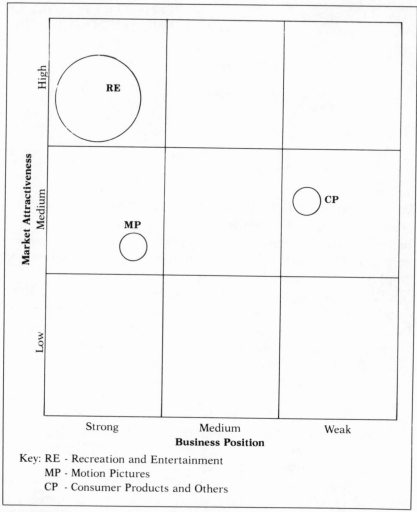

FIGURE 10
A Strategic Snapshot of Walt Disney Productions in 1983

The "Magic Kingdom" amusement theme park was the original business in this segment, but today, with Epcot, Walt Disney Productions runs hotels and camping, golf, and other facilities for tourists and business visitors.

Success in this segment depends on such factors as location, demographics, accessibility, quality of product, and quality of management. The customer must perceive that there is more value for dollar spent at Disney than on some other entertainment program. Repeat business is also an important factor.

Motion pictures. This segment contributes about 20 percent to revenues and about 10 percent to net income. Included are theater, commercial television, home video, and the Disney cable channel. These "film" products are marketed and distributed worldwide and compete with all other forms of entertainment.

Consumer products and other. This segment contributes approximately 10 percent of revenues and 24 percent of net income. Three areas comprise this segment: character merchandising and publications (books, toys, etc.), records and music publishing (LP records and cassettes), and educational media (films, tapes, and software for home and school markets with learning as the emphasis). Walt Disney Productions considers itself one of the main sources of educational products.

DOMESTIC STRATEGIC PLANNING IN PRACTICE

5

In this chapter, William Shaw (TRW)* offers his views on strategic planning. He sees strategic planning as basically a resource-allocation program, a program that permits upper management to make decisions regarding where to direct the firm's resources. According to Shaw, the strategic planning process involves looking at both opportunities inside the firm and alternatives outside the firm. And then, the allocation decisions are made.

Shaw feels that strategic planning is taking a more sophisticated role, one in which the portfolio (top-down) approach is being integrated with operational (bottom-up) planning. Such an approach permits blending the day-to-day perspective of the operational level and the broader, objective-setting, upper-management point of view. This is seen as offering a much stronger final plan than either approach taken separately.

According to Shaw, strategic plans should (1) be flexible and simple enough for management understanding;

---

*Mr. Shaw is now president of Venture Capital, Inc. in Chagrin Falls, Ohio. At the time of the interview he was with TRW.

(2) be consistent year to year to permit comparisons; and (3) require management — even CEO — commitment and involvement. The latter, in particular, is essential if planning is to become a part of the reward system and if the process is to be given serious consideration by managers at all levels. While five-year plans seem to be in vogue, Shaw finds nothing magical in five-year cycles but rather emphasizes the need for taking a relatively long-term perspective in strategic planning. He emphasizes the importance of competitor analysis — but not a competitor analysis that considers only current competitors in the company's specific industry or industries. Rather, the competitor analysis should also consider other prospective industries where the corporation's skills and technologies could be brought to bear.

Corporate planning within the very large firm often requires considerable decentralization, especially when the division itself may be a multibillion-dollar entity with independent operational status. While the division's plans must be integrated with those of the total organization, the developers of the plans have the same responsibilities for achieving objectives (and have corresponding organizational latitude) as does the overall corporate planner in a smaller or less decentralized business. Anything from acquisitions and product/unit pruning to recommendations for the long-term resource needs for the division may be included in the divisional plan.

One of the soundest and most imaginative high-technology firms among the *Fortune* 500 is TRW, Inc., of Cleveland. William Shaw, the Director of Strategic Planning for its Industrial and Energy Sector, is the epitome of the divisional strategic planner. Shaw came to TRW with experience at the corporate planning level from another firm (General Instrument) plus extensive line management (including "bottom-line") responsibilities at Gulf and Western. Therefore, he brings to this position (and to our interview) a background that is clearly able to provide all the needed planning skills *plus* insight into management and corporate planning at the central office.

Because of his expertise, we wanted not only to determine the relationship between the divisional and the overall corporate plan, but also to get his views on questions regarding the use of current planning techniques, the appropriate level of sophistication of plans, organizational dynamics, and several other issues. From Shaw's responses, it is evident that he heavily utilizes his extensive financial background in planning activities. His candid interview—avoiding, of course, proprietary information—is presented in the remainder of this chapter.

INTERVIEW WITH WILLIAM E. SHAW
TRW, INC.

INTERVIEWER: What is the appropriate role for strategic planning at the corporate level in the multidivisional company?

SHAW: Broadly speaking, I see strategic planning as a resource-allocation program. In other words, it allows management—in most cases upper management—to decide where they want to direct their resources. In theory, they have limited human, financial, and technical resources to direct, and for them to make discriminating use of those resources, they have to have some program or some plan. Strategic planning allows you to look at the opportunities within your businesses and alternatives to those same businesses and make decisions relative to where you want to flow your resources to and from. You can take that into a portfolio context or you can take that into an operating context. It works in either one. Here, being at a sector where we are very decentralized and autonomous, we do run a portfolio. But the difference that we have [sector-level]—versus, say, corporate-level planning—is that we look among alternatives and we flow resources, but we do not have the responsibility for balancing our "cash flows." We do not balance the cash flows within the portfolio, so we kind of have the best of all worlds in some respects, because we do not have to worry about that restraining hand. The way I look at a planning process—that will be called a strategic planning process—is that we work both bottom-up and top-down. From the top-down, the process is initiated by giving objectives, guidance, values, and choices. From the bottom-up, lower levels of operating management start to look within their chosen alternative at the current moment, because they tend not to be able to separate what is the best operating strategy from the best alternative strategy.

INTERVIEWER: Do you see these roles changing?

SHAW: They are changing. I think in the seven or eight years I have spent in planning it has changed dramatically; planning really operated at two poles for a very long time. You had at the corporate level the top-down portfolio approach that the BCG [Boston Consulting Group] and some of the other consulting firms used that never really integrated what was going on in the operations. When I was with my former employer, we probably ran one of the first and one of the most complete portfolio analyses of any company I've ever heard of and actually implemented it. But it was totally unrelated to anything that was going on in the businesses themselves. There was almost no input from the general managers or from the people who were creating and implementing the operating strategies. Prior to that, planning per se was really operational planning, where you had much more of an ITT, Xerox kind of approach—by the numbers. So what you had were five-year forecasts versus worrying about resource allocations and choosing between alternatives; those two ran in conflict for a long time. Initially, a lot of planners tried to get familiar with that breed [operational] or whatever it was, and then later others were coming in with the wave of portfolio planning and trying to go in at the CEO or board level. The two ran in direct conflict.

The changing of the roles is just what I was talking about—at least in a couple of companies that are relatively sophisticated. And I am not trying to pretend that we are; we just try to copy and select as best we can. We are now trying to integrate the two processes—taking advantage of the value that an operational plan has and blending it with the portfolio approach.

No one knows a particular business better than those people who are working for it. The problem is they become victims of tunnel vision simply because they have to worry about executing what they are doing on a day-to-day basis and it is very, very difficult to broaden the focus. It is the exceptional manager who can step back and say, "What alternatives do I have here? Could I do something different? What's happening in the marketplace other than the day-to-day, order-by-order, customer-by-customer, manufacturing process kind of comparisons?" The ability of planners at the top is to take that operational knowledge, integrate it, and step back and look at the alternatives themselves or get up one more tier to an upper tier of management to look at those alternatives; giving that knowledge or at least implanting that knowledge is really where strategic planning is moving. It is moving to an integrated process rather than two totally separate processes, which was the original conflict. This changing role is important. I think that it is very important, because neither of the earlier, separate approaches was right. I know when we did our portfolio study, we made some tragic mistakes. In the aggregate our decisions netted out to be very, very profitable. It was the success of the company—there is no question about that. On the other hand, I feel there were some opportunities that were missed and there were some mistakes made that would not have been made if we had understood the operations or if we could have taken some of the other alternatives and allowed the manager with the operations knowledge to explore them. I would definitely say the roles are changing.

INTERVIEWER: How formal should the various plans be, and what time horizons are relevant?

SHAW: They should be formal, but they should be flexible. There should be a formal review process. And as I just commented in a meeting yesterday, the most important things to remember about a planning process—in a group of businesses or a division or whatever it is—are actually threefold. First, to make it flexible and simple enough that the management can understand what you are talking about. Something that they can say, "Oh, I see what he is looking at. I see what he is asking. I can supply his information." It sounds very simple, but sometimes we planners just overwhelm management one way or the other, either with the numbers and their complication or in working in the multidimensional kinds of graphs. Second, keep it consistent; do not change. Keep it consistent for a number of years. Even though they [line managers] understand what they are asked for, it probably takes them two or three years to be able to get beyond just supplying information and to begin to understand some of the ramifications—to look at projections in market shares and competitors—alternative scenarios. It takes a couple of years of looking at these in order to say, "Oh, this is what he [the strategic planner] is saying. If we do this and we take this share, what is Company X or Company Y going to do?" Then the final part is to get the management involved, and I am talking about it having to start with the CEO or, in our case, a sector executive vice president. If you do not gain management commitment and involvement which finds its way into the remuneration, motivation, and reward systems—and it is clearly understood that it finds its way there—you are going to be fighting a very, very difficult battle because managers are only going to respond to those motivators. They are going to do what you tell them to do to maximize their personal income or cash flow or growth potential. Our company is as guilty as any other of saying, "Look, we are going to reward our managers based upon the long-term," but then we pay them based upon how [well] they have done for the most recent year, usually measured in performance via some operating ratio like the return on assets employed. For example, take a current manager I know who is probably the best control manager in the automotive OEM supplier business; he has actually improved his performance in the large end of the automotive business for the last three years. It is impossible to do. What he has been doing is just shrinking, shrinking, shrinking— just constantly pushing down—his assets, keeping his efficiency going at absolutely a level which is three or four times what PIMS would say he should be doing. That is great, but it may be the wrong strategy for the business, because eventually there will be nothing left. Now, there are some opportunities in that business that are going to be creamed; he is just going to take the top off and let that add to the rest. And yet he is being rewarded, told, "You are doing a good job." So how do you tell him what he is doing wrong? You can't.

CEOs and boards still worry about how this quarter is versus last quarter, what the earnings this year are versus last year. Their motivation is the same. There is just no way that you are going to be able to motivate or reward managers very easily on meeting planning objectives unless you can express that from the top. We have done a pretty good job of that here, and I think we did an excellent job at my former employer's. I participated in the way we built up our remuneration program and a bonus program that was paid off over a series of years based on meeting objectives that were set for specific plans. It was stated right there! And those objectives could be nonquantified ones. In other words, the objectives could be some specific level of operating service that you want provided—e.g., 100 percent delivery or something like that—or it could be market share or product quality, or "getting a system up" in a certain period of time. It could be such non-monetary kinds of things. They did an excellent job of motivating the right kind of long-term action programs.

Then, I guess finally, the last part of that is for these managers to see some results. The other side of reward motivation is seeing some results. If they actually see that the business itself has improved its inherent return, you can argue whether 80 percent of the return is the responsibility of the business or that it is the marketplace or the PIMS theory percentage or whatever it is—but it is obviously some mixture. (There is some part of that return that is the responsibility of how the business is structured and what industry it is in and how its managers drive it, whatever the relationship is.) So if you can prove to them or show them that by planning a business—e.g., by saying we have been going down this track and yet it is providing unacceptable results, so let us switch over and go for an alternate track and reposition the businesses or the way we are focusing our assets to meet some needs—you may put it in a position that would allow it to make inherently higher returns.

We have done that with our bearings business, which was basically a commodity business. The Japanese came in and destroyed the commodity businesses. We really said, "Let us look at our other alternatives; let us look at what we could be doing with these assets." We are very tied to the bearings industry. We obviously are not going to go out of the bearings business, but there are other alternatives even within bearings. So we decided to go into very specialized niches, provide high services, go into some distribution areas; and that business has become quite successful. Rather than being an inherent 10, 11, 12 percent ROAE [return on assets employed] business, it probably is a 16, 18, 20 percent business. It is going to make about 18 to 20 percent ROAE, which is within acceptable range for TRW. We have gotten some very-high-market-share, high-return kinds of niches that we have identified and in which we have taken strong positions that are providing harbors, very safe harbors that are not going to be easily attacked. The entry cost is going to be so great that no one is likely to risk it. So, over the last four years, bearings have demonstrated to most of the managers exactly what planning can do for them even with the short-term reward criteria they adopt. It is a positive reinforcement because they can see the inherent value. It may not be the right reason for adopting the planning criteria, but it is a part.

INTERVIEWER: What kind of time frame do you think you should be working on in terms of the planning process? How many years? What does the planning cycle look like?

SHAW: My personal opinion is that the way management should manage a business—I am really talking about at the company level or executive-vice-president level, or even sector-vice-president level—is to look at some broad, long horizon. We use five years. But it could be ten or it could be three. I do not think there is any magic in the number of years—but some long horizon—and five has just kind of been a number we have latched onto because I think it is a simple number and one that most companies have. It is beyond something short-term and it is not so long-term as to be unrealistic (even though sometimes it seems somewhat unrealistic). If you want to take it to a financial viewpoint, you check numbers, or if you want to talk about market shares and resources and requirements and programs, you are taking a general direction for certain reasons. Environmental reasons should then drive you to look at where your position is and you make choices.

Then, you take a narrower perspective, perhaps two years, where you are trying to bring the focus down from the five-year plan. You are trying to cut the planning range down. You say, what do we think this long-term direction is going to do? What requirements do we have for resources, etc., in that two-year period to meet that longer-term direction—to get where we are trying to go? And then that feeds our planning into a focus for a first-year budget or forecast. That is kind of the way we envisioned it here. We are moving to this approach slowly because this has been a highly control-oriented company, one that did an annual budget four times a year. In other words, take a five-year look, a two-year look, and a one-year look. You may be doing that one-year look twice a year, but you are moving toward that overall kind of a program. We, for example, are letting that five-

year look drive our resource allocation, then move into a narrower two-year look, which evolves into a one-year budget; and
management attention is being refocused more on the longer
five-year look than just totally focusing on the one-year look.
But, frankly, it does not happen overnight.

What the heck. Planning might be a little bit too much on
the other side [overemphasized], too. Planning is very good and
needed for growth. But it also bears the weight of criticism on
the way down. When you are in a recession you come under a lot
of weight of criticism. Planners have been somewhat their own
worst enemies, constantly projecting "onward and upward." We
have been unrealistic in a lot of our expectations of what is going
to happen. We have tended to be very positive, very aggressive,
and very optimistic people and, therefore, tend not to have the
realism that management requires.

INTERVIEWER: In fact, that really leads us into a question that I
had planned to ask later—the question of alternatives, in terms
of your planning.

SHAW: We did an interesting thing last year: we started very
heavily into our top-down process and we said we have got to
look at the relative alternatives for *all our businesses*. What we
have tried to do, therefore, is to break our business down into
units, the smallest business that it makes sense to have a strategy, one that has a definable and measurable ROA, maybe that
is a definition. It is a simple unit. It may be a $2 million business
or it could be a $20 million business. It would tend to be small.
I think we have 40-plus of those units. That is the kind of thing
[units] BCG tends to put in their circles on their charts. However, we then said, look, that is not really the level by which management or a corporation can manage a business. That level is
really what I call business areas (or we have changed what we
call them to sets of businesses just because people did not like
business areas). So we broke our sector down into these sets of
businesses, about eleven of them, and really what we were doing
was to identify those common kinds of areas [sets] where there
is a commonality of markets or competition or products or manufacturing processes, where you can really cluster them together.
And then you are able to determine what type of alternative
strategies you should be looking at; we said we can go through

and say what the environmental characteristics are, we can get position assessments, and we can identify the high-leverage points. Then we are able to define some alternative strategies, perhaps make some evaluations, and then we have got to make *the choice*.

In going through this process, we broke out some of these business sets and then we said, "Okay, let us put it down on some kind of schematic (like a flowchart)," and that is what we did last year. We asked what the alternatives for, say, our hand tools business are. Our most obvious alternative is always to hold or divest the business. We can keep it going on its current operating strategy or maybe we can sell it. Another one we felt was to fix it [change its operating strategy] because of its returns. If we fixed it, maybe we could sell it or do some other things with it later. We had different alternatives. Now, the requirement was to value these alternatives. Obviously, if you really do believe that the present value of the future cash flow is the way you value a business, you take a present value on each alternative; then if you want to look at the efficiency of that strategy, you can say what is your investment in it now related to that cash-flow strategy. This brings us to a measure we like to use—the *valuation index* or VI. If you say this strategy provides the kind of returns over that period and it gives you a present value of say $100 million and if you have $50 million invested in that business now, then, in fact, it has a valuation index of 2. In other words, that future cash flow is worth *twice* what your investment is now. You might do this same type of evaluation with an acquisition. Consequently, if you had strategies that came in somewhere around a VI of 1, where the present value of that strategy alternative is only slightly greater than the current investment you have in that business, you have to be worrying about (a) the strategy, and (b) the business.

Of course, this is a simple kind of thinking. Additionally, you have to realize how this portion of your operation fits into the whole. Is there synergy? Obviously, there are businesses that we see as *stand-alone* businesses. They have to be examined by themselves. Also, there are those businesses that have some intermingling with other parts of the company and add value somewhere. So you can look at that kind of valuation index only in the aggregate sense, and that is where business sets come into

105

play. Business sets tend to be independent, *stand-alone* operations, and therefore, you can make the simple kinds of comparisons.

In fact, this year we have become much more specific and have said, based upon how we value each of the possible scenarios for each of these businesses, these two sets are not only candidates, but *will be* divested in the next year. They are two businesses that we are now planning to sell. The criterion to sell them, of course, is obviously that they have more value to other companies than to ourselves, because of those companies' portfolios of businesses or because of their strategies. These companies may be tying themselves into something they do not want to depend solely on, and, in fact, they may like to venture into this area or this area offers them some manufacturing commonality with some market alternatives they cannot currently find. We have also said this year that there are several of our other business sets that we do not see right now in the current alternatives as providing the kind of relative return that is needed. We cannot see new alternatives, but we are not clear relative to all the alternatives and the value of all the alternatives, and also we feel that we can probably improve some of their lots in the next year and, therefore, make them eventually more attractive for us. But what this analysis does is show the way we have integrated some of our *operating strategies* with our *portfolio analysis,* and we have been extremely successful in that respect. It is to be proven if we are going to be able to execute, but we already have started.

INTERVIEWER: How essential is competitor analysis to the ongoing planning process?

SHAW: You can always say the objective of the strategic planning is to learn where to compete and how to compete. Where to compete and how to compete may be different at the sector level, where you are talking more about portfolio, than at other levels. You are really talking about where you want to channel your resources and what industries and businesses you want to be in—given that you are status quo. Where to compete, how to compete, however, means something different when you are talking about an operating strategy—when you are talking about a guy out there who has got a business and he really cannot worry about taking his presses and forges and going into the cosmetics business. He is not going to be able to redeploy his assets. He is going to basically be in that business he is in because he knows that his skills and assets, both variable and fixed, are pretty much tied to one general area. He has just got to point them into the most attractive alternatives. On the other hand, our competitive analysis, I think, is twofold. We do a very good job at the group and division level of looking at all those [companies] who are immediate competitors in the markets that we are currently serving. We understand their strengths, their weaknesses—where, in fact, they would move relative to different strategies on our part. And a little bit about their strategies, as we can best perceive them, as well as where *we* are vulnerable and where *they* are vulnerable. We have done an excellent job, as has been exhibited by our ability in "down markets" to effectively produce returns. That is one of the things TRW has always done very well—understood its competition at an operating-strategy kind of level. What we have not done as well and what we are trying to do in strategic planning is understand where to compete and how to compete at a very *broad level* relative to redeploying our assets—being in other industries or other parts of industries than we are currently in. When you think about competitive analysis, immediately in TRW that is the five valve "guys" [companies] that you are working against or the four "guys" that are providing fasteners to the automobile industries or the three "guys" who are doing electromechanic assemblies. We can almost tell you every one of their foremen's names. We have a very strong understanding of that competitor.

What we do not do is say, "We are a large corporation which has a large investment base, a large debt capability (that we are not utilizing), and we can play in a lot of industries." We have some skills and technologies that will allow us to have competitive advantages or comparative advantages in certain industries in certain places in the world; maybe it is in energy, maybe it is in petroleum equipment, maybe it is in some form of capital goods, computer operations or data processing, or something like that. We have not really applied those skills and those capabilities well with our financial resources, people resources, or technological resources. We are now trying to do such competitive analysis. We have some independent studies and some in-house capabilities to do this. To say, "What do we see in the '80s and '90s as the high-growth, high-opportunity areas—things that are going to be stressed given what the world and the environment look like?" We are not just looking at what we know inside; we are looking at outside agencies, government agencies, academia, consulting—whatever we can find—to say, all right, what do they see as the big drivers of the future? ["Drivers" are events and trends that present business with opportunities and threats.] What does inflation do? What does the need to sell and buy productively do? What of the energy crunch? (Will world demand actually surpass supply in the early '80s?) What do these drivers tell us? Then let us take this filter, this screen, called TRW's skills, capabilities, technologies, and run the two together and see what that tells us, where we should be. We are not going to go into chemicals and we are not going to go into some forms of customer service, but we will go into a lot of things that are consistent with what we know how to do and do well. Where are these growth opportunities? We have set some very high financial objectives for ourselves that we will not be able to meet just solely based upon internal momentum. We have large cash capability and cash reserves, so it is obvious that we have to do it through external investments. Now, external may mean some internal development that takes advantage of an opportunity, like funding it internally or making an acquisition. But all of this is what our people are looking at as part of a much broader competitor analysis.

INTERVIEWER: What about the kind of unpredictable competitive thing that Exxon did by going into business machines or something where somebody with just sheer clout tries to enter a new market?

SHAW: They are trying to do what I think BCG's Bruce Henderson talked about and a lot of other people talked about. If you want to take a position in the market, and you are already committed but lack the talent, you have to spend a hell of a lot of money to do it. You either acquire knowledge or you just blow the bucks at it [until you develop it]. I hate to return to a financial arena, but sometimes we have to. The present value of that flow is pretty damn lousy. If I were a stockholder, I would be upset. I'd say, "Look, you either do that through inherent skills and capabilities that you acquire slowly or you go out and buy the learning curve or the experience curve." You don't try to enter through cash and force yourself upward on that curve. You can, but it is a waste. It is a poor use of cash. In my opinion, Exxon probably has been the most poorly managed from a planning viewpoint of any company I have ever seen. I have insight into that. Chuck Ames has some very interesting stories about it. But, no, I think that it is an example of a statement that Fred Crawford made. Fred Crawford is a very interesting guy. I don't know if you have any background on Fred Crawford, but he was one of the first managers in TRW. TRW has had, I think, only five chairmen of the board and Crawford was the second and lasted for about fifteen years. He was placed in the Business Hall of Fame last year and is ninety years old—and still very alive. At the ceremony, Crawford said that at the turn of the century there were only a hundred or so companies making sales of X million dollars—perhaps just a few million dollars. He added that in 1980 only two of them were still around. Crawford said that if you make another analogy and say that in the last ten years we have duplicated the technological advances of the prior seventy years, what is going to happen to those companies [high-tech] in the next ten years? Think about that one.

INTERVIEWER: Very insightful comment from a man ninety years old.

SHAW: He is sharp as a tack. He talks about when he was having a business problem with a customer, "So I would hop on my horse and go see about them." When you put that into context you can understand a man that has been in the business world for seventy or eighty years; what he understands. But, anyway, I think there are going to be more companies that get killed by the technology and particularly, they are going to get killed by their inability to see what is happening, not just by technology. They will get killed by not understanding the world that they are in and making adjustments to it. They are either going to be absorbed or they are going to default. There is no question about it. Either it will be from not providing the services or understanding the dynamics of business, from being rationalized out of the industry on a worldwide basis, or from just losing through technology. Those companies that can make the right applications and can understand what their skills and their strengths are, what their resources are, and have a feel of what the direction is going to be and continually ratchet themselves into the proper position are the ones that are going to survive. The necessity to compete and compete better is just an ever-increasing requirement. It is not by mistake that these consultants, several of your colleagues, are making great money on the competitive strategies—the Michael Porter kind of thing—because that, in effect, is the tremendous pressure that a lot of businessmen never felt before but are now feeling, and are seeking the expertise on the outside, rather than creatively using their own skills and knowledge.

INTERVIEWER: How can a company go about ensuring proper interface between strategic planning/marketing, on the one hand, and R&D on the other? In other words, how can R&D be guided by strategic issues?

SHAW: The interface between planning and R&D—actually between planning and any resource allocation is what we are talking about—in some ways might be a function of the process itself. It is difficult because it is like a marriage that you both have to work at. The planning people cannot function totally independently nor can the people who are running the research program or the functional program. We have tried to link our planning with our R&D by first saying, let us let our strategic planning drive a lot of our resource programs and point them in a direction. Let us let them also have feedback; let them have an input from these R&D units as to what strategies have been selected and what the values of the strategies are. That sounds conceptually very good, but it is, from an implementation viewpoint, very difficult. It is really a personality type of thing. If we can get the people working in the planning function with the people who are working in the other areas, then hopefully both will try to understand what the other is doing and try to understand what their skills are. A particular application may be obvious, but tying the planning and R&D together starts first with an understanding of what the need is and what the application is; second, understanding what technologies you have; and then third, bringing those people together and saying, "Look, we think this is the proper application." We cannot direct the R&D,

but we can apply some skills or capabilities and see if the application can be brought into a new industry. I truly believe that it is basically a people thing and that it is an ability to understand on both sides what, in fact, the skill is on the R&D side and the application of that skill to what is being proposed as the *market need.*

STRATEGIC PLANNING FOR GLOBAL BUSINESS

6

In many companies, strategic planning is not merely a domestic activity but encompasses international aspects as well. And the number of firms impinged upon by global business is growing at a rapid rate. For executives engaged in strategy formulation for global business, it is imperative to put country-to-country differences (read, cultural dimensions) in proper perspective: in today's more homogeneous world, a very real potential exists for transferring select domestic-learned business strategies and tactics.

Any executive with global responsibilities often finds an economic rationale underlying political actions. And it is invariably the political-risk factors that most differentiate global business strategy planning from domestic planning. So for companies doing business in more than one country, having access to well-researched and hopefully valid political-risk assessments is especially important.

If risk analyses are to be most germane and useful, they need to be company-specific, as firms' degrees of vulnerability vary by industry and form of entry. Many organizations and individuals are in the business of providing risk assessments, and they run the gamut from the very competent to the not-so-competent. Thus, the selection of the "best" data source for a particular company's needs is itself a critical decision. We see five specific steps in the selection of a risk-analysis organization to be key ones.

For critical evaluation of various foreign markets, a number of strategic planning approaches or models have been used in practice or otherwise suggested for use. We consider a few such models, which are really no more than international adaptations of the kinds of portfolio models (e.g., the Boston Consulting Group model) that we discussed earlier. The most pertinent question is, what characteristics does a workable and helpful global portfolio model need to include?

One final point. The Japanese have rightfully received a great amount of attention in recent years for their prowess in business strategy. We discuss, therefore, the major planning differences between U.S. and Japanese corporations, as well as how the British go about global strategic planning.

"Take a global perspective" may seem to be inappropriate, if not poor, advice to offer a firm doing $10 million in total sales and having less than 10 percent of its market overseas. But such advice is appropriate for *any* firm, regardless of its size or current overseas commitment level. Realistically, every company must come to grips with the international realities of today; all companies sell overseas, compete with overseas producers in their home market, buy from overseas, or engage in some combination of these activities. Even the farmer (and the agriculture sector) is influenced by overseas sales; the hospital uses foreign-made supplies and instruments; and the small manufacturer typically uses some imports in its day-to-day operations. To state it bluntly, U.S. companies can either accept this challenge or allow U.S. executives to become second-class business citizens.

It is perhaps ironic that second-class citizenry is even a pos-

113

sibility when one recalls the U.S. "world-dominating" business position less than two decades ago. In 1968, noted French businessman J. J. Servan-Schreiber issued to the nations of Western Europe what he labeled "the American Challenge." It was his view that the U.S. business threat to Western Europe resulted as much from American managerial talents and capabilities as it did from American technological competence.[1] In contrast, according to Richard Tanner Pascale and Anthony Athos in *The Art of Japanese Management,* it is the same U.S. managerial "set" that is being used by the Japanese to challenge the United States.[2]

In a sense, Servan-Schreiber overvalued U.S. management expertise, while proponents of Japanese management now tend to understate it. From our perspective, there are two extreme types of U.S. management approaches pertaining to strategic planning in international business—and both should be avoided. First, there is the approach that says intermarket differences do not matter. A 1969 study by one of us, which dealt chiefly with international advertising, showed that roughly two-fifths (39 percent) of the advertising and marketing executives polled felt that "an individual approach to each country or region is entirely unnecessary."[3] And this same extreme position appears to be held by some marketing and business planners today. A second fallacy in international business is for management to assume that each market intrinsically has different characteristics. What needs to be avoided is the downplaying of country-to-country similarities—likenesses that permit the transfer of domestic-learned business strategies and tactics to many countries. Management expert Theodore Levitt sees these increasing similarities to be part of an inevitable process in which the " . . . world's preference structure is relentlessly homogenized."[4] A few occasional setbacks aside, the authors share his view.

---

[1] J. J. Servan-Schreiber, *The American Challenge* (New York: Atheneum, 1968), p. 122.
[2] Richard Tanner Pascale and Anthony G. Athos, *The Art of Japanese Management* (New York: Warner Books, 1982), p. 25.
[3] James H. Donnelly, Jr., and John K. Ryans, Jr., "Standardized Global Advertising, A Call as Yet Unanswered," *Journal of Marketing,* April 1969, p. 59.
[4] Theodore Levitt, "The Globalization of Markets," *Harvard Business Review,* May–June 1983, p. 93.

In view of the global nature of business today, it is imperative that the international dimensions of a company's operations be incorporated in its strategic planning efforts. For the true multinational corporation (MNC), this means that the global nature of its business must be directly reflected in its ultimate plan—an integrated strategic plan that accounts for intermarket synergy and is not merely a collection of national plans. At the other extreme, for the basically domestic-oriented firm whose only overseas activity is importing/exporting, the international dimension may be merely reflected in its alternative scenarios, competitor analysis, or other components of its plan.

Before indicating the global dimensions that will be covered in this chapter, however, it is important to recognize that many U.S. CEOs and senior corporate officials feel extremely uncomfortable with the international issues of business. Their training and experience have been domestic-related, and despite bridge-up efforts via seminars, current periodicals, and the like, they perceive international business as highly complex and replete with financial and personal risks—something for the specialists. Further, the dangers of international business have been widely chronicled in such popular books as *Big Business Blunders* and *On Wings of Eagles*;[5] the latter describes how Ross Perot, the Texas computer genius, put together a Green Beret–like rescue team to spring his key executives from an Iranian jail. Yet it is essential for the CEO and senior company executives to be sufficiently acquainted with global issues to place such concerns in their proper perspective and to learn about international issues themselves rather than merely relying on specialists. (The latter often leads to either ignoring or overemphasizing the impact that global issues can have on the firm.) One of the authors is reminded of the time he chided a top executive of a medium-sized U.S. manufacturing concern for his company's lack of international export involvement. The serious response from the executive was that he was concerned about the dangers of *expropriation* overseas. Since the company would be merely exporting its products, such a fear was obviously unwarranted, but the

---

[5]David A. Ricks, *Big Business Blunders* (Homewood, Ill.: Dow Jones-Irwin, 1983); Ken Follett, *On Wings of Eagles* (New York: William Morrow & Company, 1983).

executive's response did signal the widespread misconceptions and misinformation about international business operations.

Thus, the authors hope to help CEOs and senior executives to place the complexities and risks of international business in proper perspective, as well as to indicate the international dimensions that should be considered. These dimensions include sundry issues:

- How much weight should the CEO or senior executive assign to the obvious cultural differences one finds in moving from country to country? Are Theodore Levitt, Dean Peebles, John Ryans, and others correct in saying that cultural differences are often "blown out of proportion"?[6] In other words, is it necessary to plan for each market separately, or can an interactive model be employed that indicates the market-to-market tradeoffs required to achieve the optimum plan for the firm as a whole?
- Concomitantly, what kind of global synergy or intermarket strength is potentially lost by decentralizing strategic planning to the local areas and making no attempt to integrate strategic planning?
- How does the fact that the corporation operates under multiple sovereign governments, each affected by its own attitudes toward business—especially foreign business—affect the firm's planning abilities and horizons?
- Can a firm effectively conduct long-term strategic planning in an era in which currency fluctuations (and oftentimes inflation) are rampant? And can strategic planning ever account for political uncertainties like those associated with the overthrow of the Shah in Iran, the spilling of the Iraq-Iran war into the tanker traffic in the Persian Gulf, the kidnapping of a seemingly endless number of corporate executives, and the British-Argentinian Falklands "dispute"? In light of such possibilities, how much emphasis needs to be

---

[6]Levitt, "Globalization of Markets," pp. 92–102; Dean M. Peebles and John K. Ryans, Jr., *Management of International Advertising* (Boston: Allyn & Bacon, 1984), pp. 274–280; Mo Drake, "It's Product Culture That Matters," *Advertising Age's Focus*, April 1984, p. 36.

placed on foreign risk analysis and how does one select a risk-analysis firm?

- What are the appropriate factors to use in comparing market-to-market opportunities and to consider in ultimately establishing priorities for these opportunities?
- What impacts do actions of the U.S. federal government have on U.S. corporations? To what extent can U.S. government positions, which often seem unpredictable, be anticipated? How important is nationalism in the federal government's position?
- Can an understanding of Japanese strategic planning benefit the U.S. executive? That is, to what extent is the Japanese management process regarding planning country-specific to Japan, and to what extent is it "exportable"?
- Is global strategic planning in point of fact really global marketing planning? What are the "right" roles for production, finance, and other functional areas of business in the global planning process?
- What are the most widely tested international strategic planning approaches? And do they recognize that a firm may employ different forms of entry (licensing, joint venture, etc.) in various markets? Is the portfolio approach the one still offering the greatest potential to management?

These are all sound queries and each has contributed in its own way to the reluctance of many international firms to give more than lip service or token attention to strategic planning in international business.

Somewhat parenthetically, a 1980 study by Noel Capon, John Farley, and James Hulbert explored the question of to what extent corporate and strategic planning practices have diffused internationally.[7] The study specifically looked at the degree to which leading U.S. and foreign international managers are aware of the various strategic planning techniques. The findings indicated that, even among the most successful executives,

---

[7]Noel Capon, John U. Farley, and James Hulbert, "International Diffusion of Corporate and Strategic Planning Practices," *Columbia Journal of World Business,* Fall 1980, pp. 5–13.

slightly less than two-thirds are aware of the business portfolio methodology for evaluating products and divisions. While this proportion could be viewed as rather rapid diffusion, it does nevertheless indicate that, even among the best-read and up-to-date overseas executives, the type of strategic planning we are discussing is quite *new*. Further, the study's results revealed that only one-third or less of the firms asked were actually using such planning techniques—and these were most often subsidiaries of transnational companies.

CULTURAL DIFFERENCES

Cultures do differ. The peoples of the world are simply not all alike. Fortunately, cultural anthropologists and international business researchers have helped to identify many of the most significant differences. While language and racial differences are most apparent, any list of "how peoples differ" would also include religion, social class, and, in the more modern parlance, lifestyle.

In estimating the specific product-acceptance potential for a consumer good in a foreign market, for example, culture can be a consideration of great magnitude. Obviously, the market potential for Seagram's products in Kuwait is influenced by the Moslem attitude toward alcoholic beverages. Yet in some instances a cultural "taboo" for one company becomes a market plus for others. It is small wonder that the cola-beverage companies have seen the Middle East as having high potential demand for their products.

Thus, when a company is evaluating what importance it should assign to cultural differences, a very significant consideration is the *type of product or services* it sells. Industrial companies often find few meaningful differences among their various international customers; that is, the customers all tend to have similar technical expertise and product usages. On the other hand, a consumer-products manufacturer may be able to identify certain taste differences among its markets. This kind of experience has led companies like Nestlé to treat each national market as singular. Yet such an individualized approach has not been followed by Barilla, Italy's leading pasta maker. Barilla's managing director is quoted as having said, "Our company does not believe there are insuperable cultural barriers to the acceptance of foreign food products."[8] Interestingly, support for Barilla's position is offered by the Swiss-based International Research Institute of Social Change, which has found that national cultural differences within the European Community tend to be overstressed; it sees an increase in shared "lifestyle" traits today.[9] Similar minimizing of international cultural differences in other areas can be expected with the growing worldwide influence of satellite television.

The pattern for service businesses has many similarities to the industrial product vs. consumer product distinction. Some service companies, such as advertising agencies and public accounting firms, deal with other businesses and, thus, can often give minimal attention to culture. Others, like Kentucky Fried Chicken, McDonalds, and the Sheraton chain, deal directly with the public and so may have to assign greater importance to culture in their international operations.

From a corporate strategic planning point of view, most lists of cultural "dos and don'ts" can be seen as little more than "light reading" and offering nothing more than a few travel caveats for those going to another country. What is really of concern in strategic planning is the identification of the kinds of cultural differences that would, for example, allow a religious leader to take an Iran from a rapidly advancing technological state back toward the Middle Ages. Fortunately, for predictive and planning purposes, most political actions have an underlying *economic* rationale; for example, neither Britain nor Argentina seemed overly concerned about the Falkland Islands until the possibility of offshore oil reserves was identified there. Similarly, most monetary actions are relatively predictable: the devaluation of the Mexican peso, for example, has tended to revolve around the country's national elections. And from a strategic planning perspective, it is the political-risk factors and political actions that most often

---

[8]Quoted in Elizabeth Guider, "Barilla Pushes Pasta Faster," *Advertising Age's Focus,* March 1984, p. 7.
[9]Joel Steatte-McClure, "Now Divided but United by Lifestyle," *Advertising Age's Focus,* January 1982, pp. 12, 13, 15.

make for differences in international and domestic planning. Then, given the importance of political risk, how can managers cope with it in their international planning efforts?

POLITICAL-RISK ANALYSIS

It is imperative for international managers to keep political risk in its proper perspective. Franklin Root has said that "it is possible for the U.S. company to manage political risk in the same objective way it manages the usual business risks."[10] But, too often, American firms have missed exceptional opportunities overseas because they have been *unduly* concerned about political risk.

Our goal is to look at the nature of political risk and to suggest ways for the manager/strategic planner to go about evaluating the importance of various risk factors. Take terrorism. After conducting considerable original research on this topic and its impact on the multinational corporation, we found that international corporate executives rank terrorism second only to inflation among the problems of doing business overseas.[11] In fact, terrorism alone has caused many firms to adopt separate business strategies for some nations. Yet we also found that multinational managers have learned to cope with terrorism in a variety of ways, ranging from the direct avoidance of certain high-risk countries to the establishment of personnel policies that permit making greater use of nationals. In other words, firms have employed tactics especially designed to respond to terrorism in a matter-of-fact, businesslike way, rather than emotionally.

Just what are the political risks that should be considered in making international decisions? Expropriations, trade bans, profit repatriation restrictions, and the like may be the imme-

---

[10]Franklin R. Root, *Entry Strategies for Foreign Markets: From Domestic to International Business* (New York: AMACOM, a division of the American Management Associations, 1977), p. 10.

[11]John K. Ryans, Jr., and William L. Shanklin, "How Managers Cope with Terrorism," *California Management Review*, Vol. 23, No. 2, Winter 1980, pp. 66–72.

diate causes of business problems, but ultimately these events are the consequences of political actions. For long-term planning purposes it is beneficial to identify the various underlying political problems that produce results actually or potentially detrimental to the firm.

F. T. Haner has suggested a framework for political-risk assessment that focuses directly on root causes and thus allows the planner to make judgments about individual countries[12] (see Figure 11). It is helpful for management to attempt to determine the extent to which various internal and external risks are present in a country. Even just the recognition of the presence of symptoms can be useful. For example, Haner indicates that the frequency of violence and general strikes in a country reflects societal conflict. And societal conflicts often result in a poor business climate or even restrictions on profit repatriation. Therefore, the simple process of carefully reading daily newspapers and the business press can provide a good idea of social conditions in a country. Alert multinational executives maintain newspaper clipping files on selected markets and include other international and local country writings that reflect political and social climates of concern. The best-selling book *Megatrends* was based on content analysis of newspaper stories across the United States.

Political-risk assessment lies at the very core of strategic planning in international business. Such risk can be either mitigated or exacerbated by a number of company specifics, notably the nature of the product or industry and the form of entry the firm chooses.

Type of Company

Methods for determining political risk have become increasingly sophisticated, and a number of organizations specializing in risk assessment have been started. A consideration often ignored in this evaluation process, however, is the type of company that needs the information for planning purposes. In practice, the

---

[12]F. T. Haner, "Rating Investment Risks Abroad," *Business Horizons,* April 1979, pp. 18–23.

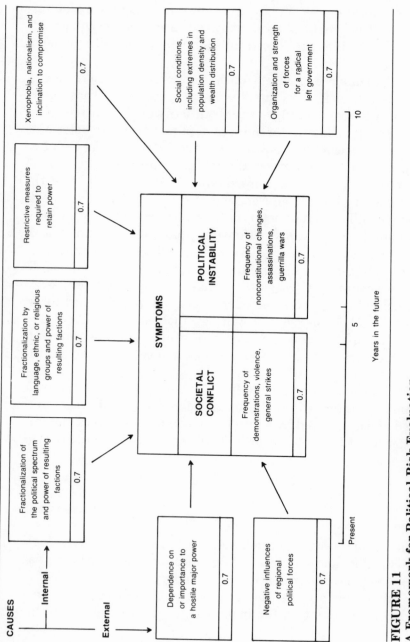

FIGURE 11
A Framework for Political-Risk Evaluation
Source: Reprinted by permission from *Business Horizons*, April 1979, p. 20. ©1979,
Foundation for the School of Business at Indiana University.

risk-assessment organization often provides a general "rating for Peru" rather than, say, a "rating for Peru for a specific elevator manufacturer." Why should country risk ratings be company-specific? Because, clearly, certain types of companies or industries have a greater likelihood of running into political difficulties in countries where they operate. For example, foreign companies in the raw material or extractive industries, such as petroleum and bauxite, have generally had more problems in developing countries than have companies engaged in local manufacture. Similarly, foreign firms in the communications industry have been very vulnerable to expropriation whenever relevant political coups have occurred. Therefore, if a firm is in a politically sensitive industry, it might opt to export or establish licensing arrangements in higher-political-risk countries.

Chapter 1 emphasized the importance of the external environment to a company's planning process and suggested the need to monitor the environment continually. In particular, the use of alternative scenarios in planning was recommended. While not specifically stated in Chapter 1, much of the discussion implicitly related to planning within the company's domestic market.

However, environmental monitoring and the use of alternative scenarios have become increasingly important—and difficult—in international facets of strategic planning. Not only is the firm concerned with happenings within a country such as Peru, it is equally concerned with broader regional and worldwide situations that impact on Peru. Haner has suggested this latter point in his risk-assessment framework, and its importance needs to be reiterated. If a company is doing business in fifteen markets, then it must develop environmental forecasts of activities within each market and for broader regional and worldwide happenings that might externally impact on each market. And, again, these environmental forecasts must be company-specific. If, for instance, the company's only involvement in three of the markets is through exporting to them, then the environmental scenarios for each of the markets might be less detailed than if the company had manufacturing subsidiaries in each of them. There are exceptions to this rule, especially if the company's long-term objectives include the possibility of expanding foreign direct investment to markets currently served only through exports.

Given the recommendation that country-by-country and international or intermarket scenarios need to be developed, just what should they include and what sorts of likely future developments need to be included? To begin with, the kinds of information typically collected in the environmental scanning (see pp. 5–8) need to be obtained for the individual foreign markets. These include cultural, legal, economic, technological, and political kinds of information. It is often in the political area that the firm must be most careful in its assessment. Frequently, plausible political contingencies relate to international political tensions—for example, a return to the Cold War mentality, heightened conflict in the Middle East, or major disruptions in the world economy, as might occur if a number of developing countries defaulted on their commercial debts or a potent new economic group emerged. The number of these contingencies appears to be endless and could keep the strategic planner occupied forever in dysfunctional pursuits. This need not be the case. What is important is for the firm to consider only plausible events and then to develop realistic scenarios. This point has been made most effectively by Selwyn Enzer of the Center for Futures Research, who says:

> Causality suggests that current trends and conditions contain the harbingers of tomorrow's changes, and that tomorrow's changes are the monitoring signals of subsequent changes, and so on. To be effective for strategic planning, a scenario must be sufficiently detailed to trace the causality chain from the present to the new future state—it must be "explicitly plausible." One of the more common weaknesses in scenario generation procedures is their failure to emphasize the importance of developing the evolution of a scenario in sufficient detail so that its plausibility can be evaluated better. . . . items such as defaults by some Third World and Western nations on debts held by the large international banks are widely discussed by strategic planners today. However, one rarely encounters a scenario that plausibly describes how those events evolve from current conditions, or the follow-on state of the world economy if these defaults were to occur.[13]

---

[13]Selwyn Enzer, "Exploring Long-Term Business Climates and Strategies with Interax," *Futures: The Journal of Forecasting and Planning,* Vol. 13, Number 6, December 1981, p. 471.

Enzer continues by describing a "plausible scenario" whereby Brazil, South Korea, and Turkey find themselves unable to meet their minimum foreign exchange needs as a result of ever-increasing interest rates and oil prices.

Political-risk factors are the overriding environmental ingredient and provide the basis for the development of plausible alternative scenarios regarding the future. Recognition of this lesson from multinational business history is central to effective strategic planning for world markets.

Forms of Entry

Since strategic planning is rarely conducted under conditions where the firm is a complete novice in the foreign arena, another consideration that needs to be evaluated is the current "forms of entry" it is employing in the various markets overseas. Franklin Root has described the "transition from domestic to multinational enterprise" as an evolution through three stages: (1) the export stage, (2) the foreign production stage, and (3) the multinational enterprise stage.[14] During this process, the typical international firm uses several different entry strategies, depending upon particular markets. To illustrate, the company may be exporting to Canada, employing a licensing arrangement in Australia, producing through a joint-venture facility in Mexico and Brazil, and operating a wholly owned subsidiary in Belgium to serve the European Community (E.C.). Strategically, the company's plan might call for changing the current form of entry in any or all of these countries. But it is essential to recognize that the obstacles to doing so tend to be much greater than the obstacles to making similar changes domestically. Mexico, for example, requires that the foreign firm hold only a minority interest in its Mexican operations, so any long-term strategy must accommodate this requirement. In the same vein, Belgium has rigid restrictions regarding plant closings. This constraint would be a very pertinent consideration to a company that might otherwise decide to switch production to Ireland, where the same

---

[14]Root, *Entry Strategies for Foreign Markets,* p. 10.

access to the E.C. is available and the investment incentives are more favorable.

Realistically, any strategic planning effort must take into consideration the firm's present form of entry and allow for national differences (and nationalism), access to economic groupings, other intermarket trade patterns, investment incentives, and so on. We might add that corporate rigidity regarding form of entry (e.g., U.S. firms have historically preferred wholly owned subsidiaries) is not apt to be a formula for success overseas in the coming decades.

Political-Risk Analysis Selection

A growing number of firms have entered the field of foreign-risk analysis and, as might be expected, have varying degrees of expertise to offer (and different track records). Business International and the Economist Intelligence Unit Ltd. have provided a variety of information for many years. Purchasers of these and like services are aware of the firms' monitoring of markets throughout the world and the high quality of their financial and economic data. For example, the Economist Intelligence Unit Ltd. advertised a special report titled *South Africa: Business Prospects Reassessed,* which looked at business opportunities "in light of slower world growth, possible trade sanctions, mounting labour unrest, the oil embargo and an oscillating gold price."[15] This is just one type of data available from the group. Other organizations specialize solely in risk assessment, and it may be a bit difficult for the firm newly engaged in international business (or just exploring) to judge their qualifications.

What are the suggested steps an international business executive can take in order to determine the value of different risk-analysis organizations? (The names of organizations may be obtained from sources such as U.S. Department of Commerce regional offices; the international divisions of multinational banks—Citibank, Bank of America, Chase, etc.; world trade

---

[15]Economist Intelligence Unit Ltd. advertisement, *The Economist,* July 3, 1982, p. 86.

organizations—located in most major cities; the International Chamber of Commerce; or from a local multinational already engaged in doing business abroad. Most of these sources are likely to list several organizations rather than recommending a specific organization.) We suggest the following five steps:

1. Contact several risk-analysis organizations and ask for samples of their work, as well as for a list of firms currently using their services. (Most will be reluctant to list all their customers because this is proprietary information, but they will be able to indicate a few.)
2. Specifically, ask the organizations to demonstrate how accurately they forecasted a recent political or economic event, such as a coup or an important currency devaluation.
3. Contact (telephone) an international executive in one of the MNCs that are listed among their clients and determine his or her degree of satisfaction with the firm's services.
4. Determine what firm appears to best meet your requirements.
5. Find out exactly what the political-risk analysis firm charges for the services your company needs. (Your costs will be reduced if you can minimize the amount of company-specific information and individualized studies required.)

Undoubtedly, the executive who subscribes to several business journals has already received literature from one or more risk-analysis organizations. (It is easy to get on such mailing lists.) However, it is advisable to follow the steps we have suggested. Remember that poor-quality risk-assessment information is likely to be less valuable than just reading *The Economist, Business Week, The Financial Times* (London), *The Wall Street Journal, The Asian Wall Street Journal,* and similar publications. For example, each week *The Economist* features one country and thoroughly examines it current political/economic situation. Further, the U.S. Department of Commerce's biweekly magazine *Business America* and its *Overseas Business Reports* on individual overseas markets are valuable information sources. However, while all these publications offer useful insight, the value of the risk-analysis organization is that it can provide specific company and industry data and it offers comparative assessments among various countries—for instance, Chile is a better location for direct investment than Peru or Bolivia, because. . . .

Finally, we hope it is obvious from our discussion in this section that a good rule to follow in selecting a risk-analysis organization is *caveat emptor*. By following the steps suggested, the international executive can avoid the charlatans who have unfortunately been attracted to the field.

FEDERAL REGULATIONS/POLICIES AND THE COMPANY'S GLOBAL OPERATIONS

For years, U.S. companies engaged in international business have undoubtedly been frustrated more by their own country's policies than by foreign restrictions. In early 1984, *Business Week,* reporting on the Harris Poll of American business leaders that it sponsored, found growing support for a "national industrial policy."[16] This unexpected finding perhaps resulted from the state of the economy, the growing trade deficit, increased foreign competition, or unemployment—or, for that matter, from any combination of these. But management's attitude might instead have reflected growing frustration over the seeming lack of direction in U.S. foreign trade policy that has prevailed for decades. In a 1983 study by the Congressional Budget Office entitled *The Industrial Policy Debate,* a reference was made to the "myriad of proposals [that] have been made to establish a consistent industrial policy."[17] Further, the study indicated that those who wish to merely reform current policy, rather than establish a new government policymaking body, are motivated by what they see as the necessity to *free* American business from its domestic restraints in order to make it competitive internationally.

Obviously, the kinds of inconsistencies that have been pervasive have made the need for global planning greater, but at the

---

[16]"A Cautious Nod to Industrial Policy," *Business Week,* March 19, 1984, p. 15.
[17]Congressional Budget Office, *The Industrial Policy Debate* (Washington, D.C.: U.S. Government Printing Office, December 1983), p. xvii.

same time have made the international business planner's job more difficult. Let us consider several quite recent examples that add to the corporation's dilemma regarding international strategic planning. For years, the United States has championed the cause of freer trade and through the Department of Commerce has encouraged, even chided, American producers to export. More recently, the federal government appears to be giving a new signal: it has established "barriers" to the export of high technology. Initial U.S. concern for the export of computer equipment with potential military applications was broadened to cover biotechnology and other high-tech items. The complications regarding clearances and related matters began to make exporters wonder if the U.S. trade policy had become one of protecting technology rather than free trade. The U.S. government has also been criticized by its foreign partners for employing an extraterritoriality policy: that is, imposing domestic-related legislation on U.S. companies' overseas subsidiaries and customers (and attempting to force economic or trade rules on global business allies). The U.S. government's actions in Europe regarding the controversial Soviet pipeline deal offer a case in point. Then, of course, the United States' use of grain and foodstuffs as a bargaining tool has also caused concern. And not all of these confusing policies have had to do with U.S.-Soviet relations.

To the U.S. executive attempting to plan for his or her company's future opportunities overseas, these mixed signals dramatically impact on the executive's ability to predict the future. Further, federal government agencies themselves have rather consistently failed to operate in concert. Two actions that gave considerable hope of a reduction of inter-agency squabbles were the increased role of the Department of Commerce (DOC) in the selection of commercial attachés for U.S. overseas embassies, and the clear delineation of duties between the DOC and the Justice Department regarding the approval of charters for export trading companies. However, the more recent conflict between the DOC and the Department of Defense (DOD) over the control of high-tech products indicates that a consistent trade policy may continue to be an unfulfilled hope. In late April of 1984, *Business Week* reported on the feuding between the two agencies and particularly cited the strong *and opposing* positions being taken by DOD's Assistant Secretary, Richard N. Perle, and

DOC's Under Secretary for International Trade, Lionel H. Olmer. DOD's Perle felt that even the sale of Apple IIs to the Soviet bloc should be prohibited, as the computers could be used for military purposes. Olmer reportedly countered that controlling the sale of personal computers would be "wildly impractical" and even dysfunctional—that is, would direct DOC resources away from monitoring the sale of a "truly strategic technology."[18]

Controversies of this nature are not new, nor peculiar to any particular political party. The point is that upper management must consider such conflicts when contemplating and planning for the future in the global business arena. Further, it must be recognized that not all federal actions will be negative or unpredictable. For example, even in the most protectionist of times, the U.S. government typically has a most positive overall export orientation, and legislation is often formulated to improve our trade posture. The Export Trading Company Act (ETCA) is a case in point. The ETCA is primarily enabling legislation designed to permit the establishment of "Japanese-style" trading companies in the United States and is seen as a boost to trade. In other words, the ETCA creates exclusions from antitrust laws and banking regulations that would allow, among other possibilities, the blending of a commercial bank with competing manufacturers and an export specialist. Regardless of whether or not the legislation is successful in achieving increased trade, it represents the continued U.S. policy theme of supporting exports.

How can the global executive anticipate changes arising from Washington that might impact on his or her international strategic planning efforts? While we have tended to focus here on U.S. efforts to stimulate or prohibit exports, there are many other federal actions that directly affect global strategic planning. These include a host of regulations and policies related to taxes, monetary issues, environmental issues, foreign aid, and government-to-government relations. For instance, a few years ago a change in federal income tax laws dealing with American

---

[18]"Reagan's East-West Trade Muddle," *Business Week,* April 30, 1984, p. 151.

expatriate personnel led some companies to make a mass shift of U.S. employees back to the States and to rely increasingly on local managers. Similarly, any change in the level of foreign aid directly affects U.S. manufacturers, since well over 90 percent of foreign aid stipulates the purchase of American goods and services. To fully monitor *all* of these potential influences in-house would require an extensive staff, and indeed many large corporations maintain a Washington office or employ lobbyists for this purpose. Others rely on information from their trade associations or the business press (*The Wall Street Journal, Business Week, Business Marketing,* etc.), or they may purchase one of the many Washington newsletter services.

The amount and timeliness of information needed, of course, depend upon the extent of the company's level or planned level of global involvement. In any event, a lack of correct information can have enormous repercussions on a company's operations. The authors are reminded of a medium-sized industrial company's reaction to the so-called Arab boycott legislation (and the confusion that surrounded it) a few years ago. Thinking that *any* company dealing in the Middle East might be censured, the company withdrew from what would have been the largest sale it would have ever made to that time. Management believed that since it could not get a clear reading on the Arab boycott legislation, signed into law by President Carter in June 1977, it would be more prudent to avoid the deal entirely. In fact, as the reader might have guessed, the transaction in question would have been entirely legal. This company was not alone in its withdrawal action. A 1978 study of major U.S. companies operating overseas indicated that roughly one-half were similarly discouraged from doing business in Arab markets, because of the confusion over the legislation.[19]

Usually, the types of information needed are really quite company-specific. Key issues are the amount and type of the company's foreign commitment, the percentage of its current and planned sales overseas, and the nature of its business. As a

---

[19]John K. Ryans, Jr., and James R. Wills, Jr., "The Arab Boycott: A Real or Psychological Barrier?" *Akron Business and Economic Review,* Summer 1978, p. 33.

guide to determining its federal informational needs, a company must consider a number of questions. For example, it should ask itself:

1. Are we engaged (or will we become engaged) in the production or sales of products or services that have possible military applications?
2. Are there current (or likely) regulations regarding the exportation of our products or services?
3. Are our international sales an essential component of our total or projected operations?
4. Are we currently assigning U.S. nationals to our overseas operations?
5. Is our own government (or are foreign governments) included among our customers?
6. Are there significant import restrictions that impede the sale of our products/processes/services in our current and potential markets?
7. Is the sales level of our products/applications/services in foreign markets sensitive to the value of the dollar?
8. Do we have licenses or joint ventures with foreign companies, either for the sales of products/services in the United States or in a foreign market(s)?
9. Are we engaged in joint research assignments with foreign companies or laboratories?
10. Are we dependent on foreign sources for products, raw materials, components, and so forth?

If one or more of these questions is answered affirmatively, then the company needs to monitor current and pending U.S. actions—legislative, judicial, and executive. As an illustration, would a presidential executive order concerning trade with Country A or a ruling by a federal district court that one of our foreign suppliers was guilty of dumping in the United States have significant impact on our company's operations, both domestic and foreign? We need to anticipate the possibility and probability of such occurrences and build them into our global as well as domestic scenarios. Further, to determine potential problems and their likelihood of occurrence, a company needs to have regular and reliable information sources—just as with its foreign risk-assessment efforts.

PUTTING CURRENT GLOBAL PLANNING APPROACHES INTO PERSPECTIVE

A decade ago, two authorities provided this metaphor to describe the problems of "practicing what we preach" in planning for foreign markets: "like the fat person and his weight-watcher program, multinational planning has been difficult to implement despite the fact that all the necessary skills seem to be known and available."[20] Earlier still, William Cain cited implementation hindrances ranging from language differences to the domestic orientation of most U.S. firms' top management to the lack of cooperation from foreign unit managers.[21] Today, many critics and more than a few practitioners of strategic planning for international markets would share these pessimistic views and certainly confirm the difficulties. Nonetheless, a few international strategic planning approaches/models have been suggested; most relate to marketing planning and strategy and employ modification of the product portfolio approach described in Chapter 4. Particularly instructive is a method recommended by Gilbert Harrell and Richard Kiefer, based on Kiefer's experiences at Ford Motor Company's international tractor operations.

The Harrell and Kiefer Market Portfolio Approach

To begin with, Harrell and Kiefer focus on *market conditions,* rather than *products,* as the principal unit of strategic endeavor. Thus, although they employ a portfolio methodology, they feel

---

[20]S. Prakash Sethi and Jagdish N. Sheth, *Multinational Business Operations: Long-Range Planning, Organization, and Management* (Pacific Palisades, Calif.: Goodyear Publishing Company, 1973), p. xviii.
[21]William W. Cain, "International Planning: Mission Impossible," *Columbia Journal of World Business,* July–August 1970, p. 58.

it is more appropriate to make international decisions about *market portfolios* than about portfolios of products. To illustrate their approach, they use Ford's overseas tractor operations and point out that some of Ford's greatest opportunities "were due to broad potential profit variations across market areas" rather than within national borders.[22]

Further, Harrell and Kiefer tell us that a difficulty in using the basic product portfolio approach (discussed in Chapter 4) is that the various overseas markets often are in markedly contrasting stages of the product life cycle. To avoid this problem, they examine each market in terms of a given country's attractiveness on the one hand and the company's competitive strength in the country on the other.

As with any use of portfolio analysis or some variation of its grid schema, the quality of the model is derived largely from the quality of the inputs employed in assigning the relative positions on the grid—that is, in determining whether the country has low or high attractiveness and whether the company is highly competitive or not in the country. Herein lies the value of the Harrell and Kiefer approach: they suggest the appropriate factors for determining a country's attractiveness and a company's competitive strength in the market. Factors recommended for ascertaining a country's attractiveness include market size (company-specific), market growth (annual, company-specific), government regulation (price controls, etc.), and economic and political stability (inflation, trade balance, political turnover). For competitive strength, Harrell and Kiefer use market share, product fit (Ford's subjective assessment of how its product characteristics match local needs), contribution margin, and market support (dealer representatives' quality and Ford's necessary level of market support). This evaluation procedure incorporates some items that are generally factual (e.g., market share) with the company's own singular qualities such as market fit, which are more subjective.

To better convey the approach that Harrell and Kiefer suggest, we are presenting three illustrations from their article (see

---

[22]Gilbert D. Harrell and Richard O. Kiefer, "Multinational Strategic Market Portfolios," *MSU Business Topics,* Vol. 29, No. 1, Winter 1981, pp. 5–15.

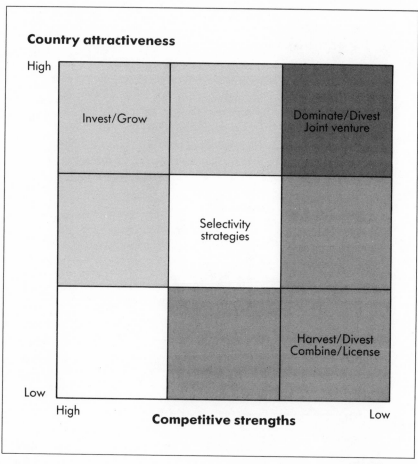

FIGURE 12
Matrix for Plotting Products

Figures 12, 13, and 14).[23] Figure 12 is quite similar in appearance to the portfolios we described in Chapter 4. It depicts the company's situation in a single country and, based on where the company's product(s) are located on the grid, would recommend a strategy to follow. Plotted on the two axes are the country's

---

[23]Tables from Gilbert D. Harrell and Richard O. Kiefer, "Multinational Strategic Market Portfolios," *MSU Business Topics,* pp. 7, 12, 13, Winter 1981; reprinted by permission.

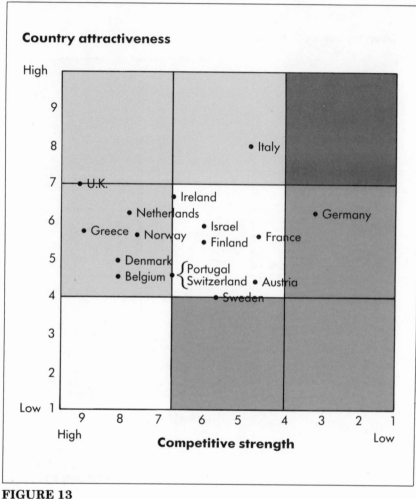

FIGURE 13
European Matrix

attractiveness as a market and the company's competitive position in the market. For example, if it were felt that Ford Tractors were located in the lower right block for Country A, the recommendation would be to divest or license its product(s) *in that country*. (This position is akin to "dog" in the traditional Boston Consulting Group portfolio model.) Naturally, the considerations that give rise to the rating for the particular country/mar-

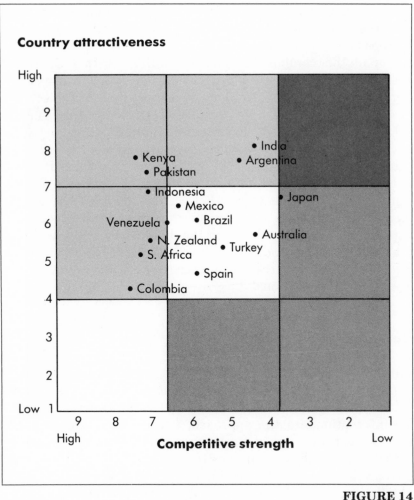

FIGURE 14
Key-Country Matrix

ket might be unique to the company: Ford Tractors might consider "product fit" to be more important to competitive strength than would another company. Therefore, each company must determine for itself the factors underlying different positions on the two axes. The only caveat we would offer is that the same factors be considered for *each* country that is analyzed. This becomes most apparent as we next turn to Figures 13 and 14.

137

In Figure 13, all of the countries in a particular region of the world are compared. Whether a company may choose to compare Europe, as is shown in this figure developed by Harrell and Kiefer, or another combination such as South America or Southeast Asia, is a company-specific decision. The advantages of the approach shown in Figure 13 are that executives can objectively (1) establish priorities for countries within a given region, and (2) identify any synergy that may be found in the region. Alternatively, the company may choose to compare *categories* of countries—for example, newly emerging industrialized, developed, or less-developed nations, as shown in Figure 14. For the Ford Tractor example, we see that Harrell and Kiefer have rated Kenya and Pakistan as being in the invest/grow blocks and Japan comes closest to being in the divest/license blocks. Thus, they would recommend Kenya and Pakistan as having the highest priority among the key countries shown in Figure 14 for the Ford Tractor operations.

Our Comments

Initially, therefore, the Harrell and Kiefer market portfolio approach indicates for a given market or country the relative value of various products and suggests actions for that market. To internationalize the approach, further steps are required: that is, the firm can now aggregate the various markets for individual products by directly positioning all the countries considered on the *same* matrix. Again, using Ford Tractor as an example, the matrix could include all European countries or cover a broad spectrum of countries. Such comparisons offer a basis for long-run planning in terms of which markets need further investments, which should be divested, and so forth.

However, while this approach provides an excellent tool for strategic and tactical decisions, it does imply that each market can be viewed alone. This is not always the case and, in fact, many intermarket decisions are required if a firm is to optimize its overseas efforts. For example, in Western Europe there is extensive media overlap among countries. Therefore, certain marketing advantages may be gained through a more all-Europe approach. Also, a production location in one European Community country offers the producer tariff-reduced access to the entire ten-country economic group. For instance, a decision to withdraw from Ireland because the country has become unattractive to the company may cost the firm all the Western European markets it has been reaching via exports from its Irish plant. So any possible or actual synergistic effect needs to be taken into account in a firm's overseas planning.

Another Portfolio Approach

A second portfolio approach has been suggested by Yoram Wind and Susan Douglas.[24] While their method has not been fully operationalized (as has the one offered by Harrell and Kiefer), it has promise to overcome the lack of intermarket analysis that we just referred to.

Wind and Douglas recognize the need to integrate the firm's international operations "across national boundaries in order to take maximum advantage of potential synergies and leverage arising from operations in multicountry markets."[25] And they too recommend a modified (and much more complex) version of product portfolio analysis as the framework for analysis. In their view, international portfolios "should be considered at various levels (such as corporate, strategic business unit, and even product group) and for various units of analysis including countries, modes of entry, specific products, and market segments."[26]

In particular, Wind and Douglas call for a resource allocation that takes into account the projected outcome of each course of action on the "relevant management objectives." For example, they correctly point out that the R&D required for developing or modifying a product for a single market may be uneconomic. But for several related markets, such expenditure might be quite economic.

Their suggested approach to designing a system for portfolio

---

[24]Yoram Wind and Susan Douglas, "International Portfolio Analysis and Strategy: The Challenge of the 80s," *Journal of International Studies,* Fall 1981, pp. 69–82.
[25]Ibid., p. 70.
[26]Ibid.

analysis will not be detailed here. However, it combines what they call the Analytic Hierarchy Process with Stochastic Dominance Analysis. The former is a conceptual and measurement approach that relies on the subjective judgments of relevant managers to develop alternative international portfolio options. This process involves the assessment of a large number of portfolios "of countries by mode of entry, products, and market segments based on their opportunities and risks."[27] Thus a combination of qualitative and quantitative methods is utilized to determine the best allocation of the firm's resources across markets. We expect to follow the further development and testing of this model, as it may offer a very useful planning tool for the future.

WHAT CAN BE LEARNED FROM FOREIGN STRATEGIC PLANNERS?

Recently, much attention in the U.S. business community has focused on how foreign companies manage their operations. This interest is undoubtedly due to the successes that Japanese producers, as well as some from other countries, have had in the U.S. market. The thinking goes that if "they" can dominate our own marketplace, they must know something ... have some secrets for success. And, if this assumption is correct, then we need to consider what are the characteristics of Japanese or German or British strategic planning that might be useful to U.S. companies.

The Japanese

Japanese management style and culture have been popular topics for authors. Recently, we have seen *Theory Z, The Art of Japanese Management,* and *From Bonsai to Levi's,* to name but a few books on the subject. Each attempts to offer a better

---

[27]Ibid., p. 76.

understanding of the Japanese society in general, and most explore the Japanese corporation in some depth.

In particular, an article by Warren Keegan has effectively captured the essence of the strategy employed by the top-performing Japanese companies and has described the critical differences between the goals and objectives of U.S. and Japanese firms.[28] Keegan cites the fact that every Japanese firm has a well-developed business philosophy and ensures that it is understood throughout the company. This business philosophy becomes the essential ingredient for the company's planning efforts. This principle is basically what is followed in the most successful U.S. firms. More important lessons may be learned from the comparison between Japanese and U.S. companies' goals and objectives for the business. Unlike U.S. companies, Japanese firms tend to set goals that are more truly *aspirations*—that is, something to be sought, but possibly never fully attained. Their objectives are more pragmatic, more akin to what we commonly refer to as goals. But, whereas in most all U.S. companies the short-term measures (quarter-to-quarter) receive the bulk of the attention, the Japanese give simultaneous attention to the short-term and long-term.

It is perhaps this issue of long-term/short-term objectives that provides the greatest contrast between U.S. and Japanese businesses (and strategies). One of the authors recalls a visit to Kenya shortly after its independence in the late 1960s. While Western companies were scurrying to "pull up stakes," Nairobi and Mombassa were crowded with Japanese executives looking for tomorrow's opportunities. While there are many underlying reasons for the differences between U.S. and Japanese planning horizons, ranging from business-government relations to CEO-job lifespan, the typical American company can benefit, especially overseas, by taking a longer-term perspective à la the Japanese.

Overall, however, we recommend that U.S. companies not be too quick to totally accept and follow Japanese management

---

[28]Warren J. Keegan, "Strategic Market Planning: The Japanese Approach," *International Marketing Review,* Autumn 1983, pp. 5–15.

style and philosophy. What may work in a highly homogeneous society may not be appropriate in a U.S. company's heterogeneous world. Rather, a sounder approach is to merely draw on the best the Japanese offer, a tactic well-conducted by the Japanese themselves.

The British and Europeans

While Great Britain and Europe provided some of the early planners, such as Michael Brooke and H. Lee Remmers,[29] perhaps the most useful recent contributions have been specialists in international management and in organizational design. Here we would consider, for example, Lawrence Franko, John Stopford, and Louis T. Wells.[30]

In Great Britain, Malcolm McDonald has studied the global marketing planning practices of some 200 industrial companies.[31] (Like Keegan, McDonald has focused on the marketing planning process, but his comments and insights are useful for corporate strategic planning.) Based on his study, McDonald realistically concludes that many firms have confused market planning and sales forecasting, while others seem unaware of the need for nondomestic planning. However, his major contribution, from our perspective, is his discussion of the role of the CEO in planning; he stresses the need for the top official to see the need for a *formalized* market planning system, to understand it, and to show an active interest in it. This is a perspective we heartily endorse and add that the failure of CEOs to demonstrate interest in planning is a common problem in the States as well. (Because McDonald's presentation highlights so many common strategic planning problems that senior company offi-

---

[29]Michael Z. Brooke and H. Lee Remmers, *The Strategy of Multinational Enterprise* (London: Longman, 1970).
[30]Lawrence G. Franko, *The European Multinationals* (Stamford, Conn.: Greylock Publishers, 1976); John M. Stopford and Louis T. Wells, *Managing the Multinational Enterprise* (New York: Basic Books, 1972).
[31]Malcolm McDonald, "International Marketing Planning: The Gap Between Theory and Practice," *International Marketing Review*, Autumn 1983, pp. 42–58.

cials should be aware of, we have included his article in the Appendix at the end of the book.)

PERSPECTIVES

From our discussion of international planning, we hope to convey that only limited attention has been given to this topic to date. Even so, we feel that the market portfolio model offered by Harrell and Kiefer—the one employed by Ford Tractor's overseas operations—is quite workable. It allows the planner to compare multiple markets and make long-term decisions regarding research allocations. It is limited, however, because it does not consider synergies and leverage arising from operations in multiple markets. Of course, the development of alternative scenarios based on the actions suggested by Harrell and Kiefer's market portfolio approach might offset this limitation—for example, "if we close the Irish plant what will happen to our E.C. competitiveness?"

Clearly, a firm can determine just what measure (competitive strength, R&D efforts, etc.) is critical to its overseas decision making. And this measure can be employed along with country or market attractiveness for each of its products or its total product line or mix. Then the country-by-country results can be aggregated à la Harrell and Kiefer. This step will identify those markets ripe for future investments and those that should be handled by licenses or eliminated altogether. Before adopting such actions into long-term strategy, however, the firm needs to develop alternative scenarios to get at whether these proposed moves will have negative intermarket results.

In summary, the type of portfolio model we recommend:

- Permits evaluation of individual country markets
- Allows for intermarket comparisons
- Recognizes product-life-cycle differences between markets
- Accounts for political risk and economic change
- Successfully meshes diverse types of salient market/corporate information

If the model merely focuses on local market factors, it could be ignoring such concerns as the value of the dollar across markets or a current U.S. foreign trade policy that could impact on several markets. Matrices like those in Figures 12, 13, and 14 could be developed under worst-case and best-case longer-term scenarios—for example, one in which the dollar is quite weak overseas and one in which it is quite strong. This procedure would provide the company with a realistic understanding of the potential, as well as the downside risk, of following a particular strategy.

STRATEGIC PLANNING APPLIED GLOBALLY

The views of Robert T. Spahr (American Motors/ Renault) on strategic planning are presented in this chapter. Spahr feels strategic planning is a function historically considered to be the sole responsibility of the CEO. Therefore, the strategic planning department's objective is to aid the chief executive in his or her long-term strategic positioning and planning. As a relatively new activity, strategic planning is evolving and its parameters are changing.

Speaking specifically of international strategic planning, Spahr sees its basic role as similar to that of domestic planning. However, he points out that the international environment is more complex and filled with more uncertainty. As a result, the planner must accept higher risk tolerance; the assumptions are more tentative. Spahr considers portfolio analysis and other strategic planning techniques to be useful; however, he notes that their role in planning must be kept in perspective. They are tools. (And the same must be said for risk-analysis techniques.) While such tools are valuable, Spahr says,

145

there is always a "seat of the pants" judgment to be made in international strategic planning.

According to Spahr, there are several problems inherent in international strategic planning. These problems relate to (1) multiple environments and multiple product uses; (2) cultural differences, especially fundamental differences in "ways of looking at things"; (3) fluctuations in the currency exchange rates; (4) difficulties in obtaining information (and processing it); (5) communications flow weaknesses; and (6) regulatory concerns. With this number of problems, it is not surprising that Spahr feels that there should be more flexibility in international strategic planning than in domestic planning and that the international strategic planner needs to have some overseas experience.

There are numerous problems associated with international strategic planning and a number of possible approaches to follow, including the ones recommended in the preceding chapter. Faced with the dilemmas, but needing to develop actual short-, medium-, and longer-term plans, how does the international planner respond to this challenge?

To obtain the views of a practicing international strategic planner, we interviewed Robert Spahr, the Director of International Strategic Planning at American Motors/Renault. Not only are Robert Spahr's credentials impeccable for such an assignment, he is also able to speak from the perspective of someone employed by an innovative American industrial concern—one willing to enter into a joint operation with a major government-owned organization in Europe. However, we have asked Spahr not to offer a company position (for obvious proprietary reasons) and not to limit his views to those of the auto industry. Rather, we are interested in seeing how he copes with questions of cultural differences, nationalism, and multi-nation (developing and developed) opportunities and problems.

Further, we wanted to know how, if at all, international strategic planning differs from domestic strategic planning. And how he, as a strategic planner, has worked to develop credibility for strategic planning within his organization. In addition, we explored various aspects of the strategic planning process with Spahr and obtained his opinion on such activities as scenario development and competitor analysis. Finally, just how sophisticated can international strategic planning be today and is there a tendency to rely too heavily on quantitative models, rather than on judgment?

INTERVIEW WITH ROBERT T. SPAHR AMERICAN MOTORS/RENAULT

INTERVIEWER: What is the appropriate role for strategic planning in the firm, especially an international corporation?

SPAHR: Let us first examine what strategic planning is, as I see it. A short definition is that it represents a business equivalent of "planning moves ahead in chess." A more specific definition would be that strategic planning is a planning process undertaken in recognition of the fact that a company's future competitive position will be affected by the evolution of both fundamental and competitively generated long-term trends in all aspects of the business. To an extent, these trends (1) are predictable; (2) are addressable through consistent, intelligently formulated, and properly timed short and long lead-time actions; and (3) will *not* be as effectively addressed through a series of short-term actions solely based on short-term focus.

Strategic planning represents to me the latest in a spin-off of departments accorded functions that were historically considered the sole responsibility of the CEO. The objective, therefore, is to assist him or her in long-term strategic positioning and planning; that's right across the board, involving products, markets, methods, policies—virtually anything of strategic significance. That's a rather broad view. The field is still new. The scope of its responsibilities is still evolving, still being tested. For now, CEOs must make their own decisions on what their strategic planners should do.

In addressing this issue, I think the CEO has to take into consideration that the following factors are rather important: first, what the CEO feels he needs perhaps as a supplement to his experience, or perhaps in an area of complexity that he

147

doesn't have time to address. Second, what the CEO is willing to delegate. He may have a preference on what he'd like his strategic planning people to do and what he'd like to keep for himself, because, after all, these are his sole responsibilities before he sets up this office. If he feels he's an expert on something and he isn't going to take any direction on it, then there is no sense in wasting time or setting up a conflict situation by assigning it, in name only, to strategic planning. Third, what objectively does he actually need; and in that sense, it may be somewhat different from what he feels he needs. A CEO who wants to address that question should go to his organization, because collectively, they know, perhaps better than he does, what is needed. Hints have probably been dropped or questions raised in meetings that might give some suggestions as to what the corporation needs.

I think that the functions of strategic planning should start small, generally speaking. Make initial objectives clear, and let the strategic planner you have selected help you decide where to go from there. I think you have to resist the tendency to over-extend because results are not immediately evident, easily measurable, or highly conspicuous; hence the excessiveness of an overly large organization will not be readily identified or corrected except in the long term. The CEO should continually evaluate whether the function is helping him or not, and if he comes to the conclusion that he has some problems, he ought to ask himself if it's the strategic planning process as he's trying to do it or if it's the person he has chosen for the job, or a combination of both.

INTERVIEWER: Do you see this role changing for the strategic planner?

SPAHR: Yes, I do. I see it slowly, over time, becoming more focused, more narrowly defined, and evolving toward more effective approaches in many ways. Don't ask me how it's going to ultimately resolve itself. I am not sure, other than for the fact that I expect it to grow in use. I think it is a little bit too soon to tell. However, I want to say that it's not a be-all and end-all. New functions often tend to become regarded as panaceas. This is really just another tool. I suppose there will be a period of euphoria and then a period of disillusionment. Organization planners will feel compelled to define, restrict, pigeonhole. Ulti-

148

mately, the field definition will be much more cut and dried, and then it will be probably restricted from delivery on its full potential and promise, and academia will have to invent a new field to cover the next spin-off from the CEO. However, there is a potential danger that I see, and I think it could lead to a very serious mistake. I feel that with the increasing focus on "let's get a bunch of charts together that follow certain patterns" and so forth, it could become a function robbed of some of its more demanding, creative aspects. If you boil it down too much in that direction, it becomes very logical at some point to say "let us put strategic planning under finance or marketing because they do a lot of numbers." At that point, I honestly feel the concept is blown. It is necessary for this office to operate in the perspective, not of a financial person, not of a marketing person, but of a CEO who is thinking of the entire sphere of business operations. If you stick it in one of those other departments, I think that it will just go away or become ineffective.

INTERVIEWER: What type of individual makes the best strategic planner, especially on international strategic plans?

SPAHR: I believe that it is very important to look for a person who is very much a generalist, very experienced. This person doesn't have to have experience in every aspect of the business, but I think you are almost better off getting an individual from your own international organization, because there are so many complexities particular to the international sphere to cope with that it takes a long time to train people.

INTERVIEWER: Do you feel international strategic planning differs significantly from domestic strategic planning?

SPAHR: The basic role of strategic planning is essentially the same, but for any given type of business I think you will find that the international environment is generally of much greater complexity and significantly greater uncertainty. There are more competitive variables. There is a broader variety of issues, cultural implications, and so forth. There is usually less information available, and it is generally not as good. In general, you do not have as much volume in any given international market versus a home market, which means that you cannot spend as much money gathering information. This typically dictates, therefore, a different approach. It is less intense—i.e., you have to accept higher risk tolerance. The assumptions you make are more tentative. The time frame tends to be shorter-term. And you have to face the fact that your international strategic planning person is going to look somewhat less professional than his or her domestic counterpart because the international planner is coping with a more complex problem and cannot speak with as much certainty.

INTERVIEWER: Now let us consider the question of just how formal this strategic plan should be?

SPAHR: I'd say that the most significant consideration here depends upon one's analysis of one's own business and the requirements one has for that business. First, in terms of the formalization of the plans, let me say that the strategic planning process in itself isn't just limited to the production of formal plans. It's obviously necessary for formal plans to be generated, and these plans, of course, are not just ones that deal ultimately with the financial side of the business, i.e., generating expectations in the future of certain cash flows and so forth. Nor are they just product plans for what model of your product will be launched in what country and in what year and so forth. They are long-term plans and programs for the overall operation of the business. They are obviously coordinated in a certain sense, but they don't necessarily have to relate to one another into an integrated whole, as long as they do not interfere with one another. In other words, you can have a number of different strategies that you are implementing all at once. The reason you have to have them formalized is that unless you put something down on paper, people forget, they modify the plan a little in their own minds, and over a period of time they will tend to lose sight of what the objectives are, why and how you were planning on getting there, and what the background considerations were. If there is a change in the environment and you have not documented what your environmental assumptions were, there is the possibility you may miss the necessity of changing that plan. Strategic plans should not be changed very often, but obviously sometimes circumstances change and you have to change plans with them.

150

On the other hand, another part of the strategic planning process that I see is a need to keep the things bubbling, to keep bringing up ideas, bouncing them off people. It's a formalization of, to an extent, what gets discussed in the executive washroom or at the old boys' club perhaps in past days; the need for formalization is very important to get things documented and to assure consistent attention to the issues. You see, the reason you set up the strategic planning department, or one of the major reasons, was that you decided that you needed *consistent* attention being paid to *forward strategy*. The CEO himself is often not capable of giving it that consistency because he is distracted by other, shorter-term considerations.

INTERVIEWER: What time horizons appear relevant for strategic planning?

SPAHR: Again, this depends very much on circumstances. One of the key circumstances is what kind of thing it is that you are trying to forecast. If you are trying to forecast, say, macroscopic changes in product trends, you may be able to rope out a scenario that would be fairly predictive of the types of products that might be desired in the year 2000 on the basis of the fact that food production is probably going to become much more subject to crisis conditions or that incomes are going to increase in certain areas at generally a certain rate. Even if major changes occur that would affect those directions, you would not be so far off that you would not have a fairly good idea of the types of products that you would want. For example, in vehicles, fuel economy is a long-term trend of significance and, for the moment at least, appears to be of significance through the year 2000 and beyond. The horizons on some other things are very much shorter, particularly when you get down to very detailed assumptions affecting plans that certain numbers of dollars will be generated by certain kinds of business. In that particular case, my experience would suggest that for many industries, even a five-year time frame would be too long to really be very indicative of actual circumstances. Three years perhaps is more meaningful. It all depends on how much variation you can tolerate in the answer. If you can't tolerate very much variation, then you had better not look too far in the future because so many variables exist in international business that you'll probably be wrong one way or the other.

INTERVIEWER: Let us now turn to the question of some of the various strategic planning approaches that have been suggested, such as portfolio analysis, and see how valuable you see these as being in international strategic planning.

SPAHR: My first reactions to that would be that there is nothing wrong with tools such as portfolio analysis (or various other tools that might be at the disposal of the planner), but it is important to recognize that portfolio analysis and things like that are, in fact, just tools to strategic planning. They are not strategic planning itself. Now, whenever a new concept like portfolio analysis is developed, there is always a risk of placing too much reliance on that new tool. However, there is always a "seat of the pants" judgment to be made and we should not kid ourselves about that. I'd like to use an analogy to point out what I think is an example of a tool that has been used improperly. I do not know when the concept of return on investment was developed, but it became very much the focus of American industry. All you had to do if you were in a hurry was to look at two proposals on their ROI basis and take the one that was better—without thinking about it—and I believe that we are now finding out that this sort of focus (and the short-term profit focus that goes along with it) has very much damaged American business in international competition. There is no one single answer. I think we have to examine portfolio analysis—and the same comments would apply to services that evaluate political risk, business risk, social risk, etc.—some other things that work on the basis of weightings—coming up with an index. What you have to ask yourself right at the outset is, "Does this weighting of the factors; the weighting that's being used; does that *illuminate* or *conceal* the true facts of the matter?" Do not let your judgment be violated in this point, and, by all means, do review the assumptions behind the weighting and see if you agree with them. Perhaps you know that there is a single condition in one country that is the overwhelming consideration. I don't care what the index number is, a country on the verge of revolution is not a good investment candidate at this point in all practical senses; you have to look at what the really significant problems are on a country-by-country basis. In one country it is poverty, and in another country it is political suppression or whatever.

The question of whether to use product portfolio analysis versus market portfolio analysis depends on whether your current situation is more product- or market-oriented. You might want to consider the possibility of using both if you have the time to do them, if you have the information to do them, if you have the judgment necessary to come up with the weighting factors and so forth that are required, and if both might actually be useful. I think a lot depends on your business, your environment, and your present positioning also in terms of what kinds of tools will be most useful to you.

INTERVIEWER: How essential do you think competitor analysis is to the ongoing planning process?

SPAHR: I think it is definitely important. As a matter of fact, I would say that it is essential. Immediately as I say that, let me tell you that the problem is going to be getting the data, at least in many industries. Some of it is closely guarded, a secret of the company that you are attempting to compete with, and, in general, international statistics are somewhat less extensive than they are in the U.S. If you can successfully predict your competitor's actions on a consistent basis, you've got it made. For example, if you are involved in competitive bidding, you might have your financial guy study very closely to see if your competitor is following a generally consistent practice. This is not strategic planning in a sense, it is just good business judgment, but it is very good to find out what your competitor is doing, and if you can do that, you can start beating him. Now, of course, he will probably sooner or later shift his strategy. If you can find out what he is doing then and again and again and again, you'll find at some point he sort of runs out of strategies and starts returning to the earlier ones. All you have to do then is attempt to predict what strategy he is using at the present time. The same thing applies, I think, to strategic planning, only on a considerably longer-term basis. If you can find that your competitor is spending a lot of time on developing his productivity capabilities, for example, you may decide that you have to spend some more investments for equipment or plant. If, on the other hand, he is developing new products, then that tells you that perhaps your products will have to be updated, so I think it is very important. I think it is important to remember that one's future environment is affected by fundamental trends and competitors' actions. It is not only what long-term macroeconomic factors and social trends are doing but also how your competitors are responding and, to an extent, how you are responding because your response in and of itself will have some environmental impact.

INTERVIEWER: Do you think overseas markets should be viewed singly and/or in some intermarket approach? Is something of an intermarket approach more viable?

SPAHR: I think again it depends on the situation. There are certain cases where you have to take intermarket approaches. For example, most companies will not have international markets large enough to bring out different products for every market. Also, at some point you are going to have to integrate these things into some sort of an overall general plan, and your overall general plan will deal with a companywide perspective as opposed to a market-by-market perspective. There are cases where differences between a group of countries are not really so great, so for certain purposes you can take an intermarket approach to those. You may, in fact, have to take such an approach not only in planning but also in actual business implementation. For example, you may have just one distributor in Benelux or in the Scandinavian countries if that is a limitation of your business because of its size or whatever.

However, I just want to say that every time you ignore country differences you lose something of value because, over time, every country is essentially different from every other country, and I heartily caution against resisting the tendency to assume that it does not matter. You may come to the conclusion after you have studied it for some time that it doesn't matter, but please make that step. Definitely, at some point in the planning process, each market should be viewed singly, even though for purposes of your overall, more formal plan it has to be pulled together in some more condensed shape. Considering differences, however, does not mean you should close your mind to similarities. That's also very important, I think, as a predictive tool.

There are similarities in religions, say between various Arab countries. Gosh, they never seem to be going in the same direction, but the threat, say, of fundamental Islamic insurrection that is so prominent today in Iran threatens to spread to other nations that have the Shiite religion as a significant religion in their country. If you assume a spread, you can predict what the general effect of it will be on the nations that it spreads to.

INTERVIEWER: Just tying into that as a practical matter, would you recommend keeping a file on every country that you have an interest in?

SPAHR: Definitely. I would keep a file on every country. I would also keep a file on every product, and I would also keep a file on every issue of strategic importance, which means sometimes you are filing one letter in three different places. I think it is highly desirable.

INTERVIEWER: Do you see a role for formal strategic planning in the small or medium firm as well?

SPAHR: Yes, the function has to be done. It is just a question of who does it. If strategic planning does not do it, then the CEO, by definition, will have to. The question is, I think, "Is it being addressed?" If so, how effectively? How much time does it take (which is not necessarily the amount of time that is being devoted to it) and what are the other demands on the CEO? How strong is the competition in this respect? What are the potential benefits or penalties of not doing this on a more formalized basis? I think it is also significant to again address this point: Can the CEO reconcile himself to "sharing his function," because the smaller the company, the more the CEO tends to feel that it is his company and does not want to let that kind of control, perhaps even in part, out of his hands. Also, I don't think you want to hire a strategic planner and make him half a strategic planning manager and half responsible for Latin American operations, or pretty soon his day-to-day business will blow off the strategic planning aspects. Get an individual who is going to address strategic planning totally. Problems won't go away as a result of having a strategic planner. You'll always have problems. Hopefully, however, they'll be better identified. As a matter of fact, you may even identify more problems, but in the final analysis you will know about them, and hopefully as a result of this process, you will be able to cope with them better.

INTERVIEWER: What do you see as the major problems or difficulties that are inherent in international strategic planning that may not be as relevant domestically?

SPAHR: First thing, there are obviously many more things to consider. You'll be dealing with multiple environments, different uses for your product. There will be different laws and different cultures. I suppose it's appropriate to follow up on this cultural point at this juncture, because often when the issue of different cultures comes up people tend to regard it lightly, and it's not something to be regarded lightly. It is not just a matter of the fact that when you are selling pork sausages, you do not try and sell them to, say, Israel and the Islamic countries. It is not a question of strange little quirks. It is a question of fundamentally different ways of looking at things. Let me give you an example. If fifteen years ago or twenty years or maybe even longer ago than that there was a strategic planning chap in an automotive company attempting to look to the future and specifically in that context evaluating Japan and what they would probably do, I think that he would have concluded from a U.S. perspective that the Japanese would not go heavily toward automation. They had by far the lowest labor rates of any automotive-producing country in the world. Even on the assumption of changes in exchange rates and the normal progression of salaries in Japan versus the other countries—assuming even that was somewhat higher than in other countries—it would be many many years, if not decades, before Japan's labor costs would be as high as the labor costs in other countries. Furthermore, there was not clear evidence of any other lower-cost country emerging as a significant automotive competitor for perhaps decades. So Japan had a tremendous advantage in labor costs; hence why spend money in automation? Also, part and parcel of that would be that the strategic planner would have been able to analyze the automation trend in the United States and come to the conclusion that it was not proceeding all that quickly either, so we were not really going to close the gap on the Japanese all that much. Nonetheless, the Japanese automated, and even while they were doing this over a period of years, they did so with relatively little attention being paid to it. I suppose when a guy would pick up an article in the U.S. that said something about automation being put into a particular operation in the Japanese company, he would say, "Well, there's an oddball thing," and throw it in the wastebasket. It's only in the last few years that we have suddenly realized that they have automated a lot and in fact, under the guise of robotics, which is just another description of automation, have now reached the point where they are very much in the forefront of robotics leadership in the automotive industry and perhaps in some other industries. Why did they do that? I do not know, but I think it might have had something to do with two very significant cultural differences that a person in the United States who had not had exposure to these cultural differences could not begin to appreciate or plan for. One cultural difference I sense is that the Japanese are rather paranoid about the way they were treated in international trade. I believe it is quite possible that when they decided to build an automotive industry they said, "The other countries of the world that make automobiles are not going to want to see us succeed, and at some point they are going to place all sorts of barriers and obstructions in our way." So rather than approach the question of what they should do to build an automotive industry, as it is typically approached in the U.S., I think they were more inclined to say, "Let's envision the absolute best that could be done with technology and let's make that our criterion. Let's try to make the edge so great that no matter what reasonable actions the other companies take, we are still going to be in the fray." Since automation does reduce the cost of making vehicles even though the labor cost per hour is less in Japan, it obviously follows that, using that perspective, they would still consider automation.

Second, I would like to share with you something of my experience. I have noted in speaking with people from Asian companies and from personal dealings with Asian companies that there is a tendency for Asian cultures to view assets or, shall I say, to view plants, facilities, and equipment as assets in a different context than we traditionally view them in the United States. When you facilitize for a new plant, you say, "What am I going to need in order to do the job that has to be done" and if you build a plant and have facilitized it for considerably more production than you get, you've got a problem. If your plant never even gets going, if it's sitting there, you do not consider that an asset, you would consider that a liability. Asians, on the other hand, having been very poor, having experienced catastrophic periods in their national histories, and often having been in the position of having to "make do," seem to regard a plant as having essential value whether or not the thing is operating. I believe they feel that might be the only plant they will ever get to build and sooner or later they will need the output that that plant can give them, and when the time comes, they'll have it. So I think that the Japanese were probably thinking that the automotive plants they built might be the only shot they would ever have and the plants might have to last a long time— so they better be as good as they possibly can. Under those circumstances, if my perception is correct, it makes sense for the Japanese to automate even though their labor costs are lower than anybody else's.

Next, we have foreign currency exchange rate fluctuations to concern us. There have been a lot of comments made in strategic planning publications that you really do not have to worry about these on the basis that they simply reflect certain other fundamental factors, internal inflation rates and so forth, and through the process of the inflation and other changes that will occur over a period of time, it does not really matter what the foreign exchange rate will be in the future. You will be in about the same competitive position. That is not true at all. You see, when we elected President Reagan, he said he wanted a strong dollar. Now, I do not think that any of us thought that the yen would be at 257 to the dollar, which is about what it is today. When we elected him, it was under 220, I think. But there has not been a whole lot in the fundamentals that has changed over that period of time. Most of this depreciation of the yen or growth in dollar strength relative to the yen has come about for reasons other than those basic fundamental factors. That means that right now if you are competing against the Japanese, you have just received a price increase of maybe 20 percent or so and you have not had any adjustments in your costs, your product is not inherently worth any more, and there are not any other factors to explain it. But you are going to have to sell at 20 percent more relative to Japanese products. It is very important and, unfortunately, foreign exchange rates are not very forecastable. There are many people who forecast, normally services; they charge quite a bit, but they have had a horrible track record—not only in terms of trend, but direction—over the last few years. It would lead you to make the absolute wrong decisions. I believe the best advice in this area would be to take into consideration the fact that there will be currency movements for other than fundamental reasons and to make contigency plans where possible.

International is also different in that you need to be able to quickly adopt the perspective of another culture or another operating environment *without losing sight of your own.* You have to be thinking when you are talking to people overseas, what is he really saying, what is he really thinking, what does he really want, what would I expect him to do or say under the circumstances of the environment as he sees it? You have to be able to shift mental gears very quickly because you will be bounding back and forth between considerations in one country versus another. This calls, I think, for a lot more experience than would be true in the domestic environment and you should consider that in your selection process.

We have talked about the difficulty of getting information. The statistics are not uniform, if they are even available at all. Sources are inconvenient, scattered, and in foreign languages. Not only is there a problem in getting the information, but there is a very great problem in digesting it. If you are involved in many countries, the mass of information that is *potentially* available to you becomes enormous. But the bits of information are buried in inconvenient locations and the mass of data from which you must extract the information is unorganized and often seemingly unmanageable. At some point it will tax your ability to use it, even considering the use of data processing or outside services that might be available. Communications are particularly difficult. If you want to check your strategic plan assumptions or get feedback from foreign locations, that will be a problem.

A lot of the strategic planning function, I think, calls for the generation of concepts and ideas for testing them, the discarding of those that are not so good, and the further development of those that are. One way I think you can do this is to develop a very free-flowing exchange of comments between the strategic planning office and the various other functional heads and the CEO if you are capable of operating that way. Send the letters out in a continuous flow, raising questions like "What about this?" or "I have noticed that...." I'm not sure you even have to worry a whole lot about the follow-up. The comments that end up in nearly everybody's wastebasket are probably not that good anyway. But in this process of raising questions, certain issues will emerge. You can then do second and third iterations until finally, lo and behold, I have often found that when you finally get into a meeting to discuss the formalization of the approach, the decisions that have to be made are already decided.

Another big difference between international and domestic strategic planning is that one has to understand and take into consideration in the international sphere things that restrain trade. In the domestic environment, if there is a law passed, it is going to affect everybody the same, but it does not always work that way in the international environment (i.e., a law affecting you may not affect a competitor). Of course, there are duties—taxes and things like that—but there is also a category which is best described, I think, as nontariff trade restraints that are very significant. In evidence of that I saw an interesting little article recently in *The Wall Street Journal* quoting Jim Tumir, Director of Economic Research and Analysis for the Secretariat of the GATT, who estimates that 40 to 48 percent of all international transactions are subject to nontariff trade restraints.

INTERVIEWER: In talking about the qualifications of the individual, to what extent do you think having had a foreign assignment, or let us say direct overseas experience for an extended period of time, is important to an international strategic planner?

SPAHR: I think it's very desirable. As a matter of fact, I'd say it was almost essential. I would not think that the major criterion would be having one major assignment—a long term in another country. Obviously, a person whose only overseas experience has been four years in Brazil would understand the Brazilian perspective very well but might not understand anything about Asia or Europe or any one of a number of different areas. It would be best if you had a person who had been overseas on relatively short-term assignments in many locations and who perhaps had the opportunity to address problems not of a "nitty-gritty," day-to-day sort, but rather of a high management focus, say, perhaps a participant in negotiations.

INTERVIEWER: What is your view on the question of how standardized your strategic program should be?

SPAHR: Standardization for standardization's sake is pointless in my view. In the final analysis, there is a job to be done and it is not going to be done simply because someone adopts a certain standardized approach. There will be a need for some standardization. For example, if you have an international division that reports to the corporation, the corporation will structure a certain standardized approach, but let us not get hung up on the form of the "bloody" process. Let us concentrate more on what it is designed to address and the underlying philosophical concepts and approaches that are leading to that goal. That would be my advice to both the CEOs and other people considering the field in an actual practical environment.

INTERVIEWER: Another point that you made is the recognition that we probably need to be a lot more flexible in international strategic planning than we perhaps are in domestic strategic planning. Is that your feeling?

SPAHR: I could not have said that better myself. It is simply the combination of generally less "adequate" data coming in from overseas, the fact that if you are involved in very many countries, there will just be an immense amount of information available. You simply cannot spend infinite amounts of time or personnel resources addressing it, if only because your overseas markets individually will probably tend to be quite small. As a matter of fact, I think it would be interesting to note that by comparison with the domestic organization, the entire international part of your business will tend to be quite small unless you are a member of a very small group of truly international companies that have made outstanding success in the international business. I am quite confident that 95 percent or more of all the companies operating internationally have domestic business that is greater than all their international business put together, and that piece of international business is then broken down between many countries. Of course, that is highly variable. There are some companies that have operations in, say, the United States and then have three or four affiliates in places like Brazil, West Germany, and Singapore. They are dealing with essentially four different environments. But I don't even think that is too typical. What happens is that your products do tend to flow into other countries, and sooner or later you establish distributorship operations there and so forth. Many of those will be marginal, will be small over a long period of time, and you just cannot spend all that much time addressing them in detail. On the other hand, you cannot ignore them either. Furthermore, there are many more different types of considerations involved in international business than there are in domestic business if only for things like culture and potential foreign exchange rates and their implications and so forth.

INTERVIEWER: One question comes to mind that is perhaps a little more controversial. Some people concerned with strategic planning say that political reality has become the key factor in international planning and that such considerations supersede anything else. Do you have any comment on this view?

SPAHR: I think that is a very perceptive and a very interesting question. Let us introduce a concept. Let us introduce the concept of hierarchy of pressures, pressures that tend to affect long-term strategic considerations. I suppose, in most cases, political environmental considerations, political realities, would be at the top (or very near the top) of the hierarchy of these pressures, because in essence the political environment and the political policies that accompany that environment—the political sphere in general—tends to dictate a downflow throughout all the arms of a particular country's government, its public viewpoints, and so forth. And it affects the policies of the country in terms of its economic policy, it affects its market expectations and the feelings of its citizens, and affects the ability of your company to operate there. So generally I believe that the point you have brought up is true. Of course, there will be a need for aspirins and shoe polish around the world that transcends the requirements of any one particular market, so to an extent the political adjustments, the political realities that occur in any particular country may not have that much impact on the company. However, in the final analysis, then, yes; in the ultimate perspective, the political reality would be the overwhelming factor. I am reminded of Bismarck's statement, "Politics is the art of the possible." Politics sets the scene in which subsequent events take place.

INTERVIEWER: We hear a lot about the value of developing alternative scenarios as part of the strategic planning process. Do you have a comment on that?

SPAHR: I think that the scenario analysis approach is very worthy of consideration in the context of its providing the flexibility of alternative contingency plans—alternative contingent strategy plans in the event that circumstances change from a most likely condition. However, I would like to point out that you have enough problems attempting to develop even the first scenario due to all the uncertainties of the business environment internationally—all the difficulties of getting information and so forth. Therefore, it is a very extensive process to develop multiple scenarios if only because they take a lot of time and the economic realities of the size of your international market are that they may not support a staff large enough to develop very sophisticated scenarios. In the final analysis, none of your scenarios is apt to come through as structured. That does not mean, however, that the contingency plans you develop to deal with these scenarios will necessarily be impractical. They will often be practical. Most companies, let's face it, because of the need to keep things rather simple and stay flexible would benefit from scenario planning, but only in terms of very general scenarios simply because it is just *not economically feasible* to be more detailed.

INTERVIEWER: One of the problems that you seemed to allude to earlier was the problem of developing credibility for the strategic planning process itself. Would you want to comment on what we might call the problem of strategic planning credibility within the organization?

SPAHR: Yes, I think that is a very important question. Whenever there is a new field there is a certain question of credibility until it's established just what that field will address and generally how it will go about addressing it. So that part is understandable. There is always a credibility problem when functions previously handled by a CEO are now being addressed by some other per-

163

son. It almost suggests a favoritism or something of that nature and this can be a real hindrance. There is also a potential credibility problem if someone within the organization at a relatively high level does not happen to like the idea of a strategic planner nosing around into things which he regards (at least in part) as his business. I believe a strategic planner has to have a defined ability to rove to an extent, but I think he has to exercise this power with very subtle diplomacy. When you are thinking of filling the strategic planning slot you ought to give real consideration to choosing someone from within the organization who has tended to do things like that before and has gained an acceptance already in similar roles. That solves a lot of your problems. But it is still something that has to be approached with subtlety, and the field over time does still have to prove itself. It has not really proved itself yet, but I believe that it is going to, and very convincingly. A lot of the credibility issue too depends upon which strategic planning organization you are talking about. If you are one of the larger companies that has one at the corporate level and then has them further down at the division level and so forth, it is like any organizational issue, any policy issue, any problem practically at all that you are addressing. If you have a lot of visibility at the top, your corporate strategic planning staff may be accepted very readily, but perhaps paid lip service to an extent. As it funnels down through the organization, if you impose it on people at lower levels, if they don't really feel that they need it—but that they have got to have a strategic planning guy because it is the thing that the corporation expects them to do—I think that fellow at the lower level could have a real credibility problem.

STRATEGIC THINKING FOR THE FUTURE 8

In this final chapter, Stanley C. Gault, the Chairman of the Board and CEO of Rubbermaid, Inc., offers his insights on strategic planning—especially what the future holds for strategic planning. From his earliest interview remarks, it is obvious that Gault places high importance on the planning function; he feels it should receive appropriate and continuing attention from top management. In many (most) organizations, this means having strategic planning report directly to the CEO.

As Gault indicates, the CEO sets the tone for the way the planning process is seen, accepted, and regarded throughout the organization. Without the obvious support of the CEO, i.e., his or her personal commitment, the strategic planning process will not succeed. And, according to Gault, that means starting the process at the very top through the establishment of the corporation mission and objectives.

Regarding two strategic planning issues—board participation and the use of division strategic planners—Gault offers specific suggestions. First, he sees the value of selective participation by board members: "the board should have appropriate involvement . . . in order to prevent the common 'after-the-fact' approach." Next, he feels that every SBU in a large multidivisional company should have its own plan and planner (the latter reporting directly to the SBU manager and indirectly to corporate strategic planning).

Gault feels that the CEO can and should evaluate the contribution of the strategic planning group. To him this means establishing objectives for the unit and then judging the contribution, the performance, and the realizations of the objectives; it is no more difficult than evaluating R&D. In other words, it means comparing what you have now with what you had prior to the strategic planning function.

For the future, Gault foresees the strategic management concept making greater use of the contribution of functional components other than finance in the allocation process. These other functional components include technology, human resources, marketing, and so forth. Also, Gault raises the possibility of there being a committee of the board responsible for strategic planning. And Gault sees more and more CEOs becoming involved in the planning process — a role that he feels they should assume.

What is the future for the corporate strategic planning function? Strategic planners, and the business schools that train them, have recently drawn considerable criticism. In fact, it has become popular to blame many of the economic problems of the late '70s and early '80s on strategic planning, with the charge being that companies devote too much attention to planning and too little attention to implementation and decision making.

In their best-selling book *In Search of Excellence,* Thomas J. Peters and Robert H. Waterman, Jr., indicated that business schools have spent too much time training analyzers and quantifiers, while not devoting sufficient attention to developing managers who can make the difficult decisions that today's world requires. And, undoubtedly, one can say that many business schools have become enamored with tools and techniques at the expense of operational processes. In fact, management's focus can be so much on risk reduction (and aversion) that the passage of time ultimately makes a final decision occur through default.

Despite these criticisms, it is not surprising that the firms that Peters and Waterman judged to be "excellent" can be characterized as having superior corporate planning groups. Thus, it is not planning per se that creates problems, it is the failure of execution or shortcomings in the content of the plan itself. For example, in planning, managers must have the ability to reach closure; their desire to employ just one more technique or to involve one more "expert" must be tempered with reality and a sense of urgency.

The question that now remains for us to explore concerns the future of strategic planning in the business firm. To provide a perspective on the future and to suggest the new directions this future will take, we felt it most fitting to turn to one of the true strategic planning pioneers, an individual who was intimately involved in the initial General Electric strategic planning efforts and who has remained an active champion and practitioner of the planning function. This individual is Stanley C. Gault, currently Chairman of the Board and Chief Executive Officer of Rubbermaid Inc.[1] We visited Gault at Rubbermaid's headquarters in Wooster, Ohio, and obtained the following interview. In addition, we have received Gault's permission to print a paper on strategic planning that he has used in speeches to business groups. This paper serves as the appendix to this chapter.

---

[1]Prior to joining Rubbermaid Inc., of Wooster, Ohio, in January 1980, Mr. Gault spent thirty-two years with the General Electric Company. Among his extensive number of top management assignments with GE, Mr. Gault served as Senior Vice President and Sector Executive, Industrial Products and Components Sector (1978–1980) and as Vice President and Sector Executive, Consumer Products and Services Sector (1977–1978). As Vice President and Group Executive, Major Appliances Business Group (1970–1977), Mr. Gault became critically involved in GE strategic planning and has been actively concerned with strategic planning ever since. A graduate of the College of Wooster, Mr. Gault is a director of International Paper Company, PPG Industries, Inc., and the National Association of Manufacturers, as well as Rubbermaid Incorporated.

INTERVIEWER: What role should the CEO play in strategic planning?

GAULT: The chief executive officer's role is one of great importance in the strategic planning process and it can vary relative to the organization structure. In order to answer your question, I need to know where strategic planning is positioned on the organization chart.

I assign high priority and importance to strategic planning. Therefore, as a general rule, in small and mid-sized companies, it should report directly to the chief executive officer. I do not mean to give the impression that I suggest this reporting relationship in *just* small and mid-sized companies. In theory, there is reason to have it report directly to the CEO regardless of the size of the company. However, I realize this may not always be practical because of the complexity of the business and types and numbers of special and outside assignments and the total responsibilities held by a CEO.

For example, in a large corporation where the board encourages or asks the CEO to devote substantial time to a specific area of the business or to outside involvements, that can cause the organizational alignment for the strategic planning function to be different. But the reporting relationship should be such to assure that the planning function receives appropriate top management attention and receives it on an ongoing basis.

I am usually suspicious of those cases where the strategic planning function has intentionally not been placed on a direct reporting basis to the CEO, but where outside involvements and/or special assignments do not require a substantial amount of the CEO's time. In too many cases, the reason for such a nondirect reporting relationship is that the CEO does not want to devote the time or assume the degree of responsibility for strategic planning that is inherent on a direct reporting basis.

INTERVIEWER: Why is that?

GAULT: There are a number of reasons: a lack of interest in the subject, the absence of commitment to the process, or the inability to know how to handle it properly. Also, they want to avoid the confrontation that will develop when implementing a strategic planning process and in maintaining it subsequently.

Therefore, to avoid any internal strife, which is natural with the concept, the CEO will withdraw and assign it to a line or staff officer.

INTERVIEWER: Where should it be assigned if it does not report directly to the CEO?

GAULT: In some cases—again, it will depend upon the size and complexity of the corporation—it is assigned to the chief operating officer, to one of the top operating officers of the company, or to one of the staff functions; for example, the chief financial officer or vice president, administration (if various staff functions report to such a position).

I do not believe that strategic planning belongs within an administrative staff group. Under an administrative staff alignment it can lose much of its visibility, and the ability to perform the assigned responsibilities of the function can be compromised. The point being, the farther it gets away from the CEO, the less effective it will probably be.

Of course, strategic planning is not a totally independent function within the organization. It is a function responsible for integrating the total planning process or system for the entire enterprise, and this responsibility is a very important point to remember. It goes without saying that it must be able to work effectively with all components, both operating and staff.

Unfortunately, many view the role of strategic planning to be that of an adversary—a challenging, threatening factor. However, being an adversary or threatening factor is not the mission of strategic planning, either conceptually or functionally.

Now, let us discuss strategic planning in terms of the CEO's role in the strategic planning process.

First, there is no question that whether or not it is on a direct reporting basis to the CEO, the CEO does indeed set the tone for the way strategic planning is seen, accepted, and regarded throughout the organization. He must provide the leadership. The CEO must be perceived and recognized as being the parent of the corporate strategic plan. He is not the writer of the plan, but he sets the tone, sets the pace, provides the direction and leadership.

But on the other hand, caution must be exercised to be certain the plan is not viewed as being a "one-person" plan. If so, the business components will have the tendency to respond to their preconceived, predetermined opinions of the CEO's desires rather than independently developing their own individual pieces of the total plan.

The success of the strategic planning process in any organization is directly related to the commitment—the CEO's personal commitment—to the process and system. That commitment must mean the direct involvement of the CEO in the formulation of the basic plan. Whether or not the strategic planning function reports directly or indirectly to the CEO, the CEO must have a close working relationship with that component and, above all, the CEO must assume the responsibility for the corporate strategic plan.

INTERVIEWER: I see, it is really signaling to all concerned its priority in the organization and the steps to be followed. Is more involvement by the CEO required?

GAULT: Yes, we are talking about starting the process at the very top of the organization with the establishment of the mission and the objectives of the corporation.

From that point, it moves down and across the organization (regardless of size or structure), and in the process soliciting and receiving the understanding and acceptance of those objectives.

The next step is the development of the strategies needed to fulfill the corporate objectives.

Finally, under the strategic elements [strategies] come the specific plans and programs that respond to the strategies. It is a basic four-step program: mission, objectives, strategies, and plans.

INTERVIEWER: What, if any, is the role of the board of directors in the firm's planning beyond its traditional informational role?

GAULT: In my opinion, there is no question that the chairman should seek and give serious consideration to the suggestions and inputs from the members of the board, both individually and collectively. In order for this to happen, board members must feel such requests for participation are genuine and that their observations and suggestions will be thoughtfully considered. Therefore, the board should have appropriate involvement in the overall process in order to prevent the common "after-the-fact" approach.

Too frequently, board members become aware of the elements of the overall strategic plan, have questions/suggestions about them, but this occurs after the plan has been completed. When this happens, the plan is really being presented to the board, not for constructive evaluation and comment, but simply as a matter of information only and to receive its stamp of approval. In other words, under such a scenario, the board is approving something where it probably did not have the opportunity for any appropriate level of involvement.

Again, going back to the individual board members, some observations will be made on a general overall basis. Others will be more specific. These responses reflect the personal, professional expertise and business experience of the members.

The board is not responsible for the development of strategic plans, but it should be informed about the planning direction of the business and the major elements [strategies] of the strategic plan. For example, board members should know and bless the mission of the business, the basic objectives, and basic strategies to be followed. I do this annually with Rubbermaid's board. However, the plans to fulfill the strategies are the responsibility of management.

To a lesser degree, the board could have interest in participating in the development of strategic plans as requested by management. But regardless of its involvement in the plan, the board must hold management accountable for developing the recommended strategic elements and the successful implementation of the plans.

INTERVIEWER: I am very interested in your comments on the board. I think that is something that has really not been sufficiently considered in discussions on strategic planning. I was also just wondering, what if we have a case in which there are board members without business experience—a college president or a cleric—someone like that?

GAULT: That is a very logical question. Some board members can make a greater contribution in the planning area than others. However, regardless of the composition of the board, all members should be able to make an input and certainly have an

171

opportunity to make comments and suggestions on the strategic approach and direction recommended by the CEO.

I believe the CEO should take advantage of the capabilities within the board structure to penetrate deeper into the basics of the plan—not just read or show objectives and strategies to them. If the CEO does not believe it would be meaningful to have board involvement on a collective basis, then the CEO could approach certain members and request their individual input and contribution.

INTERVIEWER: Suppose you have a large multidivisional company: Do you recommend strategic planning at the divisional level *and* the corporate level?

GAULT: Strategic planning is a part of every component's responsibilities. If you mean should it have its own strategic plan, the answer is yes, providing such a division is a legitimate strategic business unit.

INTERVIEWER: And the divisional planner would report to both the general manager of the division and to the strategic planning unit at the corporate level, is that correct?

GAULT: Yes, the strategic planner should report directly to the strategic business unit manager and report indirectly (dotted-line basis) to the manager, corporate strategic planning.

To me, this two-way reporting relationship is paramount. For example, if you were a business manager and I was your strategic planner, I would report directly to you because you have the responsibility for the performance of the division or business unit. By the same token, I would have a dotted-line reporting relationship to the manager of corporate strategic planning in order to optimize communications and effectiveness on a corporate-wide basis.

INTERVIEWER: Functional type of responsibility?

GAULT: Right. I also believe that this two-way type of reporting relationship for the strategic planning function should be the same for other components of functional expertise: legal, finance, human resources, marketing, engineering, technology, etc.

INTERVIEWER: The next area that I would like to get into is the question of what the critics have said about strategic planning;

one often hears that the field has been "oversold" and, can the chief executive officer evaluate the contribution of the strategic planning function. I think that has been one of the things that we have heard most in terms of the critics is that the plans—at least the long-term plans—make it very difficult to evaluate the strategic planner.

GAULT: Certainly it is more difficult to evaluate their contribution to the company if you want to measure them in terms of the historical measurements used to measure performance of operating units. Measurements for operating units in most cases have really been measurements pertaining to realization of financial objectives. Also, they have been measured on short-term business performance.

In my opinion, it is not more difficult to judge the performance, the contribution, and the realization of objectives in the strategic planning function than it is to measure the contribution made by R&D, who normally do most of their work on a longer-term basis. It also relates to being able to measure someone on the basis of the documented roles, expectations, and objectives for the individual or component before the year begins.

If we are rating someone after the fact, on the basis of only an earlier verbal discussion of objectives and expectations, meaningful measurement is going to be very, very difficult to accomplish. It is unfair to the component and it is certainly unfair to the business. And it is unfair in another way because others [business units] will know that they [strategic planning] are being evaluated on a different basis than the operating components. And so the tendency will be to view them [planning functions] as having lenient objectives and a more modest grading system. It is perceived as a double standard and it does not need to be that way.

The annual operating plan for the strategic planning component is just as important as the annual operating plan for any other component of the business, staff or operations. It is not difficult to evaluate performance when there has been an open discussion and understanding of assignments, expectations, and methods of measurement.

Provided he has assumed his proper role in the system, the evaluator is the CEO. Also, by assuming his proper role in the management system, he has asked for an operating plan from

173

the planning function and he has shared this plan with other staff and operating components of the business. Therefore, the other components will know how the strategic planning function is to be judged. Likewise, the strategic planning function knows how the other functions and operations are going to be evaluated.

However, a word of caution in this regard. One must guard against becoming overly sophisticated in the development and implementation of the strategic planning process. It must not become overly complex. If it does, it will generate horrendous amounts of unused, unmeaningful data. If this happens, it is self-defeating and demeaning to the planning process. It is the responsibility of top management to be certain that this over-sophistication tendency is not allowed to develop.

In too many instances, it appears that people have the misconception that sophistication equates to effectiveness. Realism is what is essential in a successful strategic planning role. This need for realism is why it is desirable to have people in the planning function who have had previous experience in operations.

There is no question that strategic planning in many ways has been, to use your word, oversold.

Strategic planning is a concept that really had its genesis for all practical purposes in the early '70s. It has become a recognized process and component in many businesses today. But unfortunately, not much has really changed in many of these businesses that adopted the so-called strategic planning process.

In such cases, the component was probably established because the CEO, after reading many business publications, considered it to be the popular thing to do. To establish strategic planning in the business was an indication of being up with the times.

It was not unusual to establish such a component with the assistance of outside consultants. When the announcement of the creation of a strategic planning function was made to the board, the board members were pleased because they too liked the sound of it. But unfortunately, most board members had very little meaningful knowledge of the topic.

Strategic planning became a business buzzword of the '70s. I understand that the consulting services for strategic planning and work associated with it exceed $100 million; also, that it is growing at a rate in excess of 20 percent annually. I am always curious to learn what companies have paid for their outside strategic planning services. The numbers usually are very large. In my experience, I have found these charges to be higher—significantly higher—than clients anticipated they would need to pay for such services. Also, these fees can be multiplied when a few associated and follow-up studies are added.

Most members of senior management have endured their fair share of entertaining presentations by self-labeled strategic planning experts talking on the subject of strategic planning— and sometimes far in excess of their knowledge of the subject. It is startling what some of the consulting organizations have charged their clients for their strategic reviews, studies, and recommendations, particularly when they leave these clients with a myriad of graphs, charts, text, and recommendations to implement on their own.

There are knowledgeable people who do not believe much progress has been recorded toward strategic planning. Therefore, they are more critical and negative than I about what was accomplished in the '70s. Admittedly, I am not negative by nature, but I believe there is significant evidence to show that many good strategic plans were developed and implemented in the '70s.

Of course, the progress recorded in this area varies greatly among the many companies that undertook it. Although many of these companies are not as far along in the implementation process as they had intended to be at this time, they are substantially better off than they were before they initiated their planning program.

In order to evaluate and determine the accomplishments recorded under the banner of strategic planning, you need to go back and compare what existed prior to the introduction of strategic planning.

In earlier days, if there was any organized planning program, this planning effort was known as the long-range business plan or words along that line. In most cases, it was a document that represented the aggregate of the plans that had floated to the top from the various operating components of the company. Also, the numerical projections were based on economic assumptions that were seldom questioned and the future was always optimistic. It was commonly known as the old "hockey stick" forecasting approach, where every year of the long-range planning period was forecasted to be better than the last. It usually covered a five-year period.

Now, what really made strategic planning different? The answer is quite simple. Strategic planning is strategic thinking. The old long-range-business-plan approach did not embrace strategic thinking.

First, the old long-range planning approach did not include adequate evaluation of competition. Second, it did not develop and document sufficiently the objectives of the company and scrutinize them for reasonableness and viability. Third, there was an absence of an effective system to allocate resources. Fourth, compensation plans were not developed to support the strategic assignment given to the various business units. Fifth, the old forecasting approach did not give sufficient consideration to international issues and the political issues and policies, actual or projected. Sixth, the plan did not present well-developed strategic alternatives.

Therefore, when you have a professionally prepared strategic plan that does incorporate these elements, and more, you do move from an outdated business planning/collecting information approach into a strategic thinking mode and process.

INTERVIEWER: Mr. Gault, we say that there is no such thing as a company strategic plan. We believe that it has to be plural.

GAULT: Plural?

INTERVIEWER: Because of the contingency approach.

GAULT: No, I prefer to consider contingency planning as a separate part of the planning process. Contingency plans are usually a part of the annual operational plan or budget.

But, returning to the strategic plan: strategic plans can be developed by different groups within the company if they are SBUs, but there is only one overall or master corporate strategic plan. We are talking today, at least up to this point in our conversation, strictly about the strategic planning process, the strategic planning function, and the implementation of the process. But, before you leave today, I do want to discuss what I call the next step—the future of strategic planning.

At the outset, I don't want to leave the impression that the

176

basic strategic planning work in most companies has been accomplished; therefore, they are ready to move on to the next step. I emphasize this point because the majority of businesses have not completed their basic strategic planning work and therefore are not ready to move to the next step. I realize that I am being repetitive, but one needs to understand and accept the concept of strategic planning if it is ever to make a meaningful contribution to the business.

We see and hear about too many corporate officers who do not understand the process nor really accept it although outwardly they profess to understand and support it. These people still believe that day-to-day, quarter-to-quarter execution is their sole responsibility.

Realistically speaking, one cannot be overly critical of their perception because in many cases they are being judged only on the basis of whether or not they have successfully met their financial objectives [budgets] for the quarter and the year.

Admittedly, this attitude is derived from the management reward system which is chiefly, if not totally, determined on current year's operating performance rather than having a part of total compensation [be] the result of their progress made toward planning for the future.

The words "strategic planning" have frequently been used inappropriately. We tend to incorporate these words into our regular business vocabulary. We use them proudly and authoritatively, but realistically speaking, nothing much has happened in many cases other than to just introduce these new words into our business conversations because we are still following the old "hockey stick" forecasting approach.

In my mind, there is a serious lack of understanding by many of those individuals who by their positions should have heavy involvement in the total strategic planning process.

Let me return to your point on contingency planning. The one point I would like to underscore is that here again, as in strategic planning, people believe they are doing a good job of contingency planning when they may be only scratching the surface. Most operations do not have documented, detailed, and viable contingency plans with execution points and dates. Many companies who said they had contingency plans learned that when it came time to implement them, the plans were not realistic and were not effective.

177

For contingency plans to be meaningful, there must be full participation in the development of these plans by all levels of management. This involvement obviously brings authorship to the plans and it assures that management (broad management) understands *what* is to be done, *why* it is to be done, and *when* actions should be taken.

Frequently, contingency plans are developed, but management procrastinates on the execution points/dates to such an extent that when they are finally triggered, they are much less effective than originally contemplated. Also, most contingency plans are negative in design and are predicated upon the business encountering adversity.

The word "contingency" has been used as a synonym for poor performance. I want to discuss the other side of contingency planning: the contingency actions that are documented with execution dates of actions to be implemented when the business experiences a more favorable climate and is registering a better performance than budgeted. A contingency plan must include contingency actions in both the downward and upward directions.

INTERVIEWER: Again, is this possibly due to the oversophistication problem that you mentioned earlier?

GAULT: Yes, the words "sophisticated" and "effectiveness" are not interchangeable. We have many corporations who claim they have a strategic planning function operating successfully, but when all the smoke is removed, they are performing the same old business planning exercise that I described earlier. They are not examining all essential strategic elements in depth, and that must be done.

I mentioned the business buzzwords of the '70s and that strategic planning was high on the list. In looking back, one remembers how strategic planning was heavily publicized and promoted. It was to be the panacea for many troubled businesses. The concept was accepted quickly and widely as a new, supereffective management tool.

Why hasn't it been more successful? Well, strategic planning is a tough assignment. It is time-consuming, frustrating, complex, and it can be dull by comparison to other functions of the business. Some find it to be a painful experience that demands time that they just do not have to spare because they need all of their working time to produce the required day-to-day operating results. The truth of it is, businesses cannot maximize day-to-day results indefinitely without having a basic strategic plan to use as their road map.

INTERVIEWER: We read the *Wall Street Journal* article on Rubbermaid [June 9, 1982, p. 52] that suggests that you have made a number of changes—personnel, diversification, new products, etc.—since becoming CEO.

GAULT: Yes, we have made many changes. However, these changes were not made quickly or emotionally. They were strategic decisions.

In my case, and I believe the same is true for most people coming into an organization from the outside, there are situations where decisions have been deferred or postponed because prior management did not want to make them due to emotional involvement, the presumed adversity within the organization, etc. And, of course, there are some actions that were postponed because prior management believed it best for the new management to be given the opportunity to make those decisions, but usually it is because they did not want to do it. Also, there are changes that should have been made, but prior management did not view such changes as being necessary. Finally, there are those cases where prior management knew something should be done but did not know how to do it. So you have several reasons why changes may be warranted but actions are not taken.

During 1980, we thoroughly evaluated each of our eight businesses. As a result of those detailed studies, four of the eight businesses are no longer a part of the company, product lines have been pruned, product lines have been added, and we have acquired a new business.

There were some exceptionally strong sections within the existing businesses, and as a result of our evaluation we had a better appreciation of these strengths as well as their legitimate needs. We had some businesses which deserved far more support than they had received previously. The way to give these good businesses such additional support was the result of the strategic decisions we made to unload the poor-performing businesses that were not producing profits or generating cash and had very

179

little chance, if any, to be successful over a reasonable period of time, even with better talent and more resources assigned to them. Or, in some cases, they simply did not represent a strategic long-term fit.

For example, we determined that our car mat and automotive accessories business did not represent a strategic fit. Many reasons led us to such a conclusion. The market was not growing, it was a commodity business with slim margins, there was nothing in car mat manufacturing technology that was transferable or related to the rest of our product lines, and we did not need to have that business in order to help us sell other company products. It was the type of business where our highly accepted name and our reputation for quality meant nothing to the OEM [Original Equipment Manufacturer] purchaser and very little to the retail consumer. Also, it would have required significant management time and additional financial resources to correct our problems, and the projected results were not impressive, even if our corrective actions proved to be successful.

By selling the business, we were able to take the cash and human resources and reassign them to areas of more rewarding opportunity. We actually used these funds to purchase a new, profitable business that had a good growth potential.

The actions taken to sell our automotive accessories business and to purchase a self-adhesive decorative covering business represent strategic decisions. They resulted from thoroughly evaluating both businesses and critically evaluating our abilities to participate in these two different business environments and how we could employ the associated resources more effectively. We are trying to practice in real life what we have professed to understand in strategic theory.

When I was responsible for the Major Appliance Business Group at General Electric, we were the first business to undertake a strategic planning review. GE has received favorable publicity for its progress in strategic planning and it was rightfully earned. I say this because what was achieved in the strategic planning area benefited the company significantly in subsequent years.

However, my point is that being involved at the head end of the planning process was highly beneficial to me as I went on to other responsibilities within the company. I had more involvement with the process, at least for a longer period of time, than most. I have been involved with it, both in depth and in time, to know what difficult work it is when performed properly.

It distresses me greatly when I hear executives throwing around the words "strategic planning" when they do not comprehend what is truly involved to undertake and install a complete strategic planning system and to make it work. For example, people who have spent many years in the planning field say that the implementation time takes one to one-and-a-half years per level of organization. Therefore, if you have five organizational levels, you are talking about more than five years before you have an effective planning operation throughout the company. In other words, you may have it in place theoretically, but it will not be in place effectively in just a matter of one or two years.

As I mentioned a few minutes ago, there is a next step for those who are ready for it. The next step is moving from what has been basic strategic planning to what I will refer to as strategic management.

INTERVIEWER: That really gets us into looking to the future. I wonder if you might amplify these thoughts about the future a bit.

GAULT: Yes, we are talking about aligning operating management and strategic planning at all levels of the organization as the step following the successful implementation of the basic planning process.

You asked earlier about a division having its own strategic planning as a result of moving the "planning function" downward in the organization. At General Electric, we started with 43 SBUs. That number was reduced subsequently and the review process was changed as other organizational levels were created. When the company became too difficult to manage from the historical group executive structure (arrangement), a sector organization level was established (five of them) and then the sectors had their own strategic plans.

In looking at the future, the strategic management concept will make greater use of the contribution from the functional components of the business in the resource-allocation process. I say the other functional positions and components because stra-

181

tegic planning initially focused on the allocation of financial resources and on financially oriented issues. I don't mean to imply that strategic planning excludes the other areas of functional expertise, but I am talking about the other functions now having involvement in recommending the allocation of corporate resources. I'm including such functions as legal, human resources, technology, marketing, etc.

For example, with the changes taking place in technology today, the functional component [technology] must have an integral part in the overall strategic planning process and it must be positioned at a level in the organization where it can make such a contribution. [Functional components] must not be at the bottom of the plan feeding upward, but inputting at all levels of planning.

Next, I believe it is conceivable that you will see companies considering the formation of a committee of the board for strategic planning. Today, there are board committees for nominating and directors' activities, compensation and management development, auditing, public affairs, social issues, technology, etc. Therefore, a committee on strategic planning is a possibility.

Whether or not it is established will depend upon CEO and board member interest and the popularity among other members of industry. I will not be surprised to see it develop because many boards could select a committee from their constituency who have both the interest and ability to contribute in this area. This would, of course, constitute added value to any organization.

There is no question that in the future there will be more and more CEOs who will assume their rightful position in the strategic planning process. This will happen because more of the CEOs of the future will have had involvement in the strategic planning process earlier in their careers. They will recognize that it is essential to show the commitment and have the appropriate involvement in the planning process if the business is to be successful and in some cases if it is actually to survive.

STRATEGIC MANAGEMENT SYSTEM

Stanley C. Gault
Chairman of the Board and Chief Executive Officer
Rubbermaid, Inc.

Many companies that implemented strategic planning success-fully during the 1970s either have made, or plan to make, addi-tional changes and revisions in their planning system. These modifications generally include some organization restructuring and the installation of a strategic management system. The objective of such changes being to take a further step in the pro-cess to build strategic planning principles into management roles at every level in a company, adding value all along the way.

I would first like to review some of the concepts underlying these changes. Then I'll describe the strategic management sys-tem with special emphasis on the planning elements. And, finally, I'll summarize the implications of these changes to a company's future growth and profitability.

From the perspective of history, adapting a company's orga-nization and systems to new and changing internal and external challenges should be a continuous process. During the '60s, thanks to a favorable economic climate, businesses experienced almost explosive growth. But in the process, many companies encountered a phenomenon at that time called "profitless growth." Sales continued to grow, but earnings were erratic.

Companies had recorded significant growth in sales, but earnings per share and return on investment were unsatisfactory. It was not uncommon to make investments in areas that didn't produce profitable growth. It became painfully obvious that greater investment selectivity was required along with a plan-ning system that would allocate financial resources according to the earnings potential of a company's various businesses.

183

To accomplish these objectives, many companies introduced the strategic planning concept during the '70s—overlaying their traditional organization structure of groups, divisions, departments (or whatever) with another structure for planning based on the identification of strategic business units, or SBUs. These SBUs were defined as self-contained businesses with identifiable external competitors whose general manager could implement appropriate short- and long-term business strategy. In other words, he could personally get his arms around and manage the business or group of businesses.

To help determine resource and investment allocation at the corporate level, a planning process was designed to surface each SBU's strategic plans.

To encourage the evaluation of investment selectivity at both corporate and business levels, a now-familiar approach was adopted called the "business screen" or "matrix," where investments in businesses are determined according to two major considerations—"industry attractiveness" and "business strengths."

Under such an evaluation, very simply, those businesses that fall into the invest/grow area are given investment priority because of their more attractive future earnings potential. Businesses in the selectivity/earnings area need to selectively balance their reinvestment needs with potential earnings generation.

Businesses in the harvest/divest area are less attractive and are asked to produce more short-term earnings and cash with the thought that they may be exited in the not-too-distant future or sold to another company where they would represent a better product fit.

One thing that made this approach different in successful companies from other approaches was that instead of using simply numerical projections based on uncertain forecasts, a multifactor assessment was made for each business.

Another thing that made this approach work was tying the strategic assignment of each business to the incentive compensation of the respective SBU manager. Based on its position on the matrix, performance objectives were set and agreed to in advance.

Invest/grow managers were more heavily rewarded for actions and programs geared to future benefits than for short-term results. The incentive bonus for a harvest/divest manager was based more on short-term earnings. For example, I remember a business a few years ago where the compensation was higher for a manager who successfully implemented a harvest/divest strategy than for other managers who were assigned an invest/grow strategy. This compensation arrangement helped overcome the natural tendency for any general manager to want to dig in his heels and make his business grow regardless of its realistic earning potential. It also further emphasized the fact that a company wanted strategic plans implemented—not just written and placed on a shelf—and would reward those general managers who accomplished their individual strategic objectives. As a result of implementing this basic strategic planning approach, earnings growth more closely tracked sales growth and return on investment improved.

I might point out that the "what if" contingency plans, an essential part of the strategic planning process, that were implemented by these companies during the 1970s proved to be highly beneficial.

Now, if all of this worked so well in reversing the profitless growth pattern of the '60s, it begs the question, "Why tinker with the system in the '80s?"

The answer lies in the challenges one sees during the years ahead. Based on the past few years, the expectations are for a continuation of economic uncertainties, aggravated by a general slowing of economic growth worldwide. The CEOs of the future will face expanding scopes of responsibility as they must increasingly consider the impact of social, political, and international issues on their businesses as probably never before.

Consequently, the accelerated pace of decision making will require more contingency planning, more flexible organization structures, and the strategic positioning of businesses for opportunities as well as threats.

The lessons learned from the past indicate that:

- A decentralized organization motivates both company and people growth.
- Planning systems that help management in making investment decisions can make that growth profitable.

- The evolving strategic business management style can be applied successfully to all levels of general and functional management.

So, judging from the anticipated challenges of the '80s, many view it to be time to move from "strategic planning" as a process designed for one level (the SBU) to "strategic management" as a concept for all levels of managers.

This concept not only recognizes the need of a decentralized organization structure for the development of managers and stimulation of company growth, but also requires an integrated system that focuses attention on the strategic utilization of a company's total resources. As a number of prominent American companies have discovered all too painfully in recent years, the total of the resources needed can be greater than the sum of the parts in terms of cash flow, debt load, etc., etc.

With those thoughts in mind, the following objectives need to be established as the basis for developing a company's strategic management system.

First, strengthen the unified company structure and retain a single company image, where desired, by combining planning and management responsibilities at each organization level.

Second, add value at every level of management by defining roles, for both line and staff, whereby each level develops business and resource strategies unique to its level.

Third, integrate planning systems at all levels—not only by vertically integrating strategic plans from SBU to division and group to corporate, but also by integrating functional planning to assure adequate investment in the development of key company resources—financial, human, technology, international, etc.

Fourth, assure continued manageability of the company and the availability of seasoned managers by providing opportunities for organizational and personal growth.

The successful implementation of these objectives requires the review of the organization structure, the roles of the various management levels, and some of the system elements designed to strengthen planning integration.

Organizationally, we are, in effect, seeing the melding of planning and management levels.

Looking at the organization structure, the corporate executive office continues to be the highest organizational and planning level. It is responsible for providing overall corporate leadership and planning direction to the other levels of management through the development and communication of the corporate plan.

The next level of management and planning will depend on the size and complexity of the company. In large, diversified companies, the level of management is usually an industry area composed of a number of SBUs with similar strategic challenges, based on such factors as markets, products, customers, or technologies. These common challenges are reflected as group strategies in a group plan if a "group" is the next level of management below the corporate executive office.

Below the group level, the SBU continues to be the basic business entity—that is, a complete business, structured to be a strategically effective competitor and producing an annual SBU plan. SBUs usually report directly to the group (group executive is the example I am using today) and may vary in size. This alignment enables an SBU to grow from a small department to a large division without changing its reporting relationship.

The merit of this arrangement is that this structure can provide for organizational growth, while keeping the overall management and group structure relatively stable. This structure makes it possible for a general manager and his functional managers to stay with a business and grow with it while moving up in levels of responsibility and compensation.

In addition, there can be specific recognition of strategic businesses within certain SBUs where strategic management is also required. These are called "business segments." A business segment is a competitive business activity which can be planned and operated independently, has many of the same characteristics as an SBU, but due to other factors, such as size, market requirements, changing environments, or management considerations, can be a more effective competitor by being part of an SBU.

Now I'd like to turn to the roles of various management levels within the organization structure, giving special emphasis to value added. Each level of strategic management should have distinct planning and management roles relative to its scope of

187

responsibility, in addition to managing the direct reporting levels.

Value added by a management level is through the development strategies and objectives unique to that level, with particular emphasis on business development and resource planning. This value added by each level will then be articulated through a strategic plan.

At the corporate level, as a result of the greater external pressures on a company from economic, social, international, and political factors, the corporate executive office will be shifting internal company direction more and more to the group executive (next level of management). For example, strategy review and resource allocation decisions that were made at corporate level for a number of SBUs can be shifted to the group executives, allowing the corporate executive office to concentrate to a greater degree on company-wide issues, both internal and external.

The corporate executive office will also review and integrate group plans and budgets, and develop a corporate strategic plan that adds the company business and resource development perspective of the corporate executive office.

The group executive adds value over and above the SBUs within his or her group by providing management direction and integrating the strategies of his SBUs into an overall group strategic plan. The plan reflects the business and resource development strategies unique to the perspective and scope of that group.

The role of the SBU general manager will not significantly change. He will continue to be responsible for the business management of his SBU. He may manage product lines, functions, or business segments, and is responsible for integrating their plans into an overall SBU strategic plan, adding value once again through resource and business development strategies unique to the SBU's perspective.

Turning next to the roles of staff or functional management—staffs at every level have two responsibilities. The first, naturally, is to provide staff support and expertise to the executive at that level. The second is the planning and monitoring of company resources, such as financial, human, technological, production, or other internal strengths.

In addition, staffs are responsible for integrating this functional planning or issue identification activity into the strategic plans at their level.

The system elements that support the objective of integrated planning include:

- Strategic plans
- Resource or functional planning
- Business development planning
- The annual planning cycle

Starting with strategic plans, these are prepared at every strategic management level annually—that is, at corporate, group, SBU, and if appropriate, at a business segment level.

Although plans will differ from one business or level to the next, certain common elements are required to reinforce the value-added characteristics unique to a given level. These common elements are:

- A description of the business level's objectives
- Strategies and scope
- Business development
- Resource plans or programs
- The summarization of the strategies and objectives of the lower level

Although all of these levels of plans may have different scopes and timing, the discipline of writing a plan every year encourages the kind of thinking and review of alternates which is the key to the strategic management concept.

The development of the corporate plan is a process that provides overall direction to the company's planning efforts and a comprehensive statement of scope. It communicates planning challenges to the SBUs at the beginning of each year's planning cyle and provides a basis for evaluating SBU plans.

In addition, it integrates group plans and balances corporate business strategies with the company's resource capabilities. Finally, it identifies corporate issues requiring resolution.

The development of a corporate plan is an ongoing process, with revisions in any year coming as a result of an analysis of external and internal issues, dialogue between group and corporate staff, and, of course, an evaluation of written group plans.

The group plan is probably the single most critical element in this new, updated system because it bridges the gap between corporate and SBU planning and eliminates the need for the corporate executive office to personally review a number of strategic business plans—of course, not a problem in small companies.

The group plan not only expresses the unique strategies of that segment, but it also synthesizes the plans and objectives of the SBUs within the group. It describes group-level business and resource strategies that may be beyond the scope of individual SBUs to implement. In addition, group plans provide the basis for corporate resource allocation.

Next, the emphasis on resource planning is, in effect, a recognition of the important planning and management role of each staff or functional manager. As companies emerged from a recession of the mid-1970s which dramatically highlighted the vulnerability of some of their key company resources, managers with the functional responsibility to manage a company's key internal strengths became aware that many other factors were involved in managing these resources. For example, the technologist now must not only concern himself with the soundness or applicability of an innovation, but he must also consider the environmental, political, and cultural impacts of his work and, above all, address the concern that the technologies can be successfully married to an emerging market.

The emphasis on resource planning recognizes not only the more difficult job required to manage these resources (financial and human resources), but also assures careful consideration of these resources in the strategic plans at each level. Continual reassessment of critical resource areas within every strategic plan should surface issues in anticipation of problems rather than as a reaction to them.

Business development planning is also part of the value-added role at every strategic level. It encourages the pursuit and development of options which may generate new businesses or sources of growth, including pruning out unprofitable businesses. A variety of development mechanisms and techniques are available for consideration by the strategic planners at each level.

These include internal development, acquisitions, joint ventures, venture capital, divestitures, technology transfer, and licensing.

Finally, a company's planning cycle should be such to support the objectives of the integrated planning levels I've described and it should be a closed-loop process.

The corporate plan develops planning challenges which are addressed in group plans within their unique scopes. Group plans are reviewed and the impact on corporate objectives evaluated, resources are reassessed and allocated—and finally, as the next year's budgets are being finalized, the corporate plan is being updated to reflect new or continuing corporate priorities on the planning horizon.

And now we come full cycle, because prior to the end of the year, the new corporate plan is approved by the corporate executive office and distributed to the groups.

Well, those are the major elements of a management system and they may sound more complicated than they are. But, before concluding, I'd like to emphasize the implications of some of these changes that may not be so apparent.

First, the objective of integrated levels of planning is just that—an objective. It may take several cycles to accomplish completely. However, by designing a mutual dependency between the corporate plan and the group plans, both plans should continually improve in quality and relevance as they evolve together.

As a matter of fact, the mutual dependency of all levels in the development of their strategic plan encourages a dialogue between levels that is made easier by the fact that each level is planning for its own scope of responsibility. One should recognize the inherent risk of becoming compartmentalized, getting into the narrow view and not communicating with each other.

In short, planning at each level replaces planning at one level, the SBU, and reviewing at all the levels above—which in some companies meant division, group, and corporate. A system that integrates plans requires dialogue as part of the process. This dialogue alone should improve the more timely identification and resolution of key company issues.

Next, the requirements to include business development and resource planning strategies as value-added ingredients of all

191

strategic plans build into the management system that continual consideration of growth strategies and attention to preserving and strengthening critical company resources.

Also, this constant attention to opportunities, and the perpetual assessment of internal strengths and weaknesses, should minimize the need for special programs or major fact-finding studies that often have a disruptive impact on a company and may transmit inaccurate signals of company objectives.

Finally, the primary purpose of a true management system is to provide managers with the tools, the channels of communication, and the timely information to cope with the new strategic environment of the 1980s.

The effectiveness of these supporting systems will assist existing managers at every level to absorb increasing scopes of responsibility and to provide a reliable source of top managers for the future.

These challenges will require:

- Political, economic, social, and technological awareness on a world scale.
- The foresight to anticipate change and develop contingencies.
- The judgment to seek sources of growth while still maintaining the strengths of internal resources.

In short, these elements of strategic management support a company's most important objective—that of being a unified, strong, progressive, responsive, and successful enterprise.

APPENDIX
SELECTED ARTICLES

As we conveyed at the outset, we wanted to include a number of very practical articles that can provide additional, and more specific, thoughts about strategic concepts and philosophies, as well as analytical approaches to planning. Yet we did not want to interrupt the natural flow of material from chapter to chapter; so we opted to include the articles in an appendix.

For the reader's convenience, we have listed each article's title below, capsuled what it is about, and, where we felt it necessary to do so, indicated why the particular selection was included. We view these articles as a strategic planning smorgasbord of sorts, from which the reader can pick and choose according to individual interests or can select the full course by reading all the articles.

- *"Strategic Business Planning: Yesterday, Today, and Tomorrow." This article provides historic and future looks at business expansion trends. It examines the various strategies for corporate growth that have been in vogue in recent history — and the degree to which each has succeeded or failed — and then goes on to conjecture about the nature of business expansion in the future.*

- *"An Approach Toward Successful Acquisitions." Also on the subject of business growth, this article is replete with tested insights on how top management can make better strategic judgments regarding the overall quality of potential acquisitions.*

- *"Competitor Analysis: The Missing Link in Strategy." This article discusses the salient questions to ask about competitors, how to get the answers, and, ultimately, how to turn these answers to strategic advantage.*

- *"Technology's Input Is Vital to Sound Business Planning." There has been a purported attrition in U.S. technological leadership. As a consequence, firms have been augmenting their R&D efforts and monetary commitments. Still, a poll shows that experts generally feel that many companies are mismanaging their technology and have not been effective in meshing technological efforts with corporate business objectives. This article discusses the benefits of including top technical managers in strategic planning.*

- *"International Marketing Planning: The Gap Between Theory and Practice." This article examines the validity of the widespread belief that formalized marketing planning facilitates success. It is based on the marketing planning practices of British industrial goods companies operating internationally.*

- *"Is the International Cash Cow Really a Prize Heifer?" This writing looks at portfolio analysis within the context of international business. It points out and illustrates through the use of examples the pitfalls of drawing conclusions about various lines of business based on domestic (U.S.) performance data in isolation. A "dog" in the domestic market might have "star" potential elsewhere.*

- *"Inside/Outside Director Information Needs."*
- *"Should the Board Consider This Agenda Item?"*
- *"Improving Corporate Communications with Members of the Board."*

Some comments are in order regarding the last three articles, which we authored. In Chapter 2 of the present book, we wrote, "The very essence of corporate policy-making is long-range strategic planning. Accordingly, we see the board of directors' role (indeed, other than selecting a CEO, its chief function) to be that of considering, debating, and ratifying the company's strategic plan." Too often in the past, boards of directors have been but rubber stamps for whatever actions or plans were proposed by management. Now, with boards becoming more involved, due to increased legal liability and other reasons, they often have an integral role in strategic planning decisions of the highest level. We think that a board of directors composed of truly interested and motivated individuals with top-level business experience can contribute much to the strategic plan. There is also a place on boards for bright thinkers generally, regardless of where they come from or their degree of experience in corporations. But, even if a board has the best people possible, its effectiveness is only as good as the information it receives from the company. Because of the potential value of boards of directors in matters of corporate strategy, we have included a series of three articles that discuss (1) what corporate matters are proper ones for board consideration, and (2) how the company can go about providing directors with the very best in the way of the "strategic" information they need to perform ably as members of the board.

195

STRATEGIC BUSINESS PLANNING: YESTERDAY, TODAY, AND TOMORROW

William L. Shanklin

Business planning strategies have changed perceptibly in the last decade. In the 1960s, the commonly preferred modus operandi for achieving rapid corporate growth was conglomerate diversification via merger and acquisition. After a brief lull, corporate expansion through merger and acquisition is once again in vogue, but now growth-oriented companies are generally insistent on partnerships that will produce synergies with their existing operations. So while great diversity was the theme of the 1960s, compatibility is the theme of the mid- to late 1970s.

Why did this change come about? What will be the thrust of strategic business planning in the 1980s? What kinds of growth strategies will United States antitrust policy foster and constrain in the next decade?

CORPORATE GROWTH: 1960s STYLE

In the sixties, strategic business planning in many companies meant investment planning. Conglomerates attempted to parlay portfolios of diverse subsidiaries into profits, just as individual investors often do with disparate holdings of corporate securities. The prevailing wisdom was that diversity brought vitality and hedged the risks of economic downturns.

Investment goals and strategies—mainly asset acquisition and leverage using those assets—motivated one conglomerate's management to acquire more than 350 diverse companies in a year's time. The acquisitions had in common little more than central financial control from corporate headquarters. That same conglomerate today, like numerous others whose manage-

---

Reprinted from *Business Horizons*, Vol. 22, October 1979, pp. 7–14. Used by permission.

ments predicated corporate strategy on investment rather than operating considerations, has paid dearly. Management's failure to consider how well each acquisition would meld with and complement the businesses already in the conglomerate's stable of subsidiaries led to lagging profits, negative growth, and significant attrition in the market value of its securities.

Investment planning as a substitute for corporate planning was inevitably destined to falter. In describing "the fallacy of asset management," Peter Drucker explains why:

"Asset management as it relates to nonfinancial businesses is a function and not the definition of the business ... the asset managers who acquired operating businesses [in the 1960s] performed a useful function when they closed down or sold off parts that were tying down large chunks of assets without producing returns. But once they had done this, they did not know how to manage a business—and the boom of asset management ended in predictable failure."[1]

Take the case of a well-known appliance manufacturer. Some eleven years ago, it commenced buying family-owned and operated construction companies. The acquisitions were viewed as means for participating in lucrative federally-funded projects to reclaim badly polluted bodies of water, such as the Potomac River. The parent company wisely retained family members to manage the construction companies, as the former owners knew the business. But it unwisely and too abruptly installed its own "efficiency experts" to impose "good control practices," including asset control, on the subsidiaries. Soon, a debilitating number of holdover managers resigned at least partly in disgust with interference by the parent company in day-to-day operations. The appliance manufacturer was left with a number of expensive assets, few people competent to utilize them profitably, and dim prospects for help from its own ranks of appliance-oriented managers and engineers.

In contrast, a leading wood and paper products manufacturer was vigorously augmenting its growth rate during the same period by means of vertical and horizontal integration. The company acquired a sizable number of family-owned and run wholesale plywood distributors and, like the appliance company, normally retained incumbent management. In the process, the

197

parent company inherited each dealer's customers, facilities, equipment, and reservoir of good will. Contractual agreements prudently prohibited the former owners from opening competing distributorships for five years. As holdover managers gradually left their former businesses for other pursuits, the parent company easily replaced them with capable managers from within its own executive pool. In brief, the company had managers who knew the wood products business.

CORPORATE GROWTH: 1970s STYLE

A normative or ideal approach by means of which corporate strategists can identify and evaluate potential sources of organizational growth has been discussed by Kalman Cohen and Richard Cyert.[2] Their approach, which is nearly a prototype of 1970s-style corporate growth, suggests that the strategic search process should focus initially on growth opportunities within the company. Internal search might include reviews of the firm's entire marketing strategy and of innovative possibilities in research and development. Another primary target of internal search is the cost structure of the firm, with an eye toward designing a strategy for cost reduction. If these steps convince management that the company cannot attain desired growth and profit goals by internal means, then it must turn to external search. The external environment is surveyed to identify companies which, if acquired or merged with, would bring needed resources to the firm and enable it to reach its objectives. The firm looks for partnerships that would result in economies of scale, positive externalities, or both. Economies of scale could flow from an acquisition that makes possible more intensive utilization of existing personnel and facilities, for instance, by producing or distributing a newly-acquired product line with present facilities and manpower. Positive externalities might derive from the firm's obtaining a complementary new product whose sale would boost the sales of its present products; or from eliminating overlapping facilities; or from acquiring capable managerial and technical talent.

In the wake of numerous disappointments with the external conglomerate diversifications of the 1960s, corporate planners did indeed turn inward. Product lines were pruned, unsatisfactory acquisitions divested, costs cut in the operations that remained, and growth sought by means of internal synergy-producing strategies.

Today, now that internal growth alternatives have to a large degree been exploited, companies are finding it increasingly arduous to grow as rapidly as management and stockholders would like. Accordingly, corporate policymakers are once again looking outward. A McKinsey and Company executive comments, "More companies are saying that they are not in the right businesses."[3] This thinking has resulted in a new wave of mergers and acquisitions. But the object lessons taught by the conglomerate mergers of the 1960s have not been lost on today's generation of top managers and their actions show it.

The current merger trend is structurally different from its predecessor. As *Business Week* explains it:

"The acquiring companies have been much more careful than their counterparts in the 1960s about analyzing merger candidates and assessing their potential fit. . . . The current trend is grounded in a lot more thoughtful, rational analysis . . . most recent big mergers have had sensible, often traditional purposes to them . . . such mergers as International Nickel with ESB (batteries) and H. J. Heinz with Hubinger (corn sweeteners) are classic examples of integration."[4]

Corporate planners are unquestionably eschewing the economic wanderlust of 1960s-style conglomerate growth in favor of more integrative mergers and acquisitions. They are looking for compatibility of business missions in the merging firms and for synergies from the marriages. Examples abound.

Pepsico recently acquired Pizza Hut and Taco Bell. Both companies tie in well with Pepsico's rapidly growing soft drink division and enable it to serve the types of consumers it knows best. These acquisitions make Pepsico the fourth largest fast-food concern in the United States. As a result, Pepsico is in a good position to sell domestically to the members of the World War II baby boom as they enter their thirties and forties and to expand internationally where the fast food industry is in an early stage of development. Contrast the Pizza Hut and Taco Bell acquisitions to those of previous years when Pepsico acquired companies as diverse as Frito-Lay, North American Van Lines, Wilson Sporting Goods, and the since-divested Rheingold Brewery.[5] The prolific profit-maker Frito-Lay was probably the best acquisition of this group because there are close similarities between marketing potato chips and soft drinks.

In 1972 the Loral Corporation was a financially-troubled miniconglomerate specializing in electronic warfare systems. By 1973, a new Loral chairman had divested the company of most of its nonelectronics endeavors, such as toys, copper wire, and industrial meters. Starting with the purchase of a small manufacturer of communications equipment in 1974, Loral turned outward a second time. This time, however, top management was and is careful not to assume its predecessors' proclivity for acquiring companies with missions far removed from electronics. In March 1978, Loral reported profits that were fourteen times its 1972 earnings.[6]

G. H. Bass and Company, which manufactures shoes, restructured itself in 1975 under pressure from its bank. It appointed a new president, rid itself of nonshoe acquisitions, upgraded and broadened its product line, and concentrated its resources and efforts on making and marketing shoes. Sales and profits quickly responded. Subsequently, Bass's new president refused an acquisition offer tendered by AEA, a professional investor in diverse companies for purposes of capital appreciation, because he felt that the companies' business missions and philosophies were incompatible. Bass was sold later to Chesebrough-Ponds, a consumer products company with objectives more in keeping with those of Bass.[7]

The search for synergy is by no means confined to merger and acquisition strategy alone. General Electric, for example, has found it essential to reorganize in order to accommodate its existing diversity and to promote synergies. In GE's new organizational structure, each of five sector vice presidents will direct his own multi-billion-dollar group of units with its own clearly defined industry identity. According to GE's chairman, the reorganization was implemented to avoid an "unmanageable situation" by 1980. Sector management was adopted after GE experimented with the concept for a year in consumer products "to find out what the synergies were and what the relationship would be between the sector and the corporate staff." *Business Week* has described GE's reorganization as an effort to run billion-dollar sectors as though they were small companies.[8]

The proposition that industry is consolidating its efforts in search of manageable and synergy-producing growth is more broadly corroborated by industry segment disclosures in 1977 annual corporate reports to shareholders. Such disclosures were required for the first time in 1977 by Rule 14 of the Financial Accounting Standards Board. Recently, Arthur Andersen and Company randomly selected 250 annual reports for 1977 and compiled and summarized the industry segment disclosures. More than 30 percent of the 250 companies indicated that their operations were totally in one industry segment or that they operated mostly in one dominant segment. Fewer than 33 percent reported serving more than four segments. The 250 companies operated in an average of three industry segments.[9] In its annual report for 1977, General Motors said, "GM considers itself to be in a single industry broadly defined as transportation equipment."

CORPORATE GROWTH: 1980s STYLE?

"Shoemaker stick to your last!" This is the advice given to corporate policymakers by Peter Drucker. It is based on his belief that conglomerates have time and again shown themselves to be at distinct competitive disadvantages against integrated firms. He cited the long-term track records of the erstwhile high-flying conglomerates of the 1960s in comparison to those of Eastman-Kodak, General Motors, the Swiss pharmaceutical companies, and other prominent single-market or single-technology businesses.[10] For instance, LTV, a major conglomerate in the sixties, fell from fourteenth in sales on the *Fortune 500* list in 1969 to forty-third in 1977, while the highly integrated Exxon has consistently been at or near the top of the list.

Further empirical support for Drucker's contention is provided by a 1974 Harvard Business School study by Richard Rumelt. In the years between 1949 and 1969, major companies that concentrated their individual technological and marketing efforts in one or closely related businesses were superior performers, as evidenced by both return on equity and capital.[11] Judging by the integrative nature of the vast majority of recent

201

large mergers in the United States, top managements in leading firms generally agree.

Even so, large integrated companies, particularly those operating in industries with significant degrees of market concentration, may have a difficult time "sticking to their last" in the 1980s because of U.S. antitrust policy. A company does not necessarily have to be its industry's dominant firm before it encounters difficulties.

Consider Pabst. The U.S. Justice Department has circumvented its attempt to acquire Carling Brewery, in spite of the fact that Pabst has only a 9.9 percent market share and the financially-plagued Carling a meager 2.7 percent. A Department of Justice spokesman commented, "There is no way that one national beer can pick up another and not be anticompetitive on the face of it."[12] The major beneficiaries of this action would seem to be the beer industry's two dominant firms—Anheuser-Busch and Miller.

Under the provisions of the 1976 Antitrust Improvement Act, relevant detailed statements must be filed with the Federal Trade Commission whenever one party to a proposed merger has assets of more than $10 million and the other has assets in excess of $100 million. Then there is an obligatory thirty-day waiting period before the merger can be consummated. But much more substantive antitrust restrictions may be in store. Both the assistant attorney general for antitrust of the Department of Justice and the chairman of the Federal Trade Commission have publicly criticized the trend toward industrial concentration. In Senate testimony, they suggest legislative measures which would remedy the fact that U.S. antitrust laws do not presently prohibit mergers on the basis of size alone. Possible corrective steps include an outright ban on mergers of a certain size, the prohibition of mergers that would exceed specified market share or concentration limits, a modification in the law to require merging firms to prove the benefit of their merger, and changes in the tax laws that currently allow interest deductions when firms borrow to finance acquisitions.[13]

Companies that have grown via internal integrative strategies have sometimes had their problems with antitrust, too. Three years ago, in order to settle a Federal Trade Commission complaint, Xerox opened its portfolio of 1,700 copier patents to competitors. The company was obliged to license three patents to competitors without charge—and competitors were permitted to select any three they wanted. In addition, fees for competitors' use of the remaining Xerox patents were limited by the FTC. More recently, in order to terminate a suit brought by the Department of Justice, Industrial Electronics Engineers, Inc., committed itself to grant royalty-free licenses on patents it had used to dominate the market for rear-projection readout equipment for data processing systems. Currently, the Federal Trade Commission wants DuPont to give competitors—again, royalty-free—the technological know-how to manufacture a paint pigment that it has taken DuPont twenty-five years to perfect.[14] Ironically, this action comes at a time when a high-level federal domestic policy review has been organized to explore what can be done about the United States losing its technological superiority to other countries.

Several conclusions regarding integrative corporate growth, conglomerate diversification, and U.S. antitrust policy are warranted. First, on balance, integrative business strategies have been superior to conglomerate diversification strategies, in terms of comparative growth and profit records since the 1960s. Second, federal antitrusters are resolved to fight industrial concentration—and are after more powerful laws with which to do so. This means that U.S. antitrust policy actually fosters conglomerate growth and militates against integrative growth. Third, size of market share is probably the key indicant that antitrusters rely on to identify companies that may be approaching anticompetitive positions. Fourth, what antitrusters consider to be an anticompetitive share varies from market to market. The ill-fated Pabst-Carling merger was objected to because the firms together would have had a 12.6 percent share of market. Yet, in many other markets leading firms have shares that are multiples of 12.6 percent.

The implications for strategic business planning in the decade ahead depend, to a large extent, on whether a particular firm is in a dominant or nondominant industry position. Low market share companies—however "low" is quantitatively interpreted in various markets—should continue to be able to rely, with impunity, on highly integrative internal and external growth strategies: market penetration, market and product development, and vertical and horizontal integration. Antitrusters are unlikely to construe integration in low market share firms to be anticompetitive, with one exception: a nondominant company attempting to merge with an industry leader that is in the same line of business.

High market share firms are quite another matter. For them, Tolkien's proverb is apropos: "It does not do to leave a dragon out of your calculations, if you live near him." Ponder what would result if, say, IBM were to increase its market share, even slightly, in the computer industry. Recall that in 1969 the Department of Justice charged the company with monopoly under Section 2 of the Sherman Act, and the suit is still unsettled. Thus, in the 1980s, high market share companies will have to balance growth through synergy-producing, integrative strategies against the risks of antitrust actions. To this end, two planning strategies appear promising, each of which facilitates the attainment of synergy-producing growth yet obviates market share concentration.

Concentric Diversification

This strategy is attractive because it is quasi-diversifying but, at the same time, is quasi-integrating. It requires a company to develop or acquire new products which have marketing and/or technological synergies with its existing products but which are normally not intended for sale to the company's present markets.[15] The company benefits from positive externalities or economies of scale or both, but avoids inflating its precariously large market share in its major market or markets.

Concentric strategy might well be called mirage diversification. It often gives the illusion that a company is departing radically from its original business when, in reality, it is simply transferring marketing or technological expertise from its primary line of business to another much like it. Philip Morris' acquisition of Miller Brewing Company is a textbook illustration of a company achieving marketing synergies through external concentric diversification.

Philip Morris' buying Miller seemed to be a typical 1960s-style conglomerate diversification—a cigarette company purchasing a brewery. It was in fact a mirage. There were synergies aplenty. Cigarettes and beer are distributed through many of the same retail outlets, and Philip Morris had been dealing with them for years. More importantly, both products are meant for what can be characterized as hedonistic consumer markets. Consequently, when Philip Morris applied to Miller the same merchandising, marketing research, and psychographically-oriented promotion techniques that it had used to sell cigarettes successfully, the strategy worked brilliantly. Miller moved from seventh to second in its industry in six years' time, and Philip Morris encountered no antitrust problems along the way. On the surface, cigarettes and beer are different industries. Actually, they serve a generic hedonistic market that Philip Morris had the savvy to identify and the expertise to capitalize on. With its recent acquisition of 7-Up, Philip Morris is continuing with the same successful synergy-producing strategy.

Another approach. Texas Instruments, a company that has not merged with another firm since 1959, is a case study in successful internal concentric diversification with technological expertise providing the major thread binding its diversity. The company is decentralized into some eighty product-customer centers, referred to within the firm as "little businesses." Each center has the responsibility for engineering, manufacturing, and marketing a product. Various alignments of product-customer centers constitute the firm's industry segments; for example, the digital products segment encompasses minicomputers, data terminals, calculators, and watches. Corporate sales are diffused over five segments: components, digital products, government electronics, metallurgy, and services.[16] Texas Instruments has avoided inordinately high shares in any of its industry segments, while remaining a growth-oriented and integrated single-technology firm, concentrating on what it does best.

International Market Development

This strategy also enables a high market share company to stay true to its basic business by diversifying markets instead of lines of business. By taking its existing products into international markets, a U.S.-based company is able to pursue rapid growth in

205

several foreign markets, without risking too much incremental growth and too large a market share in the United States.

Many large U.S. companies are, of course, already heavily involved in international markets. But there is virtually unlimited growth potential; U.S. firms have barely scratched the surface of opportunity, especially in the Communist Eastern bloc and developing third-world nations.

So far as antitrust is concerned, international market development is the safest integrative growth strategy available to high market share companies for two reasons. First, the Webb-Pomerene Export Act exempts American companies from U.S. antitrust restraints in foreign markets. Second, U.S. policy toward business currently looks kindly upon export strategies by U.S. firms because of the serious balance of payments problem in this country.

Companies embracing integrative growth strategies over the last ten to fifteen years have, as a group, outperformed those following diversifying conglomerate strategies. These comparative growth and profit records explain the current preference in industry for integrative growth, particularly as reflected in recent large mergers and acquisitions. Given the success of integrative growth, vis-à-vis conglomerate diversification, the former ostensibly should remain the popular growth mode in the eighties. In low market share companies, it no doubt will. However, in high market share companies, strategic business planning for the 1980s will be analogous to steering a ship through a raging storm. Their attainment of additional synergy-producing growth, without antitrust interference, will be a tedious task at best. Albeit there is no growth strategy that is antitrust proof, concentric diversification, both internal and external, and intensified international market development are the synergy-producing growth strategies best suited to the task.

NOTES

[1]Peter F. Drucker, *Management: Tasks, Responsibilities, Practices* (New York: Harper & Row, 1974): 682.

[2]Kalman J. Cohen and Richard M. Cyert, "Strategy: Formulation, Implementation, and Monitoring," *The Journal of Business*, July 1973: 349–67.

[3]"The Great Takeover Binge," *Business Week,* November 14, 1977: 178.

[4]"The Great Takeover Binge": 179.

[5]"Pepsi Takes on the Champ," *Business Week,* June 12, 1978: 88–97.

[6]"Loral: Focusing Its Expertise on Electronic Warfare Systems," *Business Week,* July 24, 1978: 168–69.

[7]"How Bass Held Out for a Better Fit," *Business Week,* July 24, 1978: 131–32.

[8]"GE's New Billion-Dollar Small Businesses," *Business Week,* December 19, 1977: 78–79.

[9]*Segment Information: Disclosure of Segment Information in 1977 Annual Reports* (Chicago: Arthur Andersen & Company, 1978).

[10]Drucker, *Management:* 679–80.

[11]Richard P. Rumelt, *Strategy, Structure, and Economic Performance* (Boston: Harvard University Press, 1974).

[12]"The Battle of the Beers," *Newsweek,* September 4, 1978: 60–70.

[13]Jack Egan and John F. Berry, "Merger, Merger Everywhere," *The Courier-Journal,* August 20, 1978: E–4.

[14]"Vanishing Innovation," *Business Week,* July 3, 1978: 46–54.

[15]Philip Kotler, *Marketing Management: Analysis, Planning, and Control* (Englewood Cliffs, N.J.: Prentice-Hall, 1976): 51.

[16]Bradley Graham, "Texas Instruments Is a Leader, Innovator," *Akron Beacon Journal,* September 3, 1978: F–8, F–12.

AN APPROACH TOWARD SUCCESSFUL ACQUISITIONS

James B. Farley and
Edward H. Schwallie

The most apparent characteristic of the changing environment for acquisitions is the dramatic increase in completed transactions during recent years. In total dollar terms, acquisitions have increased fourfold since 1975 with volume in 1980 at around $45 billion, the highest level since the merger boom of the late 1960s.

As illustrated in Exhibit 1, this increase is particularly significant for very large transactions, with more than 30 deals, each

Reprinted from *The Texas Business Executive,* Vol. 7, Fall–Winter 1981, pp. 32–39. All rights reserved. Used by permission.

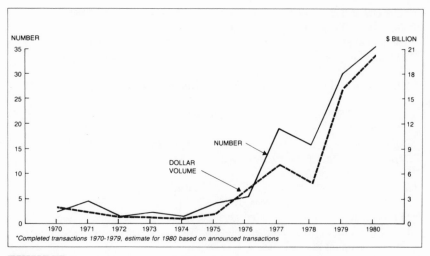

EXHIBIT 1
Number and Value of Acquisitions over $200 Million*

over $200 million, completed in both 1979 and in 1980. More-over, the first quarter of 1981 suggests that this trend will continue. This compares with five or less such deals per year during the 1970 to 1975 period, and not more than 20 in any other year during the 1970s.

As an example of the current high levels of acquisition activity it can be mentioned that the three recently announced offers within a period of seven days for major non-ferrous metals companies (Amax, St. Joe Minerals and Kennecott) in aggregate represent a purchase price of close to $8 billion. Just these three deals, if completed, would correspond to almost half of the constant dollar value of all acquisitions announced in the U.S. during 1975.

This extraordinary growth in acquisition activity reflects the combined effect of several underlying forces, including:

Low Stock Prices
While the market indices during the last month or so have approached new heights, stock prices have in general been depressed during recent years. This is a two-edged sword to the extent that the low stock prices and P/E multiples that make the

purchase price appear attractive, at the same time make it equally unattractive to use stock to pay for the acquisition. If cash is used, however, low P/E multiples only make acquisitions more attractive. As might be expected, cash is also the basis on which most transactions have been structured during the last few years.

High Inflation
High inflation frequently makes acquiring existing businesses and assets considerably more attractive than the expense and time required for developing new businesses internally.

Low Growth
Low real economic growth in many areas has generated large cash pools in well managed companies. This has resulted in incentives to acquire, but by the same token, these companies become attractive targets to be acquired.

Foreign Purchasers
There has been a strong increase in foreign buyers who, in addition to the above factors, have benefited from an until recently weak dollar, the relative political stability and overall size of the U.S. market as compared to their home countries, and frequently a technology gap that may be in either side's favor.

Aside from the increase in overall volume, another important change in the environment for acquisitions has occurred. We have witnessed a marked shift towards participation from some of the leading U.S. corporations that traditionally have not been very active in major acquisitions. Recently, companies such as General Electric, DuPont, Westinghouse and General Foods have been involved in giant acquisitions ranging from $250 million to $650 million in purchase price. In addition, almost all major oil companies are now actively using their vast cash pools for acquisitions. In fact, some 20 of the top 50 U.S. *Fortune 500* companies have made major acquisitions during the last five years.

In summary, today we are living in an environment of frequent and large acquisitions. The participants are playing a high stakes game—both the companies and the individuals involved. Success can lead to years of prosperous growth for the combined companies. Failure leads to severe problems for shareholders and often leads also to the abrupt end of a career for the responsible CEO.

THE CHALLENGE

The challenge of the corporate match-maker consists of three principal questions: how do you identify the specific company for a prospective acquisition, how do you convince the target to make a deal, and what happens when all the papers are signed?

There are both happy and unhappy marriages in the corporate world—and divorces are becoming more common. Companies such as Esmark, GAF and Richardson-Merrell have recently found it advantageous to break the ties with substantial parts of their business portfolios.

As we see it, corporate acquisitions are not getting any easier. On the contrary, there are more challenges and pitfalls than ever for the CEO that sets out to make a major deal. We believe that the following conditions and issues must be considered as a CEO embarks upon an acquisition effort.

A Competitive Market
As more and more companies get accustomed to viewing acquisitions as an ordinary rather than an extraordinary management tool, competition has increased in the market place. Also, using market research to stay ahead of the competition has diminished as computerized data banks are making high quality search and screening data available to anyone. A more liquid market has developed where more participants compete on more equal terms. New and innovative methods of search and evaluation must be employed by the companies who want to stay ahead in this tougher market.

Few Good Candidates
In many industries, the "first round" of corporate marriages has for the most part been consummated, leaving few attractive opportunities for a "second round." There is, of course, a continuing ongoing process generating an inflow of new quality candi-

EXHIBIT 2
Average Premiums Paid for Acquisitions

YEAR	PERCENT PREMIUM PAID OVER MARKET PRIOR TO ANNOUNCEMENT	
1975	41.4%	
1976	40.4	40.9%
1977	40.9	
1978	46.2	
1979	49.9	48.7%
1980	50.0	

Source: *W. T. Grimm & Company*

dates. With sustained levels of demand outstripping supply, however, these candidates will prove increasingly more difficult to find.

Increasing Price Premiums

The growing demand for acquisitions is evidenced in gradual and steady increases in premiums paid over market price. As illustrated in the table in Exhibit 2, price premiums were, on average, 41% over market price in the period 1975 to 1977 and 49% for 1978 to 1980. Several recent bids in 1981 have been substantially over the 54.6% average for 1980. For example, the initial bids in the cases of Amax, St. Joe Minerals and Kennecott were at premiums of 92%, 61% and 159%, respectively. With limited supply of good candidates this trend towards higher premiums will probably continue. The margin for error will be correspondingly reduced and the risk of overpayment will increase.

Risk of Overpayment

A common source of criticism is that companies have been overpaying for their acquisitions. With premiums paid over market price sometimes going well over 100 percent, it is not surprising that shareholders and other interested parties often wonder what great opportunities have been discovered by the buying company that the rest of the market cannot see. Unfortunately, it frequently turns out that there were no particular insights about the future at hand, and that the high price rather was the

211

result of a bidding contest or the general eagerness to make a deal.

Identifying Underlying Asset Values

In periods of double digit inflation, both the importance and complexity of identifying underlying asset values increases. This challenge is especially difficult when a potential acquisition has to be evaluated "from the outside," without access to internal data from the target company. In the case of Amax, for example, the true value of this company's vast molybdenum reserves is probably very difficult to assess even for experts within the company that can use all available financial, operating and geological information.

Finding the Hidden Risks

There is a range of "hidden risks" that needs to be clearly understood and evaluated before a deal is closed. Issues that frequently appear in this context include

- potential liabilities
- quality of management and risk that they may leave
- potential new competition
- labor issues
- requirements of new technology for success
- requirements for materials in short supply.

Penn Central's initially aborted attempt to acquire G. K. Technologies is a good example of this kind of risk. Only a thorough evaluation revealed the latter company's potential liability in connection with the tragic M. G. M. Grand Hotel fire in Las Vegas. Apparently, this issue is now resolved as Penn Central has resumed the talks and is currently in the process of concluding the transaction.

The International Environment

Most U.S. companies of any importance are today engaged in international business either through foreign operations or exports or both. Not infrequently, the international business of an acquisition target is more risky but perhaps also more profitable than the domestic operations. This makes an understanding of the internal environment facing the target company a key challenge for the acquiror. Accounting treatment, regulatory issues, currency risks and political/environmental factors can be of critical importance to the company's future prospects. The list of recent examples illustrating this challenge is long, including currency problems in Brazil and other high inflation countries, S. E. C. investigations of illegal foreign payoffs, losses due to political turmoil in Iran, and the like.

The Legislative and Regulatory Environment

While political instability and currency exposure are not major risk factors in our own country, we certainly have a legislative and regulatory environment that can provide any number of challenges to the acquisition-minded executive. With the possible exception of a more lenient interpretation of the current antitrust legislation, there is no evidence that federal and state regulations on acquisitions will be reduced under the new administration.

Technical Complexity

Finally, the technical complexity of actually making the deal happen is frequently an important challenge in itself. Different stakeholders ranging from shareholders and lenders to employees and special interest groups have to be taken into account in structuring and negotiating the transaction. Solving financial, legal and tax issues is today only one step in providing for the long-term success of the acquisition—the objectives and concerns of the investment community, the unions, various regulatory authorities and sometimes also the public at large, have to be taken into consideration.

In summary, it is a multifaceted challenge that the CEO has to face when he wants to accomplish a major acquisition. Booz-Allen has had the opportunity of working with many of our country's leading corporations in tackling these fascinating but often equally complex issues. In the concluding section of this article, we have articulated an approach to acquisitions that is based on our experience from this work. The six step discussion of the approach presented here is not intended as a detailed account for how it should be implemented. The purpose has rather been to provide the CEO with a pragmatic and brief checklist of what

213

we view as the most critical ingredients to a successful acquisition effort.

THE APPROACH TOWARD A SUCCESSFUL ACQUISITION

During his period as Secretary of Defense, Robert McNamara once asked an assistant to summarize for the benefit of the President a lengthy document dealing with the strategic defense of our country. The assistant was given four days to do the job and McNamara wanted the summary on no more than two pages. Three days later, the story goes, the assistant, in a state of considerable frustration, came to see McNamara claiming that the document was of such vital importance that it was an impossible task to summarize it all on two pages. "Precisely because it is of such vital importance we need it on no more than two pages," retorted McNamara, "otherwise the President won't focus on it."

Anyone who attempts to describe an approach to successful acquisitions within the scope of a magazine article must feel a certain sympathy for McNamara's assistant. But applying the same logic as did the Secretary of Defense, the topic is simply too important not to be summarized. Our experience has told us that the process leading up to a successful acquisition can be broken down into the following six key steps:

- Integration with the strategic plan
- "Intelligent" screening
- Evaluating of targets using both creativity and analysis
- Understanding value and price
- Anticipating the post-acquisition phase
- Efficient implementation

Almost without exception, unsuccessful acquisition attempts or unsuccessful acquisitions can be directly related to a serious mistake or omission in one or several of the above steps. Conversely, the truly successful acquisitions have in most cases been the result of a systematic process addressing each of the six issues. Let us describe briefly what we think should be done under each step.

Integration with the Strategic Plan

The acquisition process begins with a strategic plan. Strategy addresses long-term resource allocation and an acquisition should be viewed as a tool for implementing strategy, i.e. a tool for allocating resources on a long-term basis to a certain business.

If there is no strategic plan, the acquisition will by definition be opportunistic. Sometimes an opportunistic approach works, more often it does not. Many of the companies that bought first and then thought about strategy are now cleaning up their business portfolios through divestitures.

A strategic rationale for an acquisition can be generated in several different ways. Exhibit 3 presents eight generic categories for linking corporate strategy to acquisition opportunities. We have found this categorization very useful when working with acquisition oriented clients. The categories can be divided into two sets. The first is based on more conventional business strategy options. The second set requires the application of corporate strategic strengths of the acquiror to change the performance of the acquisition candidate.

The strategic rationale for the acquisition will define such parameters as industry(ies), competitive position and financial strength. Setting the criteria for a subsequent acquisition search is therefore in essence already accomplished if the strategic groundwork has been done.

"Intelligent" Screening

We make a difference between mechanical and intelligent screening. Mechanical screening usually involves the sorting out of a group of target companies through the application of some quantified criteria, such as size, location, minimum R. O. A., market-to-book ratio, etc.

The intelligent screen has to start out with a mechanical screen to get the universe of potential prospects down to a manageable number, say 30 to 50. After that the intelligent screen uses thoughtful qualitative and quantitative evaluations. It is sometimes surprising how much you can learn about companies by simply applying some rudimentary analytical skills in combination with industry experience.

An intelligent screen obviously costs more up front than the mechanical approach, sometimes a lot more. We believe, how-

215

EXHIBIT 3
Strategic Approaches to Acquisition

ACQUISITION CATEGORY	*STRATEGIC RATIONALE FOR THE ACQUISITION*
Business Strategy Based	
Acquire Synergistic Product/Market Niche Position	Achieve scale economies of distribution, production or technology.
Acquire Position in Key International Markets	Achieve scale economies for global production and technology investments.
Acquire a "Beachhead" in an Emerging High Growth Market	Anticipate high leverage business growth equations by identifying market forcing functions.
Acquire a Portfolio of Minority Investments in Companies that Represent Homogeneous Business	Apply pressure for improved short-term earnings and sell stock. Gain improved information on future potential.
Corporate Strategy Based	
Acquire a Company with Underutilized Financial Strength	Use borrowing capacity or other financial strengths, e.g. underutilized tax loss carryforwards or foreign tax credits, to achieve an immediate performance premium.
Acquire an Underskilled Company in a Related Industry	Apply superior marketing, technology or production expertise to enhance the competitive position and performance of the acquisition candidate.
Acquire an Underexploited Physical Asset	Anticipate shortages and price increases in the physical asset's value. Invest to exploit the resource using distribution capacity.
Acquire an Undervalued Corporate Portfolio	Apply more aggressive portfolio management to restructure resource allocation and upgrade results.

ever, that its overall cost effectiveness is far superior if a successful acquisition is the ultimate goal. Our experience working with "short-lists" of three to five target companies based on intelligent screens confirms this. They will be focused, well thought through and original, whereas short-lists generated from mechanical approaches basically will be a computer printout as good as anybody's that happened to use similar criteria.

Particularly the last category of strategic rationales in Exhibit 3 lends itself well to intelligent screening. We recently did a screen on this basis for one of our clients where we brought down a list of 25 companies to a short-list of five by analyzing each target company's portfolio using only publicly available data. The screen was apparently effective in spotting undervalued portfolios. Not less than four companies of the 25 were sought after by other companies during the few weeks that the search was ongoing.

Evaluation of Targets Using Both Creativity and Analysis

Corporate executives sometimes are accused of either "hip shooting" or suffering from "analysis paralysis" when dealing with acquisition opportunities. Our experience tells us that creative business thinking and good, solid analysis are both equally important ingredients in the successful acquisition program. Once the short-list is in place, the real challenge for the CEO is to balance these two extremes and stay open minded until all the necessary facts are in place on the table.

The severe time constraints that often are prevailing in acquisition situations do not imply that analysis should be put aside, but rather that the analytical work has to be highly efficient, well structured and to the point. A professionally conducted evaluation of an acquisition target should assess something like 80% of the key strategic, financial and operational issues in 20% of the time usually required for a full company analysis. The CEO who has both the appropriate creative as well as the analytical resources at his disposal will have the upper hand for rapid and well founded decisions.

One important aspect of the acquisition evaluation that frequently is overlooked is to view the situation from the target company's perspective to find arguments for why he should sell. Given the competitive environment for good acquisitions, these arguments may well be instrumental in the final analysis.

Exhibit 4 presents a checklist that we developed during a series of acquisition target evaluations for a major U.S. manufacturing company. Though the key issues vary by specific situation, the checklist may be of interest as a general guideline for

217

Key Issues	Stand-alone Analysis	Synergy Analysis
Strategic:		
● Competitive position	✓	✓
● Growth opportunities	✓	✓
● Profitability	✓	✓
● Cash flow projections	✓	✓
Management:		
● General experience	✓	✓
● Functional skills	✓	✓
Operational:		
● Raw material position	✓	✓
● Manufacturing facilities	✓	✓
● Sales and distribution	✓	✓
● R&D, product development	✓	✓
● Regulatory exposure	✓	✓
● International	✓	✓
Financial:		
● Dilution		✓
● Capital structure	✓	✓
● Tax situation	✓	✓
● Cyclicality	✓	✓
Stakeholder Perception:		
● Shareholders		✓
● Management		✓
● Employees		✓
● Lenders		✓
● Customers		✓
	Quantification ↓ Recommended	Quantification ↓ Price Range

EXHIBIT 4
Case Example of Analytical Checklist for Acquisition Evaluations

the kind of acquisition evaluations that should go hand in hand with creative thinking. Our experience is that a very good understanding of the issues raised in Exhibit 4 can be gained in as little as two to three weeks' time of analysis based on public information and other nonproprietary data sources.

UNDERSTANDING VALUE AND PRICE

As illustrated schematically in Exhibit 5, a company can be viewed as having three different values.

- **The market value**, which can be defined as the stock price of a public company or the value to the owner of a private company or division.
- **The maximum value** to the acquiror, which consists of two parts:

    First, the market price adjusted by a premium or a discount to reflect differences between the acquiror's and the current owner's perception of the company's value on a stand alone basis. This premium or discount represents the quantification of the stand alone analysis of Exhibit 4.

EXHIBIT 5
Value and Price of an Acquisition

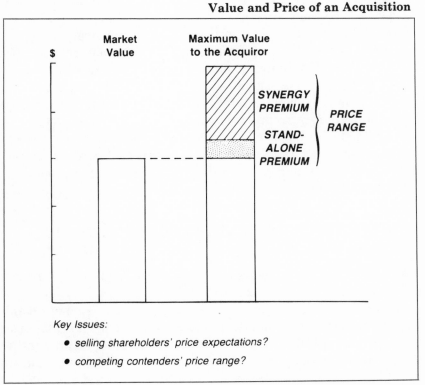

Second, a synergy premium which represents the unique value of the company as an addition to the acquiror's organization. This premium is the quantification of the synergy analysis and can include such benefits as economies of scale, savings in administrative costs, joint advertising or R&D programs, etc. When several companies seek the same acquisition, the synergy premium will vary for each contender. As discussed below, this can be a key deciding factor in a competitive situation.

- **The purchase price,** which in order to be justified should lie somewhere between the market value and the maximum value, will be a function of the negotiating skills of the two parties.

As we see it, the future will offer very few opportunities to pay the premiums that will be required without relying to some extent on synergistic benefits. The competition for acquisitions will be sufficiently intense that the contender who has the largest synergy potential, and therefore is willing to pay the highest price, will be the winner.

We believe the best approach to a pricing strategy is to go through the discipline of the analytical framework described above, thereby arriving at an affordable price range. Independent of this, an assessment should be made of what the selling shareholders' expectations may be based on P/E ratios and price premiums of recent similar transactions.

Armed with his own price and value analysis, as well as with as good an understanding as possible of the seller's expectations, the CEO will be in a position to enter the negotiating room.

ANTICIPATING THE POST-ACQUISITION PHASE

As opposed to investments in plant or property, buying another company represents a stake in a living organism. Instead of just acquiring assets, you buy assets with an accompanying organization intended to generate a return on these assets. The price you pay is typically a function of these expected returns rather than the value of the assets acquired. Because of this, the future value of the acquisition will be closely related to how well the CEO and his management team anticipate and arrange for the organizational and operational issues that will have to be addressed once the new entity is to be integrated with the parent organization.

There are almost limitless possibilities of structuring the acquisition financially, legally, organizationally and operationally. With this flexibility, there are good opportunities for designing the transaction so that post-acquisition challenges are provided for if and when they eventually emerge. Needless to say, measures that can be taken in this area prior to the closing of the deal are easier to accomplish and more effective than attempting to correct the situation once the company has been acquired.

Exhibit 6 summarizes some of the major challenges that, according to our experience, must be met during the post-acquisition phase. Many of these issues will be easier to resolve if they are anticipated and planned for during the process leading up to the acquisition. As the exhibit illustrates, the degree of business relationship (related/nonrelated) and management style (hands

EXHIBIT 6
The Post-Acquisition Phase

Major Challenges	Hands-Off, Nonrelated Acquisition	Integrated, Nonrelated Acquisition	Integrated, Related Acquisition
● Stakeholder perception	✓	✓	✓
● Financial policy	✓	✓	✓
● Capital allocation procedures	✓	✓	✓
● Executive compensation	✓	✓	✓
● Financial control systems	✓	✓	✓
● Budget and planning systems	✓	✓	✓
● Organizational fit		✓	✓
● Administrative systems		✓	✓
● R&D priorities		✓	✓
● "Company culture" issues		✓	✓
● Raw materials and supply management			✓
● Facilities rationalization			✓
● Production flow and inventory systems			✓
● Sales and distribution network			✓

off/integrated) will be important in determining the type of issues that have to be dealt with.

EFFICIENT IMPLEMENTATION

The first critical step in the implementation phase is to correctly approach the target company. There are three components of the approach that have to be considered by the senior management of the acquiring company:

- what to say
- to whom
- when to say it

The importance of carefully planning an approach strategy cannot be overemphasized. Months of search, screening and detailed evaluation can be wasted within minutes if the approach is handled in a way that puts the target's management group or key shareholders on the defensive. Our recommendation is to "brainstorm" around each of the three components mentioned above and thereby generate a number of alternative approach options. The one eventually chosen will depend on the particular circumstances prevailing when the time arrives to make the approach.

The subsequent phase of the implementation involving the negotiations of the transaction is equally important in assuring the long-term success of the acquisition. Each step of this process should be considered carefully in advance, with alternative options available if a problem arises. This will reduce the risk for confrontation between executives from the two companies during the negotiations, a common problem that subsequently can lead to high management turnover or difficulties for the two companies to work together. The risk for extreme time pressures due to poorly planned negotiations more lengthy than anticipated will also be reduced. This serves to remove any potential time bombs in the form of essential issues that were bypassed or simply forgotten during hectic negotiations.

CONCLUSION

Acquisitions, for a variety of reasons, are seen as an appropriate tool for implementing corporate strategy. They are becoming more frequent and larger. More leading companies are participating. While this trend shows no sign of subsiding, "right" partners will with increasing competition become more scarce. Our six-step approach is intended as a checklist for the CEO who has decided that an acquisition should be made. Our experience in working with major acquirors in recent years has proven the value of CEO attention to common but often overlooked issues and conditions.

The acquisition process is never an easy one. CEOs often put their careers on the line when they engage in this venturesome process. They do so because they are convinced that the rewards for their organizations can be extraordinary. While risk will be a significant part of any acquisition move, we hope that we have shown a path to minimize false steps. With this in mind we wish you good hunting or perhaps good strategizing.

COMPETITOR ANALYSIS: THE MISSING LINK IN STRATEGY
William E. Rothschild

In recent years many U.S. companies have been outmaneuvered in their home and world markets, often by unexpected rivals. A business strategist suggests that overconfident American executives have done a poor job of sizing up their competition, both domestic and foreign.

Reprinted, by permission of the publisher, from *Management Review*, July 1979. © 1979 by AMACOM, a division of American Management Associations. All rights reserved.

Over the past two decades, American companies have experienced dramatic changes in their domestic competitive environment. Small specialist competitors have exited or been swallowed up by larger multi-industry companies—resulting in often stronger, financially solvent, but more unpredictable competition. Foreign and multinational competitors have taken aim at the critical and more profitable U.S. markets, which are easier to penetrate and pivotal to worldwide success, while building and maintaining barriers to entry by the U.S. companies themselves. This foreign invasion has taken many forms, including importing, acquiring U.S. companies, and building U.S. plants. The results have been staggering since in some industries few or no U.S. manufacturers have survived.

But competitive change hasn't been limited merely to new configurations of traditional competitors, it has also included a considerable number of new companies and complete substitution by new types of products. The recent digital watch invasion of the analog dial watch market is a case in point: Electronic and integrated circuits manufacturers have taken share and position from the traditional watchmakers.

All of these facts are well-known and can be observed by merely reading *The Wall Street Journal* and other leading business publications. Even so, competitor analysis has remained an ignored managerial task. Why? If so much has taken place and if competition is a significant force in determining profitability, why hasn't more emphasis been placed on answering such basic questions as:

- Who is the competition now and who will be in the future?
- What are the key competitors' strategies, objectives, and goals?
- How important is a specific market to the competitors and are they committed enough to continue to invest?
- What unique strengths do the competitors have?
- Do they have any weaknesses that make them vulnerable?
- What changes are likely in the competitors' future strategies?
- What are the implications of competitors' strategies on the market, industry, and one's own company?

On the surface these questions appear to be logical and straightforward, and an instantaneous response would be expected. It is usually lacking, for a variety of reasons:

1. *Overconfidence*—Many managers who lead profitable businesses tend to be overconfident and give the impression that everything is under control or in their power. Because of past success in winning the competitive battle, they begin to believe that either the competitor is inept or they are superior. Such overconfidence ultimately leads to laxity, and while the arrogant managers are resting on their past accomplishments, the competitor either increases his skills or becomes more aggressive, or the void is filled by a new, more intelligent, or powerful competitor.

2. *Confusion*—Some business managers are simply confused. They are confused about what to do with competitive intelligence or confused about how to obtain it. This confusion takes many forms. There are instances where companies subscribe to clipping services or have elaborate systems to distribute data, but they never really see or understand the competitor's strategy or its implications. In other situations, companies employ analysts or consultants to write extensive competitor reports, and they never use these analyses (which admittedly often lack insight) to determine how the competitor may affect the industry in general or themselves in particular. Competitor analysis is of strategic value only if it highlights the implications and enables management to formulate or review its own strategies.

3. *Concern*—A third cause of ineffective competitor review results from concern that the company will be forced to employ illegal or unethical tactics to get the data it seeks. This concern is completely unwarranted since the strategic data required to do effective analyses is available through legal, ethical, and relatively convenient sources of data. Because of a desire to tell the world and influence investors, competitors usually broadcast their investment priorities and strategy. This occurs in a variety of ways that will be outlined later.

Another concern that sidetracks competitor review is that intelligence will be misinterpreted, resulting in wrong decisions. Of course, this is a problem with any analysis or planning—one can misunderstand, and misunderstanding can lead to failure.

But this is the price one must pay to be a leader; one must assume some *calculated* risk.

WHOM YOU'RE UP AGAINST

The first questions that should be considered are: Who is the competition now? Five years from now? Deceptively simple, these questions are usually followed only by a laundry list of company names. This list is a *first* step, but totally inadequate in itself.

Competition comes in many shapes and forms. There is competition for customers' discretionary and nondiscretionary dollars; there are many ways to satisfy the customers' needs and wants in the areas you provide. Thus, one aspect of this topic involves the questions, "What is the customer buying?" and "What are all the ways the customer can be satisfied in achieving this need or want?" If a consumer wants entertainment and you are in the television market, you should consider all forms of entertainment that could cause a consumer to spend his money in other ways. This may include radio, stereo, home movies, hobbies, games, in-home sports, and so one. (The true scope of competition here was painfully learned by radio console manufacturers when television entered the scene.)

A second way to examine competition is to do a demographic profile of the competition. Industries dominated by small single-industry specialists or small regional producers are significantly different from those dominated or led by multi-industry companies, and these, in turn, are different from those controlled by multinational or foreign companies. Thus it makes sense to use these classifications to profile the competitors. For instance, which companies are dedicated to the industry and thus can be classified as "single industry"? Which are participants in many industries and thus have the option of using one to pay for others to provide growth or to increase income levels to make earnings growth targets? Overlaying this classification, you should decide whether the competitors are domestically focused, participating abroad on a selective or opportunistic basis, foreign focused, or

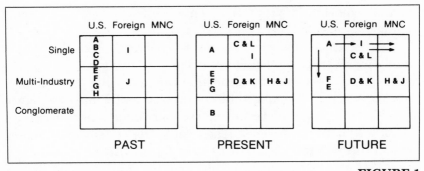

FIGURE 1
How the Competition Changes

multinational worldwide. This provides a graphic display to describe the past and the present and to anticipate the future.

Figure 1 shows the changes that have occurred over the past five years and that may take place over the next five-year period in one industry. Five years ago, this industry included a number of single-industry specialists (companies A to D) that accounted for approximately 50 percent of the market; the other major participants were divisions of larger multi-industry companies (E to H); furthermore, the Japanese were beginning to make their move with two companies (I and J) leading the way. Today, only one competitor remains in the single-industry category, and, as of the time this article was written, this competitor was under attack and could be forced to merge or sell out to another company. A number of the companies were acquired or merged into Japanese and European companies. Thus, the competitive game has significantly changed and may continue to do so, with the possibility that two companies will exit completely in the next few years.

A third view of competitors focuses on potential changes by reviewing the total interaction from supply to user. This requires asking whether any of the participants in the total system may elect to increase their role and become competitors. For example, the suppliers of components or materials may elect to move forward and compete with you. This occurred in the watch and cal-

227

culator markets with the entry of integrated circuit manufacturers.

Distributors may elect to move backward—like the Philco appliance distributors who have decided to bring back the Crosley brand to deal with the problem of maintaining product supply. When Ford announced discontinuation of Philco appliance manufacture, these distributors were left empty-handed. Since the other major producers already had independent wholesalers, or sold direct, these distributors were faced with a choice—get a new product line or quit. They decided to band together, form a buying pool, and obtain a private label line. Since the Crosley brand was defunct, they decided to reintroduce this line and have it built to their specification by other manufacturers: Rockwell/Admiral will provide the refrigerator line; Revco, freezers; Hardwick, gas and electric ranges; McGraw-Edison, air conditioners. Backward integration has offered these wholesalers a chance to survive and compete effectively against the national brands; of course, only time will tell whether this strategy will be successful.

Customers may also elect to become their own suppliers—in the manner of Ford and General Motors acquiring component manufacturers and becoming competitors in the components field. This is an excellent way to anticipate changes.

WHAT ARE THEY UP TO?

Having established the identity of the major competitors, one must ask: What are the major competitors' investment priorities and objectives? A listing or graphic display of the competition and major competitors isn't sufficient. Their total corporate situation and intentions must be understood. This task will vary in complexity depending on whether a competitor is a specialist, diversified, domestic, or worldwide in scope. In essence, we wish to know the competitors' total financial situations, determine whether they have profitable and balanced portfolios, and identify their serious problems and the opportunities they are trying to pursue.

Single-industry specialists are the easiest to evaluate since they are dedicated to one industry. Often they are "niche" oriented and distinguish themselves by innovation, quality, or dependability. Further, they often are led by an aggressive, strong willed, even autocratic, entrepreneur—which may be both a strength and limitation.

Multi-industry diversified companies have a variety of business options. Each business should have its own investment and corporate purpose, and it is important to understand each one.

It is useful to determine how a competitor describes each of its businesses to determine the balance and viability of the competitor's total portfolio. Is the competitor trying to grow too many segments simultaneously? Does it have a sufficient number of earnings and cash generators? Will the total achieve desired results? Multi-industry companies rarely have management depth sufficient to lead all their businesses effectively and, therefore, often select individuals who are unaware of an industry's peculiarities or subtleties; this may lead to wrong decisions and reduced profitability for all.

Location or market focus can also change emphasis and objectives. Foreign competitors may be influenced, positively or negatively, by their own governments. Governments may require that competitors reduce profitability to increase employment levels or to maintain the balance of trade. They may bar a competitor from obtaining supplies in low-cost areas. On the asset side, they may subsidize profits through low-cost government loans, tax concessions, or inflated profits on government projects. The key is to understand and not lapse into an emotional tirade about unfair foreign competition.

The objectives and investment priorities of multinational companies are even more difficult for an American domestic company to comprehend. Multinational companies may sacrifice profits in one country to penetrate or gain position while using profits from another country to support this aggressiveness. They have the ability to work with governments, select the least costly source of supply, and even negotiate favorable trade concessions.

Next, one must consider these factors: How important is your industry to the competitor? What is its strategic purpose?

It is essential to assess a competitor's overall goals, but you should try to pinpoint your competitor's purpose in *your own industry*. First, is it important to the competitor's future growth, earning performance, or cash flow position? If the competitor is depending on your industry to finance its other ventures, then it will fight hard to protect this cash flow position. This leads to a designation of strategic purpose and commitment. A business can:

- Provide opportunity for growth.
- Generate earnings.
- Contribute to cash flow.

It is useful to hypothesize the reason for the competitor's commitment to your industry. Commitment may be based on rational judgments or emotions. On the rational side, it may be the anticipation of growth, strong customer needs, or some unique product or market strength. A rational basis is normally preferred since the competitor's behavior is most likely to be consistent and logical and can be reversed if problems arise. Unfortunately, emotions play a significant part in decision making. The competitor's commitment may be based on such shallow reasons as:

- The CEO grew up in the industry and is emotionally attached to it.
- The business is the core from which the total corporation grew.
- The industry is considered glamorous and exciting.

Investments are therefore made that are unjustified or even detrimental—such as adding capacity when there is already overcapacity or introducing new expensive modifications prematurely or cutting prices to gain share in a declining market.

Figure 2 depicts one hypothetical multi-industry company in a way that illustrates questions examined thus far. It includes and explains the estimated commitment and position of the company along with the investment strategy that appears to be followed.

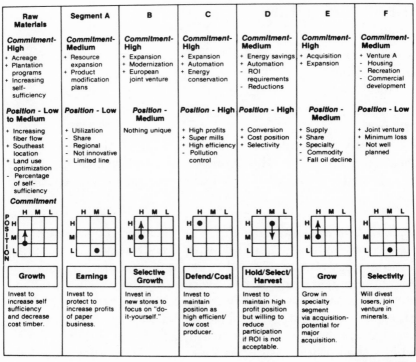

Raw Materials	Segment A	B	C	D	E	F
Commitment-High	**Commitment-Medium**	**Commitment-High**	**Commitment-High**	**Commitment-Medium**	**Commitment-High**	**Commitment-Medium**
+ Acreage + Plantation programs + Increasing self-sufficiency	+ Resource expansion + Product modification plans	+ Expansion + Modernization + European joint venture	+ Expansion + Automation + Energy conservation	+ Energy savings + Automation - ROI requirements - Reductions	+ Acquisition + Expansion	+ Venture A - Housing - Recreation - Commercial development
Position - Low to Medium	**Position - Low**	**Position - Medium**	**Position - High**	**Position - High**	**Position - Medium**	**Position - Low**
+ Increasing fiber flow + Southeast location + Land use optimization - Percentage of self-sufficiency	+ Utilization - Share - Regional - Not innovative - Limited line	Nothing unique	+ High profits + Super mills + High efficiency - Pollution control	+ Conversion + Cost position + Selectivity	+ Supply + Share + Specialty - Commodity - Fall oil decline	+ Joint venture + Minimum loss - Not well planned

	Segment A	B	C	D	E	F
Growth	**Earnings**	**Selective Growth**	**Defend/Cost**	**Hold/Select/Harvest**	**Grow**	**Selectivity**
Invest to increase self sufficiency and decrease cost timber.	Invest to protect to increase profits of paper business.	Invest in new stores to focus on "do-it-yourself."	Invest to maintain position as high efficient/low cost producer.	Invest to maintain high profit position but willing to reduce participation if ROI is not acceptable.	Grow in specialty segment via acquisition-potential for major acquisition.	Will divest losers, join venture in minerals.

FIGURE 2

Competitor X: Overall Investment Strategy

The next area of concern is: What are the competitor's *relative* strengths and limitations? Can they support its investment strategies? These are deceptively simple questions. Many managers believe they know their own resources and have a good grasp of those of their competitors. This is rarely the case. It requires an assessment of the competitor's resources in light of the strategy it has chosen to pursue.

If the competitor wishes to gain share by innovation, does it have the proper skills to do the job? These will be different from those required to hold position, maximizing earnings via a low-cost position. Thus one must look at critical resources required by the competitor and ask if the competitor can obtain what is required in both quantity and timing.

THE KEY RESOURCES

It is also necessary to establish what a competitor commands in critical resources:

Management

Who are the key leaders and decision makers? How quickly can decisions be made? Is the management team knowledgeable or experienced in the industry? Are they risk takers? Is there depth in the management ranks?

The answers to these questions will reveal managerial skills, flexibility, values, and longevity, thus enabling you to determine the competitor's managerial fit with the strategy it is pursuing. If the strategy requires flexibility and rapid decision making, but the management team is risk-averse, slow, and deliberate, the competitor will have a major problem in executing its desired strategy. If the strategy is aimed at maximizing cash flow by a slow harvest, but the management is aggressive and growth oriented, then there is a serious mismatch that may be unresolvable.

Innovation

Assessment here must identify the driving forces behind the competitor's innovation record. It isn't unusual to find a few key individuals as the driving forces behind innovation or to find the entire company's success built upon a few key patents. If such is the case, then the competitor's ability to continue this track record must be determined. Financing of innovation should also be studied to find out where the financing came from and how consistent it has been.

Does the competitor pride itself on its innovation ability? If so, it may have a difficult, if not impossible, job of accepting or implementing the role of follower. If a strategy requires applied research or "quick follow" skills but the competitor has traditionally focused on basic research and is unable to follow rapidly, then this may signal a major limitation.

Financing

This review should include the traditional assessments of debt to equity, liquidity ratios, credit availability and costs, as well as an understanding of financial objectives and constraints. Here one must attempt to understand the competitor's ability to generate financing both internally and externally at the *right time* and in sufficient *quantity*. If a strategy requires large but cyclical volumes of cash and the competitor isn't able to obtain them, the strategy won't be successful. If a competitor wants to increase its worldwide sales but isn't able to provide long-term, low-cost financing, its results will be disappointing.

Production

This requires an evaluation of efficiency, cost reduction, and capacity and supply situations, along with an understanding of their total resources for production—human and material. Some useful questions to probe are:

- Does the competitor manufacture in a high- or low-cost labor area?
- Is its plant and equipment efficient?
- Is its flexibility or response to market demands inhibited by too much integration, capital intensity, or overdependence on one technology?
- How sensitive is its break-even to capacity utilization?
- How skilled is it in maintaining quality?
- How is it affected by OSHA and EEO regulations?

Marketing

How do the competitor's marketing abilities compare to the requirements imposed by its strategy or market? Some strategies require the ability to anticipate and/or create customer needs, while others are more dependent on providing *pre-* and *post*-sale service. If the key skills aren't available, the competitor will have less than optimal results. Marketing skills must be carefully nurtured and preserved, like any other resource, and thus require consistent financing. Figure 3 provides a checklist of all these critical resources.

233

Conceive/Design	Produce	Market	Finance	Manage
Technical resources	*Physical resources*	*Sales force*	*Long-term*	*Key people*
Concepts	Capacity	Skills	Debt/equity ratio	Objectives and priorities
Patents and copyrights	Plant	Size	Cost of debt	Values
Technological sophistication	Size	Type	*Short-term*	Reward systems
Technical integration	Location	Location	Line of credit	*Decision making*
Human resources	Age	*Distribution network*	Type of debt	Location
Key people and skills	Equipment		Cost of debt	Type
Use of external technical groups	Automation	*Research*	*Liquidity*	Speed
	Maintenance	Skills	*Cash flow*	*Planning*
Funding	Flexibility	Type	Days of receivables	Type
Total	*Processes*	*Service and sales policies*	Inventory turnover	Emphasis
Percentage of sales	Uniqueness	*Advertising*	Accounting practices	Time span
Consistency over time	Flexibility	Skills	*Human resources*	*Staffing*
Internally generated	Degree of integration	Type	Key people and skills	Longevity and turnover
Government-supplied	*Human resources*	*Human resources*	Turnover	Experience
	Key people and skills	Key people and skills	*Systems*	Replacement policies
	Workforce	Turnover	Budgeting	*Organization*
	Skills mix	*Funding*	Forecasting	Centralization
	Unions	Total	Controlling	Functions
	Turnover	Consistency over time		Use of staff
		Percentage of sales		
		Reward systems		

FIGURE 3
Summary of Competitor Analysis*

*If *multi-industry*, examine portfolio of businesses (sizes, priorities, importance to company) and resources provided by parent company. If *foreign*, examine national priorities of home country; degree of government ownership; supports and incentives; home-market environment.

WHERE TO GET THE DATA

Many managers agree on the need to evaluate and anticipate changes in competitors' abilities, but seem to be at a loss on where to look. It isn't that much of a mystery. Basically, there are three sources of "secondary" data: what the competitors say about themselves; what others say about them; and what your own people have observed while monitoring their activities.

Competitors provide data about their strategy and resources in advertising, promotional materials, speeches, personnel changes, and want ads. They also provide information to the government and investors through reports, prospectuses, testimony, and required documentation.

In addition, outsiders write and speak about the competition. This includes books, articles, case histories, product evaluations, testimony in trials, and special industry studies. All of these sources can be evaluated and embellished by your own management and professionals in sales, manufacturing, finance, and engineering.

The key is to develop a profile of competitors, test for validity, and identify areas of agreement and disagreement. You will be amazed about what is known and what can be deduced from actions. Figure 4 outlines these sources of data.

AN EYE TO THE FUTURE

Another area that must be considered asks: What could cause a change in competitors' priorities, strategies, or resources? Any significant change in the "macro" environment (like government, society, or the economy) or in "micro" environment can cause a change in competitive behavior. Likewise, the acquisition of a company may strengthen or weaken it (in some cases, the merger is so disruptive that it causes the competitor to actually lose strength). At other times, a competitor changes because the chief executive officer leaves or dies. It is always important to look at the line of succession and determine if the next in line will follow the same game plan. If an outsider obtains control, you can count

	Public	Trade/Professionals	Government	Investors
What competitors say about themselves	Advertising Promotional materials Press releases Speeches Books Articles Personnel changes Want ads	Manuals Technical papers Licenses Patents Courses Seminars	Securities and Exchange reports FIC Testimony Lawsuits Antitrust	Annual meetings Annual reports Prospectuses Stock/bond issues
What others say about them	Books Articles Case studies Consultants Newspaper reporters Environmental groups Consumer groups Unions "Who's Who" Recruiting firms	Suppliers/ vendors Trade press Industry study Customers Subcontractors	Lawsuits Antitrust State/federal agencies National plans Government programs	Security analyst reports Industry studies Credit reports

FIGURE 4
Sources of Competitor Information

on change. Another key change agent is the disruption of priorities—such as a new venture causing red ink or requiring an extensive amount of management attention.

Finally, what will be the result of all the competitors on the industry, market, and your strategy? One of the major problems is that most managers stop their evaluations too soon. They analyze one, two, even three competitors and never interrelate their assessments. Thus, they never see the consequences of one competitor interacting with another.

Figure 5 outlines the commitment and position as well as the strategies of five key competitors in a given segment. Since four of the five competitors are aiming to grow and the leader has vowed to hold its position, one can expect a tough battle and

Commitment-Position	Competitor I	II	III	IV	V
Product Definition	BROAD LINE	BROAD LINE	NICHE ORIENTED	NICHE ORIENTED	COMMODITY ORIENTED
		(Specify here how competitors describe their product offerings)			
Importance		Product Lines			
% of total company salaries	24%	A 19% B 8% C 41%	29%	53%	46% of company sales
% of total company earnings	50%	.. .. 73%	..	85%	38% of company earnings
Investment Strategy	Upgrade existing equipment	Segment A Grow — Hold —	Selective Growth	Protect position	Invest to grow
Management Strategy	Opportunistically fill product line gaps	Add capacity — Line product A; Cost reduce —Line product B	orientation	Cost reduction/ efficiency	Expand capacity in advance of demand; Constrain price increases; Obtain payoff in longer term
Resource Allocation	$90 million over next five years to alter certain operations	$250 million	$120 million for 1976; Major plant under consideration for 1980	$101 million — Product A; $23 million — Product B	$165 million

FIGURE 5
Business Segment Summary

237

possibly a lot of red ink. Two of the companies plan to add capacity, which could mean there will be excess capacity. Investment will be heavy, ranging from $90 million to $250 million over five years. The combination of aggression, possibly excess capacity, and high capital investments will make the going expensive especially since this is a high break-even business and requires high levels of capacity utilization.

A complete analysis can enable you to profile needs in such areas as innovation, normal distribution and pricing practices, nature and type of manufacturing, and so on. The final step is to determine how the competitors can affect you and the worth of your strategy. If a company expects to compete in the environment just described but doesn't wish to expend heavily on capacity, then it must learn to specialize, or it will run the risk of becoming extinct. Thus, competitor analysis can help in determining and reviewing strategy.

Competitor analysis is increasing in complexity and importance, and most companies are highly deficient. If it is to have the influence it deserves, then it must become the concern of top managers, who must insist on a disciplined, comprehensive, and strategically focused effort to assess each major competitor and the total interaction between competitors and themselves.

TECHNOLOGY'S INPUT IS VITAL TO SOUND BUSINESS PLANNING
Paul Cathey

Technological advances will give your company increased market leverage—if you include technical managers in strategic planning.

Is management neglecting its technological planners, and not fitting their input into business and long-range strategic planning?

Reprinted from *Iron Age,* September 16, 1981, pp. 43–48. Used by permission.

Has top management, pinched for cash, lost interest in costly, long-term R&D projects that could have a big payoff?

Opinions differ on the answers to these two questions. Consultants, skilled in technology management, say "yes" in both cases.

Corporate technology managers, interviewed for this article, feel they are doing a fairly good job of integrating R&D planning into all phases of planning—business, manufacturing and long-term strategic planning.

But the company tech managers are concerned that a growing portion of R&D financing is directed at short-term projects that are generally related to existing products, processes and plants. They feel that, in the long run, this will come back to haunt management as the '80s wear on.

The new products, the new processes, the efficient manufacturing facilities will not be in place to keep the company alive and prospering. And, in a vicious circle, the company will—again—not generate enough cash to feed badly needed R&D.

Charles S. Skinner is vice president of the technology management group of consultants at Booz, Allen & Hamilton Inc. "The winners in the 1980s," he contends, "will view technology as a corporate asset that can be strategically managed to support the overall business strategy of their corporations."

But, while a majority of senior managers surveyed by his company feel technology will be more important in the '80s than it was in the '70s, many are ignoring that fact.

"They also view technology issues as complex and difficult to manage," he adds. "And more than four-fifths of the 3,000 senior managers questioned feel that lack of an analytical approach to integrating technology and planning is a significant barrier in managing technology.

"Another drawback," Mr. Skinner continues, "is the limited involvement of technology managers in the planning process—79 pct conceded that.

"And only 37 pct of the managers thought business and strategy were being effectively integrated in their companies in U.S. market planning. In terms of worldwide marketing, only 13 pct felt their companies were effectively integrating management and technology."

There are a few exceptions to this pattern, Mr. Skinner indicates. He cites an earlier study done by his firm for General Electric Co.

"It showed the twelve technology leaders—including AT&T, Boeing, Dow Chemical, DuPont, Hitachi, IBM, Mitsubishi and Texas Instruments—adopted a longer-term perspective, viewing technological advancement as the *most* influential factor to long-term success."

Joseph Nemec, Jr., a senior vice president at Booz, Allen, is also a consultant on technology management. Says Mr. Nemec, "Many companies are not being selective enough in funding R&D projects. They sprinkle a little money over each of a large number of projects in what I call an 'entitlements approach.'

"They are not willing," he adds, "to accept a major management responsibility—the sound allocation of resources. They are

What's Wrong with U.S. Manufacturing Technology?

"Plenty," says Robert L. Callahan, president of Ingersoll Engineers Inc., manufacturing consultants/engineers for the metalworking industries.

"Many U.S. plants are simply decrepit," he says. "There's been a lack of investment and too much emphasis on short-term returns. Even some of the new plants we put up are obsolete before they start operating.

"As an industrial nation," he continues, "we're just not adapting to the new international standards of manufacturing. Unless you plan on turning out a high quality product at the *least* cost. forget it.

"That's why the Japanese are knocking off our socks every time they enter a new market," Mr. Callahan points out. "They not only have shrewd marketing strategy, they suit it up with the factory technology to turn out good products at low cost."

Many metalworking companies who call on him for advice lack any sound overall plan, have obsolete managers who can't adapt to new ideas or are frightened by the money needed to properly modernize, Mr. Callahan notes.

"Even if you have to spend millions to meet the new manufacturing standards," he says, "you don't have to do it all at once. We describe how they can move toward it in incremental steps over a five-year span.

not willing to cut back drastically or stop altogether the less promising R&D projects and pour the money on those that are promising, keeping in mind that even some of those with high potential may turn out to be duds.

"Once you've established that you have an attractive market and that you have the potential for technological leadership in that market," he notes, "the only safe way to carve out a strong position is to be preemptive. You've got to invest at higher levels and over a longer period of time than your competitors."

Robert L. Callahan is president of Ingersoll Engineers, a consulting firm that specializes in manufacturing technology. The bulk of his clients are in metalworking.

"Too few companies have as their objective market domination or quality and pricing leadership," he says. "They're ori-

"Sometimes they grasp the concept," he adds, "and sometimes they don't. Many top plant and chief manufacturing managers, sometimes even vice presidents of operations have been around for 25 years or more and don't know any better. They're obsolete and they've got to go.

"Many, many times," he says, "they don't have any strategic plans for manufacturing. Just because they have a lot of NC equipment on the floor doesn't mean a thing. It's often stuck in anywhere it fits.

"Count the number of fork lift trucks in some plants that have a lot of computer-aided manufacturing. It tells you they still don't have the message. They're still handling material the way they did 40 years ago.

"Then," he adds, "look at the Japanese. They're running plants without fork trucks. They're running plants without material sitting all over the floor. They're running plants without inspectors, without expeditors, without work standards and without routing sheets on the floor."

Concludes Mr. Callahan: "New products or increases in volume of old products badly need a search for new processes and new technology to see if they fit. Usually the time to search is not included in the up-front planning."

ented toward short-term return on investment objectives. Today, on an international scale, this can only lead to loss of market.

"Japanese manufacturers may be the most effective users of technology. They invest *twice* as much in manufacturing technology as the rest of the world."

Mr. Callahan says many companies just won't listen to ways in which they can effectively modernize to meet today's new international standards of manufacturing. (See box on pp. 240-241.)

Corporate managers of technology lay the fault of limited funding for costly, high risk, long-term R&D at the feet of today's inflation, high interest rates and shrunken corporate profits.

Dr. Jere H. Brophy is director, advanced technology innovation, at Inco Limited. Inco is a diversified producer and manufacturer. It's the world's leading producer of nickel and a significant producer of copper and precious metals. It's a worldwide manufacturer of auto, dry cell and industrial batteries and related products. It also operates a group of companies producing rolling mill, forged and machined products.

In its R&D planning, Inco sets aside a sizable portion of funds for "seed" research into new areas and products of interest to the company.

"Throughout industry in general," says Dr. Brophy, "there has been a tendency to become more conservative in R&D funding. Lately, it's because of the high cost of money.

"What it takes to get a return on your investment—if you're putting out substantial amounts for research each year—keeps rising. You can very quickly get to the point where you'll never recoup your money. And the higher the cost of money, the higher the interest rates, the sooner you get to that point.

"It's a fact of life," he adds, "that the after tax cost of R&D is a direct substitution from what's called profit. If you don't spend a dollar on R&D, your profits will go up an average of 50¢ —in the short-term. But, in the long-term, only R&D can give you the new products, the new processes which will keep the company in a position to generate profits. And that's our philosophy here."

Dr. Brophy doesn't buy the theory that sprinkling just a little money over a lot of R&D projects can be counterproductive.

"Sure it's not the home run approach, always swinging for the fences," he says, using a baseball analogy. "The incremental advance in each of the projects may be small, but if you add up the advance in dozens of them they can have a significant impact on the business.

"It's the hit and run approach, the bunt and single approach, even, if necessary, the sacrifice at times. It's a balanced approach that will pay off," he notes.

Robert E. Gee is vice president, new technology and planning, Dravo Corp. Dravo is engaged, on a worldwide basis, in a broad range of process, technological, engineering, construction, facility operation and other services to the mining, minerals and metals, electric power, petroleum, chemical, pulp and paper, food processing and transportation industries and in the public sector. The company is also involved in natural resources development, barge transportation, manufacturing and equipment sale and rental.

"There's no question," says the Dravo chief planner, "that throughout industry there's decreased interest in spending large amounts of money on exciting new ventures. Managements today are much more aware of the uncertainties and the risks than they were 10 years ago.

"Many companies have, as we do," he says, "what's called supportive research—research that keeps existing business technology healthy. Ten years ago that averaged about 65 pct of research spending throughout U.S. industry. Today that's crept up to about 75 to 80 pct. And that's true for our company.

"But," he adds, "that doesn't mean we—and others—are not spending substantially to develop new business. One of our key objectives in the 1980s is maintaining a diversified, *technology-based* organization which will be stronger and less vulnerable as a whole than any of its component parts."

As an example he cites the research work now going on to develop a process and equipment for the extraction of oil from shale and tar sands. "When that's ready," he says, "we'll let the strategists decide what route the new business will take in the market place.

"But while this R&D is going on," Mr. Gee indicates, "we're also working to improve existing businesses—finding better ways to pelletize ore, for example."

243

Swirling around the subject of technology and its relation to strategic planning are three key questions:

- How can you blend technological planning into business, market and strategic planning?
- What's the best way to manage technological planning?
- And what sort of qualifications should a technology planner have?

Booz, Allen has come up with what it calls "an organized approach to managing technology and setting technology investment priorities." It consists of three steps:

- Defining the terms involved, tracing technology trends in the 1970s and investigating the potential impact of technology on business in the 1980s.
- Describing the emerging principles of technology management and detailing how they can be integrated into the business strategy of a company.
- And, finally, developing a technology investment strategy.

"Technology is already changing the shape of some mature and traditionally low technology businesses," says Charles Skinner. "In the auto industry, for example, we see the wide use of computer-aided design and manufacturing (including robotics), penetration of microprocessor-based control and feature sets, and manmade materials replacing the more traditional ones.

"All this has occurred in an industry considered mature by most of the business community. The same thing is happening in other mature industries, such as steel. At the other end of the spectrum, high technology industries are being revolutionized.

"Traditionally," he notes, "technology has been viewed as unpredictable, difficult to manage, and high risk. We strongly believe that the path and timing of technology development is generally predictable.

"Even breakthrough technologies, once publicly known, can generally be tracked and funded early enough for a company to get on the commercial road."

After a careful assessment of its technological stance in terms of products, processes or services, companies are ready to fit that knowledge into business planning.

244

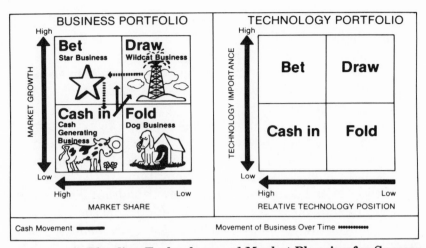

Blending Technology and Market Planning for Success
An organized approach to managing technology and setting technological investment priorities is possible. The system diagrammed above plots company's position for each product or process in terms of its market position compared with attractiveness of the market (left chart), using the familiar devices of dogs, cash cows, wildcat opportunities and stars. Then (right) the same process is used in terms of level of technical know-how compared with importance of technology leadership in that business. Then the grids are combined. If in one product you are the technology leader (bid square), but the market is a dog (fold square), it might be best to sell off the technology, if you can, and drop the product.

Conceding that managements find this difficult, Booz, Allen has come up with a grid familiar to business and marketing managers (see above). Just as the marketing grid plots market position against market potential and determines which products or processes are dogs, cash cows, promising wildcats or shining stars, the technology portfolio plots a company's degree of technical know-how in a product or process against the importance of technology to that business.

Then the grids can be superimposed and the position of each product, product line or process in the company can be plotted in terms of *both* market position and technological position.

In poker-playing parlance, dogs are poor hands you throw in and "fold." Cows are winning hands from the past which you "cashed in" and used the money for new bets. Wildcats are promising hands you are backing with bets in hopes of "drawing"

245

a winning straight or flush. Stars are winning hands on which you are "betting" the limit.

Mr. Skinner gives these examples of how it works:

"If you find yourself in the 'bet' quadrant, you're in an excellent position technologically—in a business segment where that technology is important.

"In a situation like this, it makes sense to keep investment levels high to sustain competitive advantage. Here is the business where you can afford the newest equipment, the risky R&D project and the new product experimentation.

"Products or businesses in the 'draw' quadrant," he continues, "are in an unstable 'borderline' position. The company is in a marginal position competitively, but the technology you're marginal in is *also* important. You need to make one of two decisions: Bet against the competition and invest to attain a leadership position or develop an approach to fold and concentrate technology investments in more lucrative areas.

"In the cash quadrant," says Mr. Skinner, "you're in a strong position technologically, but the technology you're strong in isn't really important. This can happen in an industry where the existing technology is supplanted by a new technology.

"Here again an approach is needed to reduce investment selectively. A company with technology positions in this quadrant may find that its strategy should be to sell off the technology. In other words, 'cash in.'

"If you're in the fold quadrant," he adds, "you're weak technologically—and it doesn't make any difference anyhow, because technology is not important. If you've substantially invested in this technology, it's a sunk cost. In any case, it's time to withdraw funds that can be more profitably invested elsewhere."

The Booz, Allen vice president emphasizes that the business portfolio is product-oriented and measures a firm's product lines in terms of competitive position and market attractiveness. The technology portfolio is technology-based and defines the firm's relative product and process technologies in terms of competitive position in the marketplace and the importance of each technology to the basic business of the organization.

"For example," says Charles Skinner, "let's assume product A is in the 'bet' quadrant—a strong position in a highly attractive market. But, in terms of technology, it's in the 'draw' quadrant—good, but not a leader in technology. The technology has to be beefed-up if product A's competitive position is to be sustained."

Companies that are technologically-oriented, such as Inco and Dravo, are constantly studying the technical state of the art, both inside and outside the company.

How this is structured within the corporation varies. In some cases (Dravo's for example), the top corporate planner is also the chief technology director. In other cases, the technology manager reports to a vice president of planning and through him to the corporate executive committee.

Inco's Dr. Brophy sees his role as having four main facets. First is his input as director of technology innovation into corporate strategic plans. He sets the overall R&D targets, how the research work should be distributed among Inco's three divisions, which projects should be financed under the corporate "seed money" concept, and how the divisional R&D objectives tie-in with the corporate strategic plan, questioning any differences.

Second, he reviews the business plans of each SBU (strategic business unit) unit by unit, and extracts the technology involved—stated or implied.

Third, he reviews each SBU's efforts in R&D, plus the corporation's R&D efforts in respect to that business unit and makes sure there is a firm, consistent mesh. If there is not, he starts asking questions.

And fourth, he takes an objective, outsider's view of what is going on in general technology that might have any value to the company.

Dravo's Robert Gee draws up the corporate strategic plan based on input from various SBUs. Then at a corporate policy meeting, which he chairs, the various operating officers are brought in and questioned about their business plans—including any aspects of technology which they involve. Again, questions are asked.

What sort of talents and skill does a top technical planner need for success, in addition to the obvious engineering or scientific background?

Both Jere Brophy and Robert Gee give similar lists.

"First of all," says Mr. Gee, "he has to have the confidence of his top management and of all the technical and R&D managers he works with. He has to be a man they can trust, understand and respect.

"Second, he must have business knowledge and understanding. That may be even more important than technical expertise. He's got to understand profit and loss. Understand marketing and finance. Understand why the company is in business."

Says Dr. Brophy, "He's got to be a practical manager with a sober eye for what the real world can use in the ways of products—and the ability to see that they get developed to make money. He can't be just a researcher swept up in the romance of science."

INTERNATIONAL MARKETING PLANNING: THE GAP BETWEEN THEORY AND PRACTICE
Malcolm McDonald

In spite of the apparent simplicity and logic of the process described in most textbooks, marketing planning remains one of the most baffling subjects, both for academics and practitioners alike. Once the international dimension is added, the very real confusion multiplies.

The purpose of this paper is to remove some of the myths which surround this very complex area of marketing management and to explain why much of what passes for marketing planning is largely ineffective. These conclusions are based on a four year study carried out at Cranfield [School of Management, in Bedford, England] into how two hundred British industrial goods companies engaged in international marketing carried out

Reprinted by permission of the author from *International Marketing Review*, Autumn 1983, pp. 42–58.

their marketing planning. Four hundred directors were interviewed, the companies being broadly representative of the complete spectrum of type and size of industrial company.[1]

Marketing's contribution to business success in manufacturing, distribution or merchanting activities lies in its commitment to detailed analysis of future opportunities to meet customer needs and a wholly professional approach to selling to well defined market segments those products or services that deliver the sought-after benefits. Whilst prices and discounts are important, as are advertising and promotion, the link with engineering through the product is paramount.

Such a commitment and activities must not be mistaken for budgets and forecasts. Those of course we need and we have already got. Our accounting colleagues have long since seen to that. No. Put quite bluntly, the process of marketing planning is concerned with identifying what and to whom sales are going to be made in the longer term to give revenue budgets and sales forecasts any chance of achievement. Furthermore, chances of achievement are a function of how good our intelligence services are; and how well suited are our strategies; and how well we are led.

IGNORANCE OF MARKETING PLANNING AND THE ASSOCIATED OPERATIONAL PROBLEMS

The degree to which a company is able to cope with its operating environment is very much a function of the understanding it has of the marketing planning process as a means of sharpening the rationality and focus of all levels of management throughout the organisation.

This requires further explanation. What most companies think of as planning systems are little more than forecasting and budgeting systems. These give impetus and direction to tackling the current operational problems of the business, but tend merely to project the current business unchanged into the future. Something often referred to in management literature as "tunnel vision".

The problem with this approach is that because companies are dynamically-evolving systems within a dynamically-evolving business environment, some means of evaluation of the way in which the two interact has to be found in order that there should be a better matching of the two. Otherwise, because of a general unpreparedness, a company will suffer increased pressures in the short term, in trying to react and to cope with environmental pressures.

Many companies, having gone through various forms of rationalisation or efficiency-increasing measures, become aware of the opportunities for making profit which have been lost to them because of their unpreparedness, but are confused about how to make better use of their limited resources. This problem increases in importance in relation to the size and diversity of companies.

In other words, there is widespread awareness of lost market opportunities through unpreparedness and real confusion over what to do about it. It is hard not to conclude, therefore, that there is a strong relationship between these two problems and the systems most widely in use at present, i.e., *sales forecasting and budgeting systems*.

The following table lists the most frequently mentioned operating problems resulting from a reliance on traditional sales forecasting and budgeting procedures in the absence of a marketing planning system:

Most Frequently Mentioned Problems

1. Lost opportunities for profit.
2. Meaningless numbers in long-range plans.
3. Unrealistic objectives.
4. Lack of actionable market information.
5. Interfunctional strife.
6. Management frustration.
7. Proliferation of products and markets.
8. Wasted promotional expenditure.
9. Pricing confusion.
10. Growing vulnerability to environmental change.
11. Loss of control over the business.

It is not difficult to see the connection between all of these problems. However, what is perhaps not apparent from the list is that each of these operational problems is in fact a symptom of a much larger problem which emanates from the way in which the objectives of a firm are set.

The meaningfulness, hence the eventual effectiveness, of any objective, is heavily dependent on the quality of the informational inputs about the business environment. However, objectives also need to be realistic, and to be realistic, they have to be closely related to the firm's particular capabilities in the form of its assets, competences and reputation that have evolved over a number of years.

The objective-setting process of a business, then, is central to its effectiveness. What the Cranfield research demonstrated conclusively is that it is inadequacies in the objective-setting process which lie at the heart of many of the problems of British companies. Since companies are based on the existence of markets, and since a company's sole means of making profit is to find and maintain profitable markets, then clearly setting objectives in respect of these markets is a key business function. If the process by which this key function is performed is inadequate in relation to the differing organisational settings in which it takes place, it follows that operational efficiency will be adversely affected.

Some kind of appropriate system has to be used to enable meaningful and realistic marketing objectives to be set. A frequent complaint is the preoccupation with short-term thinking and an almost total lack of what has been referred to as "strategic thinking". Also, that plans consist largely of numbers, which are difficult to evaluate in any meaningful way, since they do not highlight and quantify opportunities, emphasise key issues, show the company's position clearly in its markets; nor delineate the means of achieving the sales forecasts. Indeed, very often the actual numbers that are written down bear little relationship to any of these things. Sales targets for the sales force are often inflated in order to motivate them to higher achievement, whilst the actual budgets themselves are deflated in order to provide a safety net against shortfall. Both act as demotivators and both lead to the frequent use of expressions such as "ritual", "the numbers game", "meaningless horsetrading", and so on. It is easy to see how the problems listed in the table begin to manifest themselves in this sort of environment. Closely allied to this is the frequent reference to profit as being the only objective necessary to successful business performance.

This theme is frequently encountered. There is in the minds of many businessmen the assumption that in order to be commercially successful, all that is necessary is for "the boss" to set profit targets, to decentralise the firm into groups of similar activities, and then to make managers accountable for achieving those profits.

However, even though many British companies have made the making of "profit" almost the sole objective, many of our industries have gone into decline, and ironically, there has also been a decline in real profitability. There are countless examples of companies pursuing decentralised profit goals that have failed miserably.

Why should this be so? It is largely because some top managers believe that all they had to do is to set profit targets, and somehow middle management will automatically make everything come right. Indeed, there is much evidence to show that many companies believe that planning is only about setting profit goals. However, whilst this is an easy task for any company to do, saying exactly *how* these results are to be achieved is altogether a different matter.

Here it is necessary to focus attention on what so many companies appear to be bad at i.e. determining strategies for matching what the firm is good at with properly researched market-centred opportunities, and then scheduling and costing out what has to be done to achieve these objectives. There is little evidence of a deep understanding of what it is that companies can do better than their competitors or of how their distinctive competence can be matched with the needs of certain customer groups. Instead, overall volume increases and minimum rates of return on investment are frequently applied to all products and markets, irrespective of market share, market growth rate, or the longevity of the product life cycle. Indeed there is a lot of evidence to show that many companies are in trouble today precisely because their decentralised units manage their business only for the current profit and loss account, often at the expense of giving up valuable and hard-earned market share and running down the current business.

Thus, financial objectives, whilst being essential measures of the desired performance of a company, are of little practical help, since they say nothing about *how* the results are to be achieved. The same applies to sales forecasts and budgets, which are *not* marketing objectives and strategies. Understanding the real meaning and significance of marketing objectives helps managers to know what information they need to enable them to think through the implications of choosing one or more positions in the market. Finding the right words to describe the logic of marketing objectives and strategies is infinitely more difficult than writing down numbers on a piece of paper and leaving the strategies implicit. This lies at the heart of the problem. For clearly, a number-oriented system will not encourage managers to think in a structured way about strategically relevant market segments, nor will it encourage the collection, analysis and synthesis of actionable market data. And in the absence of such activities within operating units, it is unlikely that headquarters will have much other than intuition and "feel" to use as a basis for decisions about the management of scarce resources.

This raises the difficult question of how these very complex problems can be overcome, for this is what baffles those who have been forced by market pressures to consider different ways of coping with their environment.

The problem remains of how to get managers throughout an organisation to think beyond the horizon of the current year's operations. This applies universally to all types and sizes of company. Even chief executives of small companies find difficulty in breaking out of the fetters of the current profit and loss account.

The successes enjoyed in the past are often the result of the easy marketability of products, and during periods of high economic prosperity there was little pressure on companies to do anything other than solve operational problems as they arose. Careful planning for the future seemed unnecessary. However, most companies today find themselves in increasingly competitive markets, and there is a growing realisation that success in the future will come only from patient and meticulous planning and market preparation. This entails making a commitment to the future.

The problem is that in large companies, managers who are evaluated and rewarded on the basis of current operations find difficulty in concerning themselves about the corporate future. This is exacerbated by behavioural issues, in the sense that it is safer, and more rewarding personally, for a manager to do what he knows best, which in most cases is to manage his *current* range of products and customers in order to make the *current* year's budget.

Unfortunately, long-range sales forecasting systems do not provide the answer. This kind of extrapolative approach fails to solve the problem of identifying precisely what has to be done today to ensure success in the future. Exactly the same problem exists in both large diversified companies and in small undiversified companies, except that in the former the problem is magnified and multiplied by the complexities of distance, hierarchical levels of management, and diversity of operations. Nevertheless, the problem is fundamentally the same.

Events that affect economic performance in a business come from so many directions, and in so many forms, that it is impossible for any manager to be precise about how they interact in the form of problems to be overcome, and opportunities to be exploited. The best a manager can do is to form a reasoned view about how they have affected the past, and how they will develop in the future, and what action needs to be taken over a period of time to enable the company to prepare itself for the expected changes. The problem is *how* to get managers to formulate their thoughts about these things, for until they have, it is unlikely that any objectives that are set will have much relevance or meaning.

Einstein wrote: "The formulation of a problem is far more essential than its solution, which may be merely a matter of mathematical or experimental skill. To raise new questions, new possibilities, to regard old problems from a new angle, requires creative imagination."

Unfortunately, such creativity is rare, especially when most managers are totally absorbed in managing today's business. Accordingly, they need some system which will help them to think in a structured way about problem formulation. It is the provision of such a rational framework to help them to make explicit their intuitive economic models of the business that is almost totally lacking from the forecasting and budgeting systems of most companies. It is apparent that in the absence of any such synthesised and simplified views of the business, setting meaningful objectives for the future seems like an insurmountable problem, and this in turn encourages the perpetuation of systems involving merely the extrapolation of numbers.

There is also substantial evidence that those companies that provide procedures for this process in the form of standardised methods of presentation, have gone some considerable way to overcoming this problem. Although the possible number of analyses of business situations is infinite, procedural approaches help managers throughout an organisation at least to consider the essential elements of problem definition in a structured way. This applies even to difficult foreign markets, where data and information are hard to come by, and even to markets which are being managed by agents, who find that these structured approaches, properly managed, help *their* businesses as well as those of their principals.

However, there are two further major advantages enjoyed by these companies. Firstly, the level of management frustration is lower and motivation is higher because the system provides a method of reaching agreement on such difficult matters as an assessment of the company's distinctive competence and the nature of the competitive environment. The internecine disputes and frustration which we all experience so often in our business lives is largely the result of an almost total absence of the means of discussing these issues and of reaching agreement on them. If a manager's boss does not understand what his environmental problems are, what his strengths and weaknesses are, nor what he is trying to achieve, and in the absence of any structured procedures and common terminology that can be used and understood by everybody, communications will be bad and the incidence of frustration will be higher.

Secondly, some form of standardised approach which is understood by all considerably improves the ability of headquarters management not only to understand the problems of individual operating units, but also to react to them in a constructive and helpful way. This is because they receive information in a way which enables them to form a meaningful overview of total company activities and this provides a rational basis for resource allocation.

To summarise, a structured approach to situation analysis is

255

necessary, irrespective of the size or complexity of the organisation. Such a system should:

- ensure that comprehensive consideration is given to the definition of strengths and weaknesses and to problems and opportunities;
- ensure that a logical framework is used for the presentation of the key issues arising from this analysis.

Very few British companies trading internationally have planning systems which possess these characteristics. Those that do, manage to cope with their environment more effectively than those that do not. They find it easier to set meaningful marketing objectives, are more confident about the future, enjoy greater control over the business, and react less on a piecemeal basis to ongoing events. In short, they suffer less operational problems and are as a result more effective organisations.

WHAT IS MARKETING PLANNING?

Let us begin by reminding ourselves what it is. It is a logical sequence and a series of activities leading to the setting of marketing objectives and the formulation of plans for achieving them. It is a management *process*.

Conceptually, the process is very simple and, in summary, comprises the steps described below:

This process is universally agreed by the experts. Formalised marketing planning by means of a planning system is, per se, little more than a structured way of identifying a range of options, for the company, of making them explicit in writing, of formulating marketing objectives which are consistent with the company's overall objectives and of scheduling and costing out the specific activities most likely to bring about the achievement of the objectives. *It is the systemisation of this process which is distinctive and was found to lie at the heart of the theory of marketing planning.*

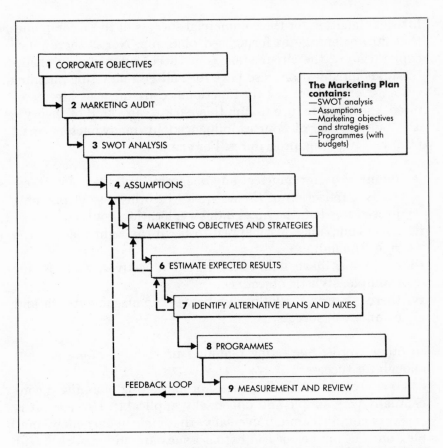

THE MARKETING PLANNING PROCESS

NAIVETY ABOUT MARKETING PLANNING

We have just rehearsed with you the notions that any textbook would offer should you care to re-read it. We have long been bemused, however, by the fact that many meticulous marketing planning companies fare badly whilst the sloppy or inarticulate in marketing terms do well. Is there any real relationship between marketing planning and commercial success? And, if so, how does that relationship work its way through?

There are, of course, many studies which identify a number of benefits to be obtained from marketing planning. But there is

257

little explanation for the commercial success of those companies that do *not* engage in formalised planning. Nor is there much exploration of the circumstances of those commercially unsuccessful companies that also have formalised marketing planning systems, and where the dysfunctional consequences are recognised, there is a failure to link this back to any kind of theory.

"Success" is, of course, influenced by many factors apart from just planning procedures. For example:

i. financial performance at any one point in time is not necessarily a reflection of the adequacy or otherwise of planning procedures (c.f. the hotel industry, location, tourism etc.).

ii. some companies just happen to be in the right place at the right time(s).

iii. companies have many and varied objectives, such as, for example, stylistic objectives.

iv. there is a proven relationship between management style and commercial success.

In other words, marketing planning procedures *alone* are not enough for success.

We have said that the process of marketing planning is conceptually very simple and universally applicable. However, it is this very simplicity and universality that make it extremely complex once a number of contextual issues are added such as (a) company size; (b) degree of internationalisation; (c) management style; (d) degree of business environmental turbulence and competitive hostility; (e) marketing growth rate; (f) market share; (g) technological changes, and so on.

It is very clear that the simplistic theories do not adequately address such contextual issues in relation to marketing planning, which may well account for the fact that so few companies actually do it.

In fact, 90 per cent of industrial goods companies in the Cranfield Study did not, by their own admission, produce anything approximating to an integrated, co-ordinated and internally consistent plan for their marketing activities. This included a substantial number of companies that had highly formalised procedures for marketing planning.

Certainly, few of these companies enjoyed the claimed benefits of formalised marketing planning, which in summary are as follows:

i. Co-ordination of the activities of many individuals whose actions are interrelated over time.
ii. Identification of expected developments.
iii. Preparedness to meet changes when they occur.
iv. Minimisation of non rational responses to the unexpected.
v. Better communication among executives.
vi. Minimisation of conflicts among individuals which would result in a subordination of the goals of the company to those of the individual.

Indeed, many companies have a lot of the trappings of sophisticated marketing planning systems but suffer as many *dysfunctional consequences* as those companies that have only forecasting and budgeting systems.

It is crystal clear that for any marketing planning system to be effective, certain conditions have to be satisfied, which we shall deal with in detail shortly.

However, there are some other points worth mentioning.

Firstly, it is possible to state that it is by no means essential for any company not suffering from hostile and unstable competitive and environmental conditions to have an effective marketing planning system. *However, without exception, all those companies in the Cranfield Study which did not have an effective marketing planning system and which were profitable, were also operating in buoyant or high growth markets.* Such companies, however, were less successful than comparable companies with effective marketing planning systems. Success was considered to be not only a company's financial performance over a number of years, but also the way it coped with its environment.

What this means is that, apart from profitability, a company with an effective marketing planning system is likely to have:

- widely understood objectives;
- high motivated employees;

- high levels of actionable market information;
- greater interfunctional co-ordination;
- minimum waste and duplication of resources;
- acceptance of the need for continuous change and a clear understanding of priorities;
- greater control over the business and less vulnerability from the unexpected.

In the case of companies without effective marketing planning systems, whilst it is possible to be profitable over a number of years, especially in high growth markets, such companies will tend to be less profitable over time and to suffer problems which are the very opposite of the benefits referred to earlier.

Furthermore, companies without effective marketing planning systems tend to suffer more serious commercial organisation consequences when environmental and competitive conditions become hostile and unstable.

None of these points are new, however, in the sense that most of these benefits and problems are discernable to the careful observer. They are, however, actionable propositions for marketers.

MARKETING PLANNING SYSTEMS: DESIGN AND IMPLEMENTATION PROBLEMS

Many companies currently under siege have recognised the need for a more structured approach to planning their marketing and have opted for the kind of standardised, formalised procedures written about so much in textbooks. These rarely bring the claimed benefits and often bring marketing planning itself into disrepute.

It is clear that any attempt at the introduction of formalised marketing planning systems has serious organisational and behavioural implications for a company, as it requires a change in its approach to managing its business. It is also clear that unless a company recognises these implications, and plans to seek ways of coping with them, formalised marketing planning will be ineffective.

Marketing planning is in practice a complex process, proceeding as it does from reviews to objectives, strategies, programmes, budgets and back again, until some kind of acceptable compromise is reached between what is desirable, and what is practicable, given all the constraints that any company has.

It has been stated that the literature underestimates the operational difficulties of designing and implementing systems and procedures for marketing planning, and that the task becomes progressively more complex as the size and diversity of a company increase. Also, the literature is inadequate in the extent to which it provides practical guidance on design and implementation.

The Cranfield research included a number of examples of companies that had been forced by market pressures to initiate procedures to help top management gain better control over the business. In all such cases, those responsible for designing the system found very little of practical help, either in the literature or in management courses. Enormous difficulties in system design and implementation were encountered in every instance.

The purpose of this section is to discuss these design and implementation problems. The most frequently encountered problems are summarised below.

Marketing Planning Systems
Design and Implementation Problems

1. Weak support from chief executive and top management.
2. Lack of a plan for planning.
3. Lack of line management support.
   - hostility
   - lack of skills
   - lack of information
   - lack of resources
   - inadequate organisation structure.
4. Confusion over planning terms.
5. Numbers in lieu of written objectives and strategies.
6. Too much detail, too far ahead.
7. Once-a-year ritual.
8. Separation of operational planning from strategic planning.

261

9. Failure to integrate marketing planning into a total corporate planning system.
10. Delegation of planning to a planner.

WEAK SUPPORT FROM CHIEF EXECUTIVE AND TOP MANAGEMENT

There can be no doubt that unless the chief executive sees the need for a formalised marketing planning system, understands it, and shows an active interest in it, it is virtually impossible for a senior functional marketing executive to initiate procedures that will be used in a meaningful way.

This is particularly so in companies that are organised on the basis of divisional management, for which the marketing executive has no profit responsibility and in which he has no line management authority. In such cases, it is comparatively easy for senior operational managers to create "political" difficulties, the most serious of which is just to ignore the new procedures entirely. Usually, however, the reasons for not participating in or for only partially following instructions, centre around the issues summarised in the table.

The vital role that the chief executive and top management *must* play in marketing planning underlines one of the key points that must be made in this section. That is, that it is *people* who make systems work, and that system design and implementation have to take account of the "personality" of both the organisation and of the people involved, and that these are different in all organisations. One of the most striking features we have observed is the difference in "personalities" between companies, and the fact that within any one company there is a marked similarity between the attitudes of executives. These attitudes vary from the impersonal, autocratic kind at one extreme to the high personal, participative kind at the other.

Any system, therefore, has to be designed around the people who have to make it work, and has to take account of the prevailing traditions, attitudes, skills, resource availability and organisational constraints. Since the chief executive and top management are the key influencers of these factors, without their active support and participation, any formalised marketing planning system is unlikely to work. This fact emerged very clearly from the Cranfield research, the worst possible manifestation of which was the way in which chief executives and top managers ignored plans which emerged from the planning system and continued to make key decisions which appeared illogical to those who had participated in the production of the plans. This very quickly destroyed any credibility that the emerging plans might have had, led to the demise of the procedures, and to serious levels of frustration throughout the organisation.

Indeed, there is some evidence to lead to the belief that chief executives who fail, firstly, to understand the essential role of marketing in generating profitable revenue in a business, and, secondly, to understand how marketing can be integrated into the other functional areas of the business through marketing planning procedures, are a key contributory factor in Britain's appalling economic performance. There is a depressing preponderance of accountants who live by the rule of "the bottom line" and who apply universal financial criteria indiscriminately to all products and markets, irrespective of the long-term consequences. Also of engineers who see marketing as an unworthy activity that is something to do with activities such as television advertising; and who think of their products only in terms of their technical features and functional characteristics, in spite of the overwhelming body of evidence that exists that these are only a part of what a customer buys. Not surprisingly, in companies headed by people like this, marketing planning is either non-existent, or where it is tried, it fails. This is the most frequently encountered barrier to effective marketing planning.

LACK OF A PLAN FOR PLANNING

The next most common cause of the failure or partial failure of marketing planning systems is the belief that, once a system is designed, it can be implemented immediately. One company achieved virtually no improvement in the quality of the plans coming into headquarters from the operating companies over a year after the introduction of a very sophisticated system. The evidence indicates that a period of around three years is required in a major company before a complete marketing planning system can be implemented according to its design.

Failure, or partial failure, then, is often the result of not developing a timetable for introducing a new system, to take account of the following:

1. the need to communicate why a marketing planning system is necessary;
2. the need to recruit top management support and participation;
3. the need to test the system out on a limited basis to demonstrate its effectiveness and value;
4. the need for training programmes, or workshops, to train line management in its use;
5. lack of data and information in some parts of the world;
6. shortage of resources in some parts of the world.

Above all, a resolute sense of purpose and dedication is required, tempered by patience and a willingness to appreciate the inevitable problems which will be encountered in its implementation.

This problem is closely linked with the third major reason for planning system failure, which is lack of line management support.

LACK OF LINE MANAGEMENT SUPPORT

Hostility, lack of skills, lack of data and information, lack of resources, and an inadequate organisational structure, all add up to a failure to obtain the willing participation of operational managers.

Hostility on the part of line managers is by far the most common reaction to the introduction of new marketing planning systems. The reasons for this are not hard to find, and are related to the system initiators' lack of a plan for planning.

New systems inevitably require considerable explanation of the procedures involved and are usually accompanied by *proformae,* flow charts and the like. Often these devices are most conveniently presented in the form of a manual. When such a document arrives on the desk of a busy line manager, unheralded by previous explanation or discussion, the immediate reaction often appears to be fear of his possible inability to understand it and to comply with it, followed by anger, and finally rejection. He begins to picture headquarters as a remote "ivory tower", totally divorced from the reality of the market place.

This is often exacerbated by his absorption in the current operating and reward system, which is geared to the achievement of *current* results, whilst the new system is geared to the future. Also, because of the trend in recent years towards the frequent movement of executives around organisations, there is less interest in planning for future business gains that someone else is likely to benefit from.

Allied to this is the fact that many line managers are ignorant of basic marketing principles, have never been used to breaking up their markets into strategically relevant segments, nor of collecting meaningful information about them.

This lack of skill is compounded by the fact that there are few countries in the world which match the wealth of useful information and data which is available in countries such as the USA and the U.K. This applies particularly to rapidly-growing economies, where the limited aggregate statistics are not only unreliable and incomplete, but also quickly out of date. The seriousness of this problem is highlighted by the often rigid list of home office informational requirements, which is based totally on the home market.

The solution to this particular problem requires a good deal of patience, common sense, ingenuity and flexibility on the part of both headquarters and operating management. This is closely connected with the need to consider resource availability and the prevailing organisation structure. The problem of lack of reliable data and information can only be solved by devoting time and money to its solution, and where available resources are scarce, it is unlikely that the information demands of headquarters can be met.

It is for this reason that some kind of appropriate headquarters organisation has to be found for the collection and dissemination of valuable information, and that training has to be provided on ways of solving this problem.

Again, these issues are complicated by the varying degrees of size and complexity of companies. It is surprising to see the extent to which organisational structures cater inadequately for

265

marketing as a function. In small companies, there is often no one other than the sales manager, who spends all his time engaged either in personal selling or in managing the sales force. Unless the chief executive is marketing orientated, marketing planning is just not done.

In medium-sized and large companies, particularly those that are divisionalised, there is rarely any provision at board level for marketing as a discipline. Sometimes there is a commercial director, with line management responsibility for the operating divisions, but apart from sales managers at divisional level, or a marketing manager at head office level, marketing as a function is not particularly well catered for. Where there is a marketing manager, he tends to be somewhat isolated from the mainstream activities.

The most successful organisations are those with a fully integrated marketing function, whether it is line management responsible for sales, or a staff function, with operating units being a microcosm of the head office organisation.

However, it is clear that without a suitable organisational structure, any attempt to implement a marketing planning system which requires the collection, analysis and synthesis of market-related information, is unlikely to be successful. A classic example of this was a large diversified multinational, where no provision was made at headquarters for marketing, other than through the divisional directors, and where divisions also generally had no marketing function other than sales management. Their first attempt at writing a strategic plan as a result of market pressures was a complete failure.

CONFUSION OVER PLANNING TERMS

Confusion over planning terms is another reason for the failure of marketing planning systems. The initiators of these systems, often highly qualified, frequently use a form of planning terminology that is perceived by operational managers as meaningless jargon. One company even referred to the Ansoff matrix, and made frequent references to other forms of matrices, missions, dimensions, quadrants, and so on.

Those companies with successful planning systems try to use

terminology which will be familiar to operational management, and where terms such as "objectives" and "strategies" are used, these are clearly defined, with examples given of their practical use.

NUMBERS IN LIEU OF WRITTEN OBJECTIVES AND STRATEGIES

Most managers in operating units are accustomed to completing sales forecasts, together with the associated financial implications. They are not accustomed to considering underlying causal factors for past performance or expected results, nor of highlighting opportunities, emphasising key issues, and so on. Their outlook is essentially parochial and short-term, with a marked tendency to extrapolate numbers and to project the current business unchanged into the next fiscal year.

Thus, when a marketing planning system suddenly requires that they should make explicit their implicit economic model of the business, they cannot do it. So, instead of finding words to express the logic of their objectives and strategies, they repeat their past behaviour and fill in the data sheets provided without any narrative.

It is the provision of data sheets, and the emphasis which the system places on the physical counting of things, that encourages the questionnaire-completion mentality and hinders the development of the creative analysis so essential to effective strategic planning.

Those companies with successful marketing planning systems ask only for essential data and place greater emphasis on narrative to explain the underlying thinking behind the objectives and strategies.

TOO MUCH DETAIL, TOO FAR AHEAD

Connected with this is the problem of overplanning, usually caused by elaborate systems that demand information and data that headquarters do not need and can never use. Systems that

267

generate vast quantities of paper are generally demotivating for all concerned.

The biggest problem in this connection is undoubtedly the insistence on a detailed and thorough marketing audit. In itself this is not a bad discipline to impose on managers, but to do so without also providing some guidance on how it should be summarised to point up the key issues merely leads to the production of vast quantities of useless information. Its uselessness stems from the fact that it robs the ensuing plans of focus and confuses those who read it by the amount of detail provided.

The trouble is that few managers have the creative or analytical ability to isolate the really key issues, with the result that far more problems and opportunities are identified than the company can ever cope with. Consequently, the truly key strategic issues are buried deep in the detail and do not receive the attention they deserve until it is too late.

In a number of companies with highly detailed and institutionalised marketing planning systems the resulting plans contain so much detail that it is impossible to identify what the major objectives and strategies are. Also, the managers in these companies are rarely able to express a simplified view of the business or of the essential things that have to be done today to ensure success. Such companies are often over-extended, trying to do too many things at once. Over-diversity and being extended in too many directions, makes control over a confusingly heterogeneous portfolio of products and markets extremely difficult.

In companies with successful planning systems, there is at all levels a widespread understanding of the key objectives that have to be achieved, and of the means of achieving them. In such companies, the rationale of each layer of the business is clear, and actions and decisions are disciplined by clear objectives that hang logically together as part of a rational, overall purpose.

The clarity and cohesiveness are achieved by means of a system of "layering". At each successive level of management throughout the organisation, lower-level analyses are synthesised into a form that ensures that only the essential information needed for decision-making and control purpose reaches the next level of management. Thus, there are hierarchies of audits, SWOT analyses, assumptions, objections, strategies and plans.

This means, for example, that at conglomerate headquarters, top management have a clear understanding of the really key macro issues of company-wide significance, whilst at the lower level of profit responsibility, management also have a clear understanding of the really key micro issues of significance to the unit.

It can be concluded that a good measure of the effectiveness of a company's marketing planning system is the extent to which different managers in the organisation can make a clear, lucid and logical statement about the major problems and opportunities they face, how they intend to deal with these, and how what they are doing fits in with some greater overall purpose.

ONCE-A-YEAR RITUAL

One of the commonest weaknesses in the marketing planning systems of those companies whose planning systems fail to bring the expected benefits, is the ritualistic nature of the activity. In such cases, operating managers treat the writing of the marketing plan as a thoroughly irksome and unpleasant duty. The proformae are completed, not always very diligently, and the resulting plans are quickly filed away, never to be referred to again. They are seen as something which is required by headquarters rather than as an essential tool of management. In other words, the production of the marketing plan is seen as a once-a-year ritual, a sort of game of management bluff. It is not surprising that the resulting plans are not used.

Whilst this is obviously closely related to the explanations already given as to why some planning systems are ineffective, a common feature of companies that treat marketing planning as a once-a-year ritual is the short lead time given for the completion of the process. The problem with this approach is that in the minds of managers it tends to be relegated to a position of secondary importance.

In companies with effective systems, the planning cycle will start in March or April and run through to September or October, with the total twelve-month period being used to evaluate the on-going progress of existing plans by means of the company's marketing intelligence system. Thus, by spreading the planning activity over a longer period, and by means of the active participation of all levels of management at the appropriate moment, planning becomes an accepted and integral part of management behaviour rather than an addition to it which calls for unusual behaviour. There is a much better chance that plans resulting from such a system will be formulated in the sort of form that can be converted into things that people are actually going to do.

SEPARATION OF OPERATIONAL PLANNING FROM STRATEGIC PLANNING

This sub-section must be seen against the background of the difficulty which the majority of British companies experience in carrying out any meaningful strategic planning. In the majority of cases, the figures that appear in the long-term corporate plan are little more than statistical extrapolations that satisfy boards of directors. If they are not satisfactory, the numbers are just altered, and frequently the gap between where a company gets to compared with where it had planned to be in real terms, grows wider over time.

Nevertheless most companies make long-term projections. Unfortunately, in the majority of cases these are totally separate from the short-term planning activity that takes place largely in the form of forecasting and budgeting. The view that they should be separate is supported by many of the writers in this field, who describe strategic planning as very different, and therefore divorced, from operational planning. Indeed, many stress that failure to understand the essential difference between the two leads to confusion and prevents planning from becoming an integrated part of the company's overall management system. Yet it is precisely this separation between short and long-term plans which the Cranfield research revealed as being the major cause of the problems experienced today by many of the respondents. It is the failure of long-term plans to determine the difficult choices between the emphasis to be placed on current operations and the development of new business that leads to the failure of operating management to consider any alternatives to what they are currently doing.

270

The almost total separation of operational or short-term planning from strategic or long-term planning is a feature of many companies whose systems are not very effective.

More often than not, the long-term strategic plans tend to be straight-line extrapolations of past trends, and because different people are often involved, such as corporate planners, to the exclusion of some levels of operating management, the resulting plans bear virtually no relationship to the more detailed and immediate short-term plans.

This separation positively discourages operational managers from thinking strategically, with the result that detailed operational plans are completed in a vacuum. The so-called strategic plans do not provide the much-needed cohesion and logic, because they are seen as an ivory tower exercise which contains figures that no one really believes in.

Unless strategic plans are built up from sound strategic analysis at grass roots level by successive layers of operational management, they have little realism as a basis for corporate decisions. At the same time, operational plans will become increasingly parochial in their outlook and will fail to incorporate the decisions that have to be taken today to safeguard the future.

Operational planning, then, should very much be part of the strategic planning process, and *vice versa*. Indeed, wherever possible, they should be completed at the same time, using the same managers and the same informational inputs.

The detailed operational plan should be the first year of the long-term plan, and operational managers should be encouraged to complete their long-term projections at the same time as their short-term projections. The advantage is that it encourages managers to think about what decisions have to be made in the current planning year, in order to achieve the long-term projections.

FAILURE TO INTEGRATE MARKETING PLANNING INTO A TOTAL CORPORATE PLANNING SYSTEM

It is difficult to initiate an effective marketing planning system in the absence of a parallel corporate planning system. This is yet another facet of the separation of operational planning from strategic planning. For unless similar processes and time scales to those being used in the marketing planning system are also being used by other major functions such as Distribution, Production, Finance and Personnel, the sort of trade-offs and compromises that have to be made in any company between what is wanted and what is practicable and affordable, will not take place in a rational way. These trade-offs have to be made on the basis of the fullest possible understanding of the reality of the company's multifunctional strengths and weaknesses, and opportunities and threats.

One of the problems of systems in which there is either a separation of the strategic corporate planning process or in which marketing planning is the only formalised system, is the lack of participation of key functions of the company, such as engineering or production. Where these are key determinants of success, as in capital goods companies, a separate marketing planning system is virtually ineffective.

Where marketing, however, is a major activity, as in fast moving industrial goods companies, it is possible to initiate a separate marketing planning system. The indications are that when this happens successfully, similar systems for other functional areas of the business quickly follow suit because of the benefits which are observed by the chief executive.

DELEGATION OF PLANNING TO A PLANNER

The incidence of this is higher with corporate planning than with marketing planning, although where there is some kind of corporate planning function at headquarters, and no organisational function for marketing, whatever strategic marketing planning takes place is done by the corporate planners as part of a system which is divorced from the operational planning mechanism. Not surprisingly, this exacerbates the separation of operational planning from strategic planning and encourages short-term thinking in the operational units.

Very often, corporate planners are young, highly qualified people, attached to the office of the chairman or group chief executive. They appear to be widely resented and are largely ignored by the mainstream of the business. There is not much evidence that they succeed in clarifying the company's overall strategy and there appears to be very little account taken of such strategies in the planning and thinking of operational units.

The literature sees the planner basically as a co-ordinator of the planning, not as an initiator of goals and strategies. It is clear that without the ability and the willingness of operational management to co-operate, a planner becomes little more than a kind of headquarters administrative assistant. In many large companies, where there is a person at headquarters with the specific title of marketing planning manager, he has usually been appointed as a result of the difficulty of controlling businesses that have grown rapidly in size and diversity, and which present a baffling array of new problems to deal with.

His tasks are essentially those of system design and co-ordination of inputs, although he is also expected to formulate overall objectives and strategies for the board. In all cases, it is lack of line management skills and inadequate organisational structures that frustrate the company's marketing efforts, rather than inadequacies on the part of the planner. This puts the onus on the planner himself to do a lot of the planning, which is, not surprisingly, largely ineffective.

Two particularly interesting facts emerged from the Cranfield research. Firstly, the marketing planning manager, as the designer and initiator of systems for marketing planning, is often in an impossibly delicate political position *vis à vis* both his superior line managers and more junior operational managers. It is clear that not too many chief executives understand the role of planning and have unrealistic expectations of the planner, whereas for his part the planner cannot operate effectively without the full understanding, co-operation and participation of top management, and this rarely happens. Often, the appointment of a marketing planning manager, and sometimes of a senior marketing executive, seems to be an easier step for the chief executive and his board to take than giving serious consideration themselves to the implications of the new forces affecting the business and reformulating an overall strategy.

This leads on naturally to a second point. For the inevitable consequence of employing a marketing planning manager is that he will need to initiate changes in management behaviour in order to become effective. Usually these are far-reaching in their implications, affecting training, resource allocation, and organisational structures. As the catalyst for such changes, the planner,

273

not surprisingly, comes up against enormous political barriers, the result of which is that he often becomes frustrated and eventually ineffective. This is without doubt a major problem, particularly for big companies. The problems which are raised by a marketing planning manager occur directly as a result of the failure of top management to give thought to the formulation of overall strategies. They have not done this in the past because they have not felt the need. However, when market pressures force the emerging problems of diversity and control to the surface, without a total willingness on their part to participate in far-reaching changes, there really is not much that a planner can do.

This raises the question again of the key role of the chief executive in the whole business of marketing planning. Without both his support and understanding of the very serious implications of initiating effective marketing planning procedures, whatever efforts are made, whether by a planner or a line manager, they will be largely ineffective.

REQUISITE MARKETING PLANNING SYSTEMS

The implications of all this are principally as follows:

i.   Any closed loop marketing planning system (but especially one that is essentially a forecasting and budgeting system) will lead to entropy of marketing and creativity. Therefore, there has to be some mechanism for preventing inertia from setting in through the over-bureaucratisation of the system.
ii. Marketing planning undertaken at the functional level of marketing, in the absence of a means of integration with other functional areas of the business at general management level, will be largely ineffective.
iii. The separation of responsibility for operational and strategic marketing planning will lead to a divergence of the short term thrust of a business at the operational level from the long term objectives of the enterprise as a whole. This will encourage a preoccupation with short term results at operational level, which normally makes the firm less effective in the long term.

iv. Unless the chief executive understands and takes an active role in marketing planning, it will never be an effective system.

v. A period of up to three years is necessary (especially in large firms), for the successful introduction of an effective marketing planning system.

In another paper for this journal we will explore in detail what is meant by the term "Requisite Marketing Planning" when we explain how to design and implement an effective marketing planning system.

For now, we believe we have given sufficient background information about the *process* of marketing planning, and why this apparently simple process requires much more perception and attention than is typically accorded it.

NOTE

1. M H B McDonald, "The theory and practice of marketing planning for industrial goods in international markets." Cranfield Institute of Technology, PhD, 1982.

IS THE INTERNATIONAL CASH COW REALLY A PRIZE HEIFER?
William L. Shanklin and John K. Ryans, Jr.

A growing number of U.S.-based multinational corporations (MNCs) are reporting higher percentage returns on sales in foreign markets than in domestic ones. Further, in absolute dollar terms, more and more of these firms are producing higher foreign than domestic operating income. And many U.S. multinationals

Reprinted from *Business Horizons,* vol. 24, March 1981, pp. 10–16. Copyright 1981 by the Foundation for the School of Business at Indiana University. Used by permission.

now appear to be relying on their foreign operations to bail out their poor domestic performances. Ford Motor Company in recent years has used this approach, but is by no means alone.

A close study of the 1979 annual reports of some 100 major U.S. corporations demonstrated their increasing reliance on overseas markets. Of this group, sixty-five firms reported that more than one-fifth of their net sales took place abroad. Forty-six of the companies had higher percentage returns in overseas than in domestic markets. For twelve of them, foreign operating income actually exceeded that earned in the United States.

At first glance, this seems like good news, coming as it does when the U.S. economy is soft. But unless the successes of international operations are placed in proper perspective, reported results can be misleading and, in fact, can endanger a firm's long-term prospects. Too often a foreign star—a prize heifer—may be treated as a cash cow with the result that hope for its continued growth and improvement is lost. Management's temptation to deplete a promising foreign market or product is especially great in the short run as the firm seeks to overcome current losses in a rapidly deteriorating domestic market.

This article considers traditional portfolio analysis and suggests how this valuable strategic planning approach, if specifically adapted to take account of the domestic/international dichotomy, can help to insure that the international side of a multinational gets the attention and resources it needs to be a major contributor in the long term. International portfolio analysis can assist corporate policy makers in firms succeeding abroad and faltering at home from forming misleading conclusions about overall company performance. We try to show how multinational management can avoid the mistake of managing an overseas star as a corporate cash cow and transforming it into a problem child.

THE INTEGRATED PRODUCT PORTFOLIO

Under the original product portfolio concept developed by the Boston Consulting Group, firms analyze the cash flow potential of their various products. Each product is seen as a star, cash

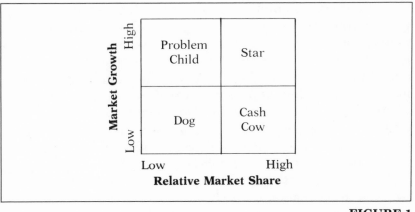

FIGURE 1
Market Growth/Share

cow, problem child, or dog, based on its individual market share and growth possibilities.

With a simple two-by-two schema [see Figure 1], this widely accepted approach to strategic market planning has allowed management to identify a particular product's role in its firm's product mix. The terms used to identify the quadrants of the matrix have become a fundamental addition to business terminology. Still for our purposes here, it is useful to review briefly the basic concepts embodied in the product portfolio approach.

Both growth and market share are quantifiable. And the products are rated as being either high or low on these measures of potential, as shown in the accompanying figure.

Growth has been referred to as a proxy for the product's stage in the life cycle.[1] Those still in the stage of ascendancy are felt to have high growth opportunity, while those leveling off or showing some decline, that is, mature products, have low growth opportunity. A basic assumption of this analysis is that a high growth product requires significant cash inputs to continue its expansion, while low growth potential suggests excess cash flow which could be used by other products.

Market share has been the easier of the two concepts for most firms to measure and requires a comparison with competitors. Those products that hold a relatively low share of the total market, regardless of market size, are considered low market share products. Again, there is an underlying cash flow assumption: market share must be bought and high market share requires significant investment. Multinational firms often have more difficulty in analyzing their products than do those firms operating domestically. In particular, it is often harder to make market share estimates for some of their overseas markets.

While the measures employed are relatively straightforward, it must be recognized that firms may view the same data differently. What may be seen as a low market share for one firm, may in fact be seen as high for another. Recently, one writer suggested that a growth rate of 10 percent or more is high, while parity with the market leader is the "cut-line" for market share.[2] This interpretation ignores the international arena where a firm may see itself as having a high market share if it has only 7 or 8 percent of all its major Western European markets.

Each of the four cells in the product portfolio matrix has its own particular definition in terms of cash flow:

Star—has the best of both worlds, a high or dominant market share and continued growth potential. It is assumed to be essential that to achieve stardom, the product's earnings are to be plowed back and not used as a net producer of cash flow.

Cash cow—has probably been a star of the past and has reached its potential. Its cash flow is used to prop up the problem child or to further R&D efforts. The assumption is that the amount of resources needed to maintain the cash cow's market share is less than the revenue it produces and that there is little growth possibility remaining.

Problem child—is often an enigma to the firm's management. Products in this category face a growing market and yet have achieved limited market share themselves. While additional investment may be warranted, the product itself may not be competitive or its market segment correctly identified.

Dog—is appropriately named. This quadrant contains those products that have neither a dominant market share nor a rapidly growing market. Depending upon the product's life cycle stage and variable product costs, it still may be able to produce a steady, if not spectacular, cash flow. In other instances, the product may be ripe for divestment or abandonment.

Since this product portfolio matrix was introduced, a number of product strategies have become associated with a product's classification. For example, once designated as a cash cow, a product is likely to receive little funding except for necessary modifications and improvements. The strategy recommended for the cash cow is "harvesting" or, as Kotler recently described it, "a strategic management decision to reduce the investment in a business entity in the hope of cutting costs and/or improving cash flow."[3] In other words, a deliberate milking.

While the basis for product analysis seems quite plausible, it now appears that the way the MNC interprets its overseas activities may lead to possible misinterpretation of its products' performances. This is especially true in two instances. First, if a product has peaked domestically but is still in the growth stage abroad, the firm is likely to place it entirely in the cash cow category. Second, if the product is entirely produced and developed by an overseas subsidiary, the firm may misinterpret a peaking in one market as being representative of its overseas potential.

An even greater concern, however, is the premature sacrificing of overseas opportunities to cover domestic disaster. Regardless of what organizational structure the MNC employs, it is still possible to isolate the contribution of the firm's overseas products and submit them to separate product portfolio analysis. Where this "harvesting" of overseas operations appears especially evident is in those firms having separate international divisions or geographic structures. Here it seems that it is the international area, which in many firms is continuing to provide profitable operations, that is feeling the brunt of domestic concerns. There are, of course, circumstances under which the apparent long-term sacrifice of potential is justifiable, but it is never justifiable to misread an overseas product's potential

EARLY WARNING INDICATORS

There are several incisive, diagnostic questions that top management in a U.S.-based multinational can ask of itself to ascertain whether the company is headed for trouble because it is erroneously handling foreign markets or products as though they were cash cows. These queries all seek to get at how the MNC has been, is now, and ideally should be managing its domestic markets and products vis-à-vis its foreign ones. The questions require top management to make both judgmental and quantitative assessments. Answers that are not in accordance with conventional management practice and theory of portfolio management are probably ominous and valuable early warning indicators that trouble lies ahead if changes of a strategic and philosophic nature are not made.

Management can take a useful first step by asking itself to judge how it views philosophically its domestic and international businesses. Is the international component an integral part of the total enterprise, or is it merely a profitable stepchild? A reliable clue to the answer is the quality of management that the MNC has been sending to its international operations.

Is the international organization mostly a training ground for executives who, once they prove their merit and gain experience, will be returned to a domestic assignment? Or is the international part of the business a dumping ground for executives nearing retirement or for those whom the company wants to relocate out of "more important" areas because of doubts about their managerial ability to function on the "faster track" of the domestic scene? If these kinds of conditions prevail, it is a clue that the domestic side of the business is thought of as the major leagues and the foreign counterpart the minor leagues where unproven, or old, or less competent executives are farmed out. The major/minor league dichotomy is significant because how a component—domestic/international—is thought of by top management is also normally how it is treated when it comes to resource allocation.

Management assuredly would want to look closely at the executive assignments to and from international operations and over a period of, say, the previous five years. Of particular concern is whether the international sector of the multinational had greater managerial turnover than the domestic sector and whether the overall caliber of executives who were assigned internationally was comparable to that of managers assigned domestically.

Quantitative indicators can also be adduced and used critically by top management in determining whether the domestic operations are being unduly emphasized at the expense of the international ones. Management needs to determine whether any of its low or negative growth and profit domestic markets are being artificially propped up by cash flows from more profitable international markets. An affirmative answer to either of the two following questions may very well indicate that a product sold in a foreign market is being milked when, in fact, it is not really a cash cow.

First, is there any rapidly growing international market in which the multinational has had a high share and profits and in which the market is continuing to grow while the MNC's share shrinks? If this is, in fact, the case, it follows that management has an early warning signal coming through loud and clear that a star performer needs attention—and quickly. Only further probing can reveal whether the star is on the decline because of forces beyond the control of management or because the market is undeservedly getting cash cow handling from domestic headquarters.

Second, is any growing international market—in which the company presently has a low but promising share of market—being cultivated financially and with competent management, so that it eventually becomes a high growth/high share market for the company? If the answer is no, but there are sound reasons why the market is not being strongly pursued, then it is time for corporate management to think seriously about cutting their losses with this problem child and withdrawing from the market entirely. But if prospects are bright for making the problem child into a star through additional resource allocations, but management's cash cow treatment has precluded such a transformation, then a signal for immediate action is unmistakable.

An example of a counterproductive cash cow treatment of a once growing and profitable international business operation is provided by Ford Motor Company. In 1974, Ford hired then-BMW executive Robert Lutz as chief executive of its West German operations—Ford's largest subsidiary. Lutz was extremely aggressive in acquiring a consumer-oriented image for Ford through such notable and innovative measures as West Germany's first one-year auto guarantee. Between 1974, when the highly capable Lutz arrived, and 1976, when he was transferred to Ford's European truck operations, the company's market share in West Germany soared from 10 to 15 percent. By 1980, four years after Lutz's departure, market share had ebbed to just over 9 percent. In an article titled "West Germany, A Ford Cash Cow Has Less for Its Parent," *Business Week* said:

281

"That slide [in market share] not only means that Ford of Germany will be less of a cash cow for its financially needy Dearborn (Michigan) parent, but it also means that the subsidiary may lose for good the market gains it scored in the mid-1970's.... Lutz's successor ... is not only less colorful but also struggling, Ford insiders say, with demands from Dearborn for cash to help headquarters meet the costly U.S. standards for pollution control and gas mileage. As a result, model innovations for the Taunus and Escort have been delayed by Ford of Germany. By contrast, Volkswagen has introduced more than two dozen new cars and variants on the German domestic market since 1975. Its Passat is also cutting sharply into sales of the Taunus."[4]

In commenting on Ford's domestic problems with its North American automobile operations, *The Wall Street Journal* states: "As recently as last fall [1979], Ford thought it had things under control. Despite red ink in the United States, it believed it could ride out the storm profitably this year [1980] on the strength of overseas sales and other operations. But some major foreign markets it counted on are weakening."[5]

Ford's attempted remedy for these problems includes the naming of Harold Poling as the new executive vice president of the company's North American car operations. Where did this talented executive come from? For several years he was the boss of Ford's then-highly profitable European operations and, during his tenure, earned huge corporate profits abroad for Ford. The transfer of Poling in 1980, and the dependence on European profits to carry North American operations, is reminiscent of the Lutz transfer in 1976 and the resulting atrophy in Ford's West German operations. What is more, both Ford's current CEO and current president—Philip Caldwell and Donald Petersen, respectively—once headed international operations.

INTERNATIONAL PORTFOLIO MANAGEMENT

The international operations of multinationals are typically structured along the lines of product or geographical areas, and most frequently on combinations of the two dimensions. Whenever the product dimension predominates, each division in the MNC may be responsible for marketing and distributing one class of products worldwide, but more commonly a separate international division is solely responsible for marketing on a worldwide basis most or all products of the multinational's domestic divisions. In contrast, when the organizational setup is geographical, each division in the multinational's international operations is charged with the responsibility for conducting all the company's business within its designated geographical sphere.

The product and geographical approaches can be and are often combined by the major multinationals. General Electric, for instance, formed an organizational structure wherein an international group, headed by a vice president and group executive, was assigned to report directly to top management. This international group—which organizationally was placed on a lateral line with ten GE product groups—was, in turn, subdivided into three area divisions (Europe, the Far East, and Latin America), in addition to the GE export division. At Dana Corporation, a similar arrangement prevails, whereby an international group consists of three major geographical subdivisions.

Regardless of the manner in which a multinational is structured, the potential is always there for top management to give cash cow treatment undeservedly, and perhaps unwittingly, to some of the firm's internationally marketed products and foreign markets—or worse yet, to the company's entire international operation. Because this threat exists, corporate policy makers are well advised to look at all the company's international markets and products marketed in them, as well as at the international operation as a whole, within the revealing analytical context of the portfolio matrix concept.

No matter how an MNC is organized for doing business abroad, appropriate matrixes can be developed to facilitate classification of the firm's international products and markets. General Electric has used a similar sorting scheme for its products. According to GE Chairman Reginald Jones, all its products have been categorized into one of five groupings:

- High-growth products deserving the highest investment support;
- Steady reinvestment products deserving high and steady investment;
- Support products deserving steady investment support;

283

- Selective pruning or rejuvenation products deserving reduced investment;
- Venture products deserving heavy R&D investment.

This kind of analysis, if tailored to depict a detailed domestic/international breakdown for products and markets, enables top management to determine readily whether an international component of the MNC is being managed correctly. Of particular interest is whether a high potential product or foreign market is being prevented from realizing its bright future because it is getting cash cow treatment from MNC headquarters. This stunting effect may not be discernible if domestic and foreign operations are not segregated and compared to one another on relevant performance indicators, such as growth, market share trends, and profits. Conceivably, a product that legitimately qualifies as a cash cow in the United States could very well be a star in an international market. Yet this important distinction, from a prescriptive managerial point of view, might be blurred by aggregated performance data. Management policy, in terms of resource allocation, naturally needs to be markedly different in the two market situations.

Domestic/international breakdowns of performance information are not hard to come by. For instance, the recent Financial Accounting Standards Board Regulation 14 already requires U.S.-based multinationals to segregate in their annual reports to shareholders specific performance data for the firm's significant foreign geographical operations.

What may be hard to come by, however, is the realization (and appropriate commensurate action) on the part of a multinational's top management that the firm is evolving away from its traditional product/market strengths. Management may be reluctant to admit that the firm's world markets are becoming more important than its domestic market, in terms of actual or potential growth and profits, or that products other than those upon which the company built its name are the wave of the future. And such reluctance is quite understandable. Management oftentimes becomes attached to products and thus is slow to modify them when necessary to meet prevailing market conditions, or in extreme instances, to give them proper burial. Then, too, there is a natural tendency for management to consider the company to be, say, a "U.S. company since 1894," even though, with the firm's vast network of world markets, this feeling may no longer remotely correspond to reality. Additionally, policy makers in large American-based multinationals work under considerable social, governmental, and political pressure to put U.S. operations first, even when more lucrative foreign markets beckon.

Understandable though it may be, management reluctance to modify radically the company's historical product/market bases can spell trouble ahead. Such reluctance can and often does lead to cash cow harvesting of growing and promising international products and markets in order to support foundering domestic operations. This sort of robbing-Peter-to-pay-Paul approach is usually thought of as a temporary solution until domestic operations are restored to health. Too often, however, the practice continues on year after year until the short run becomes the long run and the multinational ends up with weakened products and markets not only at home but also abroad.

Take the case of Singer Company. The firm's future is thought by some, including one of its own executives, to be so bleak that they have suggested that the company self-liquidate. Speaking of Singer's unprofitable U.S. sewing machine operations, which until now management has been reluctant to deemphasize or modify, another of the company's managers says:

"What Singer has is a group of high-cost factories, tooled up for a demand that existed perhaps 20 years ago, manned with union people who are not about to let the company off the hook. We're turning out machines there that cost exactly double what machines made in Taiwan cost and we're serving a [U.S.] market that is dropping precipitously.[6]

For some time Singer management has been acquiring non-sewing machine businesses to counter the decline in the sewing machine business in the United States and other industrial nations. (Demand for sewing machines has decreased 50 percent in the last seven years in the U.S. alone.) Nonetheless, Singer management continued to pursue a recovery program based mainly on the company's traditional core business—sewing machines—which resulted in a $130 million write-off on sewing machine operations in the third quarter of 1979. An earlier write-off on business machines reduced Singer's book value by half.

Now that Singer's management has literally been forced to do something more non-traditional (for Singer), it is greatly restructuring (read, scaling down) its North American and European sewing machine businesses. It then intends to reallocate $125 million in the next several years to promote its more promising businesses, including defense and the growing and profitable sewing machine markets in less developed countries.

RETURNING TO COMPETITIVE POLICIES

The focus thus far has been on the perils of management's misreading or misinterpreting the international dimension of product portfolio analysis. But in some instances, management may knowingly milk the corporate foreign star. Why are many U.S. multinationals doing so?

The answer lies with several provocateurs. It has long been fashionable to use the supposedly devious Japanese, the greedy Arab sheiks, conniving oil executives, and "cheap foreign labor" as straw men who have prevented numerous U.S. businesses from competing effectively in their own domestic markets. Yet while labor cries foul over foreign imports, it disregards its own role in diminished productivity and wage increases that go well beyond those justified by gains in worker output. And management has too often responded like the proverbial ostrich to changing consumer demands. One can hardly fault the hard-pressed American who buys the Honda or Datsun.

But the problem largely is a federal one: simply too much interference in the private sector. And the current climate for business in the United States is the culmination of years of need for redress. While not blameless, neither labor nor management can print money; or confiscatorily tax so-called windfall profits; to use inflation as a means to demotivate wage and salary earners by de facto tax increases brought about by Congressional failure to index tax brackets; or impose a staggering regulatory burden upon both business and the public.

Inflation, unemployment, and bail-outs by the U.S. taxpayer of New York City, Chrysler, and Lockheed are but symptoms of an underlying economic malady. The United States has one of the lowest savings rates among the industrialized nations of the Western world, due to federal government-fostered, spend-to-beat-inflation psychology. Understandably, then, capital formation, investment, and industrial modernization have suffered, productivity has fallen, and the competitive edge of many U.S. firms has eroded against foreign competitors.

What is more, by stacking regulation on regulation, the federal government has brought about an environment wherein management and labor can demand assistance whenever they get into trouble. The next step in this inexorable spiral appears to be an expedient like the "big wagon," the Italian government's company which purchases failing private ventures.

Significantly, influential Washington policy makers of all political stripes are now talking about a reindustrialization of America through what amounts to supply-side economics. When (or if) such talk finds its way into meaningful policy, the pressures in and on U.S. multinationals for deliberate short-run remedies, like milking the foreign star, may subside.

Coming full circle, what will remain is the need for multinational management to make certain that the product potentials in the company's foreign markets are properly analyzed. It may then even be politic to close a failing American operation or to do as Anheuser-Busch intends one day with its domestic beer business—to make current domestic products prime cash cows and then seek new opportunities at home and abroad.

The rewards for management's recognizing that a product with high growth and market share is actually a prize heifer rather than a cash cow are considerable. The long-term performance level of any U.S. multinational may well ride on its management's perceptiveness in making this distinction and resolve to act accordingly.

NOTES

1 George S. Day, "Diagnosing the Product Portfolio," *Journal of Marketing,* April 1977: 29.

2 Terry Haller, "Strategic Planning: Key to Corporate Power for Marketers," *Marketing Times,* May/June 1980: 22.

3 Philip Kotler, "Harvesting Strategy for Weak Products," *Business Horizons,* August 1978: 16.

4 "West Germany, A Ford Cash Cow Has Less For Its Parent," *Business Week,* May 12, 1980: 42.

5 "Ford's Hot Seat, Harold 'Red' Poling Has Task of Reviving North American Sales," *The Wall Street Journal,* May 7, 1980: 1.

6 "Is Singer Headed for Self-Liquidation," *Business Week,* March 31, 1980: 116.

INSIDE/OUTSIDE DIRECTOR INFORMATION NEEDS

William L. Shanklin and John K. Ryans, Jr.

The information flow between the corporation and the independent director is of utmost importance in enabling that director to satisfy his or her fiduciary duties. It is a basic responsibility of the chairman of the board to see that his directors secure information that is adequate (without being overwhelming), effectively presented, available when needed, accurate, and representative of the special needs of individual members of the board.
If the information furnished meets these tests—and if it is digested and properly queried and tested against the personal expertise of the individual director—then the board member should be comfortable in a job well done and free from unwarranted legal attack.
—Richard S. Maurer, Vice Chairman and Corporate Secretary,
Delta Airlines

The 65 Fortune-500 directors polled in this current survey of board information needs would probably agree with Mr. Maurer. Why else whould they have taken the time to answer a questionnaire which asked them to rank the interest of over 25 types of information?

Deregulation may be in store for corporate boards in 1981 and beyond, but directors' responsibility to know the company they serve will remain a formidable reality for years to come. New publics and new markets have extended the scope of management; at the same time the board's monitoring responsibilities have increased. In this larger portion of a larger network, each new responsibility has created others.

The upshot? Ever-expanding information needs for corporate boards. Directors are called upon by both law and custom to make well-informed judgments—and information, unlike judgment, can and should be tailored to board needs.

From *Directors & Boards*, Vol. 5, No. 4, published by the Hay Group. Reprinted by permission.

Rare is the premeeting information manager—chairman or corporate secretary—who can filter information to satisfy the needs of an entire board. Our survey results show one reason for this: in many cases the insider's telex is the outsider's tedium.

The directors polled here represent a highly significant population: the Fortune 500. The board information manager should find this survey useful as an indicator of dominant board opinion—or as a guide to questioning the attitudes of a particular board.

SURVEY TECHNIQUES AND RESULTS

We asked randomly selected Fortune 500 directors to assess a full range of potential board information needs. Specifically, they were asked to rate these items (on a seven-point scale) in terms of their importance to the director's effective performance of his or her duties. Of the 65 respondents, not more than two— one outsider and one insider—represented any given board.

The results of this seven-point ranking determined the *order* in which the following questionnaire topics are listed. In presenting the range of our findings, we grouped the answers in categories of high (rankings 1,2), medium (rankings 3,4), and low (rankings 5,6,7) importance.

Most of the items fell into the following interest levels for *both* insiders and outsiders:

- over 75 percent high appeal
- 50 to 75 percent high appeal
- 25 to 50 percent high appeal
- under 25 percent high appeal
  (medium appeal; exceptions mostly on high side)
  (medium appeal; exceptions mostly on low side)

Some items—notably those involving *internal corporate operations*—have a much higher appeal to insiders than to outsiders, so much so that they require separate discussion since they do not fall into the same category for both groups. Insiders and outsiders alike unanimously cast a high vote for one topic alone:

289

A Matter of Perspective

A sampling of the opinions volunteered by survey respondents points up similarities—and differences—in the ways inside and outside directors view board information requirements.

Insiders say . . .

"In general, [information should be] related to the operation, efficiency, competitiveness, capital plans, etc. of the enterprise, and not items of a cosmetic nature that can too easily divert the attention of a board."

"[I advocate] the practice followed by many companies which have each department give the board an annual half-day presentation, and in addition, have each major operating division give an hour-long report every month."

"Headline reporting—both financial and operational—is essential. Otherwise, you're buried under a mass of details and main points are missed."

"More emphasis on exception reporting on operations and more focused reports on strategies to highlight key issues."

"The board should not attempt to manage. It should judge management."

And outsiders add . . .

"The board doesn't run the company—that's the management's job. The board's job is . . . to select the CEO."

"Some in-depth exposure to individual operations is important, but too much immersion blurs the distinction between the board and executive management."

"Most directors have their own business to worry about and can only spend limited time on directors' duties."

"Management should carefully define the potential issues which the board may discuss, and provide terse information and opinions (carefully labeled as such) pertaining to the issues."

"Directors should not become involved in the operations of the company."

"I have served on one board where little interest was shown in [information] needs of directors."

annual plans and budgets for the corporation as a whole. Reviews are mixed from this point on, with outsiders exhibiting a generally lower interest level than insiders. Topics in each group, including those in the separate discussions, appear in order of preference.

Agenda items of high appeal to over 75 percent of each group include:

- long-range (5 years or more) corporate plans
- policies and strategies for dealing with the Foreign Corrupt Practices Act

Of the remaining votes for these "top" categories, all but a few—outsiders indifferent to the FCPA—were cast in the medium range.

Items ranked high by 50 to 75 percent of each group appeared in the following order:

- SEC requirements, actions
- annual plans and budgets at the strategic business unit (SBU) level
- regulatory trends (e.g., antitrust) affecting company
- long-range planning at SBU level

Some items had cumulative high votes in the 50-to-75 percent range thanks to high *insider* votes (fewer than 50 percent of the outsiders gave them high votes—and a good 10 percent of outsiders ranked them low priority):

- incentive plans for non-top-management employees
- labor relations—policies, strategies
- research and development results
- economic forecasts for industries in which company operates

Topics of high interest to 25 to 50 percent of each group included:

- tax situation and strategy
- distribution strategy
- results of company image studies
- intelligence reports on competitors
- corporate antiterrorist security measures
- affirmative action strategies

The "odd topic out" of this low-to-medium average range was *pricing strategies,* which garnered a 45 percent high vote

291

among insiders, but fell below the 25 percent mark for outsider votes. This contrast is reflected, albeit less dramatically, throughout the six topics in the 25-50 percent range: outsiders tended to find them of lower interest than did insiders.

Topics with the lowest average ranking tended to have an average of medium, but solid, minority representation on both high and low extremes, high being slightly more predominant. These "normal curve" topics of medium (skewed toward high) interest include:

- U.S. economic forecast
- EPA requirements/actions
- corporate advertising and public relations strategies
- current and proposed EEOC regulations/interpretations
- lobbying strategies
- community relations program descriptions

Lowest in average rank came topics of preponderantly medium interest with more low than high votes on the extremes:

- world economic forecast by region or country
- U.S. political forecast
- world political forecast by region or country

SIGNIFICANCE: CONTRARY TO POPULAR BUSINESS BELIEF . . .

Directors generally agree that board responsibilities and liabilities have increased over the past decade; that they need more information—even at operations levels—to meet these responsibilities in board meetings. But who would have guessed that inside directors were *more* eager than outsiders to receive such information? Whatever happened to the image—dominant in the business press for the past decade—of the inscrutable insider intent on keeping board meetings as perfunctory as possible, sedating the would-be outsider firebrand into a yes-man?

Insiders want to put everything on the agenda—accompanied by full information. Outsiders are cooler all around, especially with regard to information concerning corporate operations. Why? Do they feel they lack the necessary expertise to judge company operations—or, worse, that they are merely quid pro quo appointees? Certainly insiders do not see them that way. Indeed, the increased responsibilities of corporate officers have led them to *desire* sharing the burden of decisions at the board level. As one inside director put it: "Too many companies bring all their operating problems to the board to solve. Some executives feel a joint decision protects them." So much for the myth of the secretive insider!

But the biggest lesson learned is that those responsible for keeping board members informed beyond the quarterly-report level cannot assume *anything* about the information needs of directors, except, perhaps, that insiders and outsiders are likely to agree on only one priority: annual corporate budgets and plans. To establish priorities for other types of information, nothing short of asking directors will do. Query methods—by committee, questionnaire, or informal conversation—can be tailored to fit board needs.

What matters most is that board members—insiders and outsiders alike—receive "information that is adequate without being overwhelming, effectively presented, available when needed, accurate, and representative of the special needs of individual members of the board."

SHOULD THE BOARD CONSIDER THIS AGENDA ITEM?

William L. Shanklin and John K. Ryans, Jr.

Directors conduct a far different meeting from those in the past. Pressures—from regulatory agencies, shareholders, lenders, and the public—have practically forced greater awareness of directors' responsibilities. The board as a rubber stamp or a bastion of the

Reprinted by permission from *MSU Business Topics,* Winter 1981, pp. 35–42.

"old-boy" selection system has largely been replaced by more active, more professional boards.[1]

An adage well known to most directors of major corporations describes the role of the board: "At the board meeting, the directors need to make either one or two decisions. One, is management doing a good job? If the answer is yes, a second decision is not necessary." In the past, this saying contained a considerable degree of truth, but now boards of directors are becoming more involved in corporate affairs, largely due to their increased legal and social accountability.

The traditional thinking on board responsibility views directors as framing overall corporate policy, while management implements it. But with the recent activism of board committees, notably finance and audit, directors' involvement in operations is growing. Now that the fine line between policymaking and implementation is becoming nebulous, what guidelines do directors use to determine what matters should be brought to their attention at board meetings? Are board members at least generally in agreement on this?

To find the answers to these questions, we gained the cooperation of more than seventy directors of *Fortune* 500 companies in responding to a written questionnaire. No more than two board members from any one company were included. Morever, inside and outside directors were almost equally represented. These directors were presented with eight factually based but hypothetical matters that might warrant board consideration. The eight potential agenda items were selected to provide the directors with realistic, current, and diverse situations. The directors commented, as though they were board members in the corporation involved, on whether each item is a proper agenda item. In a sense, the way directors see these eight items provides guidance in determining the boundaries for appropriate board action—useful knowledge for today's chairperson.

Agenda Item 1: Management is considering anticipatory price increases because it is felt that there is a strong likelihood that President Carter will impose a general wage-price freeze shortly, regardless of what he says now. Is this a proper agenda item for consideration by the board of directors?

294

In the interim between the early 1950s and the early 1970s, wage and price controls were neither federally imposed in the United States nor even talked about much. It came as a shock to most people in 1971 when President Nixon mandated controls; it had been twenty years since President Truman's compulsory program—and that was instituted during the Korean war.

Ever since the Nixon freeze, the specter of economic controls has loomed large, especially in periods of double-digit inflation. Senator Edward Kennedy of Massachusetts has repeatedly asked for a short-term price-wage freeze; during the 1980 presidential primaries, he adopted the concept as a plank in his proposed economic recovery program. Various upper-echelon labor leaders, including former AFL-CIO chief George Meany, frequently have demanded a general across-the-board freeze on prices, wages, profits, dividends, and rents. A prominent business economist openly admitted in a television interview that he counsels his corporate clients to raise prices whenever economic controls seem likely.

The directors are almost evenly divided as to whether an anticipatory price increase is a legitimate agenda item. Those who answered affirmatively justify their responses in several ways, yet their reasons can be categorized easily. Some feel that any contemplated price increase involves corporate policy and thus is a board matter. One comment is typical: "Involves pricing and marketing strategy that may be related to policy issues." The public relations aspect of pricing, as well as its information importance to company policymakers, was a second category: "Any such action which might affect the company's image or standing is proper." "Clear political implications." Financial importance to the firm was another category. A number of the directors said the pricing question warrants board attention because of its implications for company success. For example: "Yes, the concept is real but absurd. If the market is strong enough to absorb price increases, why wait?" Some directors agree that, in theory, the subject of anticipatory price increases is a proper agenda item for the board, but, in practice, the importance of timely pricing action is of overriding concern. As one director said, "management judgment should prevail. Too much time is lost when requiring board approval." Another wrote: "Unfortunately, [the federal administration] vacillates so much that a decision today is out-of-date tomorrow."

A very slight majority of directors believe the topic of anticipatory price increases is not a proper board matter. The main
reason, cited time and again, was that pricing is the responsibility of top corporate management and divisional general managers; it is an operating decision. A notable warning occasionally
was provided: If any price increase is in excess of guidelines set
by the Council on Wage and Price Stability, then what normally
is a management function becomes a matter of corporate policy.

A few directors hedged. Their rationale is that it is necessary
somehow to draw a distinction between pricing policy and price
decision making. Consider these two dissimilar opinions: "Most
pricing decisions are management's responsibility. Pricing policy
would be a board matter." "The board needs to discuss
[anticipatory increases] but actual pricing decisions should ordinarily be taken by management." Another director suggested
that management should definitely consider anticipatory price
increases, but before making a decision should consult certain—
but not all—board members.

*Agenda Item 2: The company is about to hire a new chief lob-
byist in Washington, D.C. Is this a proper agenda item for consideration by the board of directors?*

Over the years, the practice of lobbying federal, state, and
local lawmakers has been used, sometimes abused, and certainly
widely lamented. Pejorative references to self-interest groups
have often been made by individuals ranging from U.S. presidents to city leaders and members of public interest organizations. In President Eisenhower's final days in office, he publicly
warned of a collusive and menacing military-industrial complex.
Since then, there has been an assortment of headlines on lobbying incidents, notably the Dita Beard, Park and ABSCAM
affairs.

A statement by the Committee for Economic Development
cogently explains the lobbying process.

The democratic process is based on the recognition that a wide
range of interest groups will naturally emerge to represent citizens.
This complex system, which permits the participation of so many
groups and individuals, can be slow, inefficient, and sometimes

inequitable. Interest groups with narrow concerns can harness the political system to promote these concerns. Such groups mobilize public opinion through extensive direct-mail and publicity campaigns. In return for political support, many are able to generate the sizable contributions and favorable publicity that politicians require for election.[2]

None of the directors question the *need* for a company lobbyist, although a few expressed regret that the need exists. One said a prospective lobbyist should be considered by the board, but added that "[it is] a sad day when corporations need defenders in Washington." Another wrote: "I wish we could avoid lobbying, but we can't."

About two-thirds of the directors do not consider the hiring of a new chief lobbyist in Washington a proper agenda item. They consider this an employment decision for management. There was hedging, however. Some said that overall political strategy should be discussed by the board, then the right lobbyist should be selected and hired by management to implement it. Others feel that if the potential lobbyist has controversial aspects in his or her background, the hiring decision belongs on the board agenda. Several directors want management to discuss the prospective lobbyist with board members who might know or know of the person, rather than bring the item up at a formal meeting. A few directors believe that, for informational purposes, the board should be advised after management has hired the lobbyist.

Among the one-third of the directors favoring board consideration of the hiring of a chief lobbyist, the reason most often cited was that someone on the board either might know the individual or might know something about him or her. Thus, the board would be called upon to perform a reference-checking function.

Agenda Item 3: Management wants to acquire, for $30 million, a company that it feels will strengthen the firm's ability to reach new growth markets. Is a discussion of the pros and cons of the proposed acquisition a proper agenda item for consideration by the board of directors?

297

Since about 1976, there has been an unprecedented wave of merger and acquisition activity on the part of large U.S. corporations. This burst of activity followed a hiatus brought about by the many unsuccessful conglomerate-type mergers of the 1960s. In those mergers, contrary to the conventional management wisdom of the time, great diversity in business operations often proved counterproductive. The strategy of the 1960s is unlike current merger and acquisition strategy.

> Corporate planners are [now] unquestionably eschewing the economic wanderlust of the 1960s-style conglomerate growth in favor of more integrative mergers and acquisitions. They are looking for compatibility of business missions in the merging firms and for synergies from the marriages.[3]

Because so many companies suffered financially from ill-advised and operationally incompatible acquisitions in the 1960s, it is reasonable to expect that matters pertaining to mergers and acquisitions would be of concern to boards of directors in large companies. That, in fact, is the case. Among all the agenda items suggested to the directors in this study, there was greatest agreement on this item. More than 95 percent of the directors said the proposed acquisition should be considered by the board. A sampling of responses follows.

"This is exactly what I think a board should do."

"The best example of a board of director function."

"Mandatory."

"Not only proper but failure by management to present to board would be serious error."

"The stockholders would have a fit if the board were not consulted."

"Management should present analysis of prospective acquisition, valuation, projection of contribution to earnings, synergy with current business."

"All major capital asset acquisitions should be approved by board."

The less than 5 percent of the directors who said the acquisition was not a proper board item did so on the basis that $30 million was not large enough in dollar terms to warrant board attention in a *Fortune* 500 firm. For example: "In a giant company, certainly this is not a board item"; and "This is a pretty small acquisition to consider." It is clear, however, that almost all the directors disagree with this point of view and feel that any proposed acquisition, irrespective of size, needs board clearance. In fact, it is fair to state even more strongly that the majority believe that management would be remiss if it failed to bring any possible acquisition to the board.

Agenda Item 4: A terrorist group has just kidnapped the company's general manager in Argentina and is demanding a ransom of $5 million for his safe return. Should everyone on the board of directors be phoned by management and asked his or her opinion on how to respond?

There is nothing more disruptive to normal multinational operations today than the threat of terrorism. The magnitude of this problem is exemplified by the kidnapping of Exxon executive Victor Samuelson in Argentina in 1973 and the subsequent payment of a $14.2 million ransom.[4] Even in firms that have taken the recommended precautions and developed extensive contingency plans, a kidnapping would command top management's immediate attention.

It is perhaps not surprising that roughly two-fifths of the directors feel that all board members should be polled in this situation. However, most directors feel that planning for response to terrorism should receive prior board approval. One respondent said the "board should have dealt with policy regarding this matter years ago." Another suggested that the "chairman should be permitted to act quickly within the bounds of the policy."

Those indicating that management should contact board members by telephone appeared to be either in firms without sufficient contingency plans on security matters or in firms in which such calls are conditional. Examples of the latter, mentioned by one director, were "(1) the amount involved is significant (very) or (2) the matter vitally affects company policy and operations."

Undoubtedly, the respondents would have been virtually unanimous in feeling that a security policy would be an appropriate agenda item. It was the immediacy and operational aspects of the question that appeared to be of concern to most of the respondents.

Agenda Item 5: In Anytown, USA, where the company has a large plant, management is thinking about undertaking a community improvement project at an estimated cost of $300,000. The project will entail the company's purchasing six old and rundown houses in a ghetto, tearing them down, and then developing a park. Is this a proper agenda item for consideration by the board of directors?

The legitimacy of business philanthropy has long been debated within the larger dialogue about corporate social responsibility. On one side of the issue are a host of individuals who feel that private sector, for-profit institutions have no place in philanthropy. This mode of thinking has been articulated by, among others, Milton Friedman, Peter Drucker, and Theodore Levitt.[5] Corporate philanthropy is objected to on one or more of several grounds: It usurps the individual shareholder's right to decide whether or not to make socially related contributions and, if so, to choose the recipient; it detracts from a company's true social responsibility, which is to produce as much profit as possible within the framework of law, so that the company will be vigorous enough tomorrow to provide jobs and pay pensions; and businesspeople should not decide what is a social good; rather, elected public representatives should make this determination. Some contend that any corporation that is able to be philanthropic is in a monopolistic or quasi-monopolistic position, else the firm would be forced by competitive pressures to use its resources exclusively for operations.

On the other side of the issue are many people of various political and economic leanings who urge corporate participation in numerous philanthropic causes. A cursory look at both the popular and academic literature of recent years on corporate social responsibility corroborates this point. What is more, cases of businesses practicing such philanthropy are not uncommon. Notably, the Five Percent Club in Minneapolis is an organization of companies that annually contribute 5 percent of pre-tax earnings to civic causes. (This is the maximum percentage the IRS code permits corporations to deduct for charitable contributions.)

By a margin of almost two to one, the directors said the proposed community improvement project should be brought to the board for consideration. Among those who replied yes, some elaborated in the vein of the corporate philanthropy controversy, as these remarks show.

"I would vote against the proposal."

"Inappropriate for a company to undertake. Paternalistic and patronizing—will hurt the company someday."

"Outside normal company business, could be criticized by some shareholders. Justification should be agreed upon by board."

"Use of stockholders' funds for philanthropic purposes should require board action."

Other directors gave less philosophic reasons for considering the proposed project a board matter. Some feel that any $300,000 expenditure, regardless of purpose, is a proper agenda item. Others want the project considered as a matter of record, solely for informational purposes.

The directors who replied negatively did so primarily because they consider philanthropic determinations to be a management function. Again, however, it is important to note that this is a distinctly minority position. Some directors believe that a $300,000 expenditure is too insignificant to merit the board's attentions in a *Fortune* 500 corporation.

Agenda Item 6: The Equal Employment Opportunity Commission has just promulgated rules defining and prohibiting sexual harassment of employees by their colleagues and administrative superiors. A female worker within the company is making serious allegations about her boss, accusing him in

301

a formal grievance of threatening to block her promotion unless she provides him with sexual favors. Is this a proper agenda item for consideration by the board of directors?

Increasing attention and research have been directed toward the question of sexual harassment of female employees.[6] Protection is afforded the employee under Title VII of the Equal Protection Act. The issue seems clearest when *sexual compliance* is added to all other job-related standards. Less clear are those instances in which the sexual compliance actually has occurred or in which the job standards are altered.

Normally, this might seem to be a personnel matter, of little or no concern to a board member. With board members' growing concern for and awareness of matters having public relations implications, however, some support for this issue's spot on the agenda could be anticipated.

As one director suggested, whether or not this could be a relevant agenda item might revolve around the boss in question. If the boss is an officer or director of the company, it *should* be an agenda item. Otherwise, the board's only role would be to develop and publish, for management guidance, a general statement on sexual harassment.

Only 14 percent of the directors considered this question a potential agenda item. In fact, only one strongly felt the issue was important and saw it having possible "far-reaching effects on public and internal relations." A more typical response was that "management has all the tools it needs to handle this problem" or that "large companies have several dozen EEO matters going at all times, most of which are frivolous."

Agenda Item 7: Management has the opportunity to sell to the Soviet Union machines that manufacture tiny ball bearings. While these bearings could be put to normal industrial use, they could also be used to reduce friction in the guidance system of a MIRV warhead and thereby give it more accuracy. Management must make a decision soon on whether to try for U.S. government clearance to make the sale. Is this a proper agenda item for consideration by the board of directors?

The question of technology transfer in defense-related areas has been a continuing corporate concern. Prior to the Afghanistan invasion and the subsequent export controls implemented by the Carter administration, trade restrictions had already been an issue. The National Foreign Trade Council (NFTC) had called upon the federal government to take a more realistic approach to its determination of sensitive technology.[7] Similarly, the Committee for Economic Development supports the need to "prevent weapons technology from falling into the hands of potential adversaries," but adds the following proviso.

> There should be sunshine provisions mandating frequent review of control procedures and categories.[8]

The NFTC has added to this position the caution that equal state-of-the-art materials are readily available elsewhere, which negates the federal position on technology transfer.

This board member study was, of course, conducted in the post-Afghanistan period. It is not surprising that 60 percent of the directors considered this an appropriate item for the board's agenda. One view was that such action "could impact on the firm's image and its government relations." Other views were that the issue had such "far-reaching complications" that board concurrence was essential, or that it would only be an issue if management wished to export "contrary to government wishes."

A solid minority held that this was clearly a management (or operations) decision. As one board respondent said, "this is almost a routine matter these days."

Agenda Item 8: Management is considering switching from the Acme Agency, with which it is dissatisfied, to the Smith Advertising Agency. More than $100 million a year of ad agency business is involved. Is this a proper agenda item for consideration by the board of directors?

Recently, an executive in a leading British advertising agency said that a corporation's board of directors must be more actively drawn into advertising decision making in order to improve advertising efficiency. He adds that too often advertising has been shifted to the brand manager level, which "does not necessarily help the company's total viewpoint."[9] Traditionally, of course, advertising matters, including the selection of the

303

advertising agency, have been the responsibility of the top marketing executive in the firm.

While firms often have long-established relationships with their advertising agencies, performance evaluations are becoming more and more common. As media and creative costs escalate and as firms become more sophisticated in establishing marketing objectives, the importance of performance measures might be expected to increase.

Yet, of all the potential agenda items discussed, this one was viewed by many as most clearly a management decision. To some extent, it tests the limits to which the new board activism is moving.

According to most of the directors, any move to shift agencies is clearly an operating decision. While 40 percent felt it should be an agenda item, they tended to want it included merely to advise the board of the change. As one respondent stated: "Let the management run the company. If you don't like the results, then the board should fire the president and CEO."

Two directors cited possible exceptions. The first would be a situation in which the board itself had expressed dissatisfaction with an agency's performance. In such an instance, "they should be a part of the final decision process." The other exception noted was the case of a retail company. One respondent said that boards of retail companies might be more apt to become involved in advertising decisions than those in manufacturing concerns. Despite these exceptions, it is evident that most board members are only interested in being informed after the fact on what they consider a purely operating decision.

PERSPECTIVES

The boundaries of issues for consideration by boards of directors are said to be expanding. *Newsweek* suggests that some of the new board aggressiveness derives more from fear than valor; stockholders increasingly are inclined to sue directors for failure to perform their fiduciary duties.[10] Undoubtedly, this heightened aggressiveness also is due in part to the new mix of directors, who bring different interests and levels of experience to the board-room. What are the limits of concern for today's boards?

In this study, each of the agenda items was carefully selected to represent one of three types of corporate matters. First, there was a strictly strategic policy category, namely, the item bearing on long-term corporate mission (the $30 million acquisition) and the one that could set a precedent for large-scale philanthropy (the community development project). As expected, since policy is involved, an overwhelming majority of directors would want to be consulted in both cases. Second, there was a strictly opera-tional classification, comprised of the advertising agency and sexual harassment items. Again, as thought, a sizable majority would not want to be asked about routine management decisions.

Regarding the four agenda items related to policy and oper-ations, the directors generally followed an expected pattern. The only question raised about the acquisitions issue concerned whether the dollar amount was sufficient for consideration. On the community improvement project, the board members seemed most concerned about the potential political and public/shareholder relations problems. There was limited support for considering the sexual harassment item or advertising agency change at the board level. Thus, except for public/shareholder relations potential, these traditional board matters remained clearcut.

The third grouping of agenda items represented a gray area, or what ostensibly are operating decisions for management to make in a giant multinational corporation, that is, pricing (antic-ipatory), selling to a foreign government (USSR), hiring a lob-byist, and dealing with a terrorist kidnapping. Yet, all these items were purposely tinged with strong political or public rela-tions overtones, given the current environment for business in the United States. It is revealing that there was considerable sen-timent in each of these cases—although not always majority opinion—for considering the items legitimate board matters. In addition, the directors are most in agreement about items that are potentially controversial.

The anticipatory price increase was felt to be a board issue only if kept within a policy framework, if the firm planned action conflicting with federal guidelines, or if it had public relations

305

concerns. The question of a Washington lobbyist produced a more diverse response. While most felt it was not an appropriate agenda item, it was obvious that a majority wanted the opportunity to comment before action.

A terrorist kidnapping was seen by some as a board issue, but not by a majority. This was recognized as a critical problem, however, and being kept informed was the minimal expectation. The board was especially sensitive to the reaction, from both a political and public relations standpoint, that the sale of technology (or even the attempt to secure approval for a sale) to the Soviets could cause. Still, although they leaned toward including this item on the agenda, some felt it was a management decision.

Our study has added empirical credence to the many observations about growing involvement on the part of corporate boards of directors. Specifically, the findings indicate that whenever public affairs considerations impinge on a corporate decision—even if it involves operations—the board of directors is taking an increasingly activist posture. This suggests that a board chairperson might better err through commission rather than omission when it comes to bringing agenda items to the board's attention. In the opinion of many sitting directors, at least, the strategic/operational dichotomy no longer defines board business.

This, of course, creates more difficulty for the chairperson, who must be able to anticipate those gray issues the firm's directors will consider potentially explosive enough to demand their involvement.

NOTES

1. Marilyn Much, "Managing the Board," *Industry Week,* 9 June 1980, pp. 53–54.
2. *Redefining Government's Role in the Market System* (New York: Committee for Economic Development, July 1979), p. 81.
3. William L. Shanklin, "Strategic Business Planning: Yesterday, Today, and Tomorrow," *Business Horizons* 22 (October 1979): 9.
4. John K. Ryans, Jr., and William L. Shanklin, "Terrorism and the MNC," *Business: The Magazine of Managerial Thought and Action* 30 (March–April 1980): 2.

5. See Milton Friedman, *Capitalism and Freedom* (Chicago: University of Chicago Press, 1962); Peter Drucker, "The Delusion of Profits," *Wall Street Journal,* 5 February 1975, p. 15; and Theodore Levitt, "The Dangers of Social Responsibility," *Harvard Business Review* 36 (September–October 1958): 41–50.
6. Catharine MacKinnon, *Sexual Harassment of Working Women: A Case of Sex Discrimination* (New Haven: Yale University Press, 1979).
7. *1979 Policy Declaration of the National Foreign Trade Council, Inc.* (New York: The Council, 1978), p. 41.
8. *Stimulating Technological Progress* (New York: Committee for Economic Development, January 1980), pp. 49–50.
9. "How to Improve Advertising Efficiency?" *Advertising Age—Europe* (November 1979): E4.
10. "Uneasy Men at the Top," *Newsweek,* 7 July 1980, pp. 54–55.

IMPROVING CORPORATE COMMUNICATIONS WITH MEMBERS OF THE BOARD

John K. Ryans, Jr., and William L. Shanklin

The role of the corporate chief executive officer (CEO) in selecting and packaging information for members of his or her board of directors is critical. Dann V. Angeloff, who is himself a director in several companies, captures with this metaphor the extreme influence the CEO has when it comes to communicating with the board:

> A chairman of the board is like an orchestra leader with his directors as the musicians. The orchestra leader decides what music to play and supplies the music he wants played. He may choose to play fast or slow, loud or soft, long or short. Let's hope [the CEO] can be influenced to play the best music with the best musicians for the shareholders.

Reprinted by permission from *Strategy and Executive Action,* Summer 1984, Bureau of Business and Economic Research, University of Mississippi.

In 1979, the *Harvard Business Review* suggested several questions that top management might ask of its directors, if it wanted to supply them with more useful information.[1] We took this idea of researching directors' informational needs and, in a year-long study, carried it considerably further. We sought the collective opinions of a broad spectrum of major company directors from U.S. industry in order to target the most needed data. The findings from the study enable us to now offer a practical, data-based prescriptive framework that can help CEOs take much of the guesswork out of selecting information for and providing information to directors.

To our knowledge, this research is the first broad data-based inquiry into corporate communications with the board. Much of what has been written or said on the subject heretofore has been either anecdotal or based on one person's limited experiences in one or a few companies.

THE STUDY

In one phase of the research project, 65 inside (employee) and outside (nonemployee) directors in *Fortune* 500 companies rated the relevance of 27 possible board agenda items.[2] These items excluded the financial and kindred performance information normally considered by boards of directors, such as operating profits and earnings per share. The directors also provided insights pertaining to facilitating aspects of board communications, such as the number of days per month needed to assimilate and act on corporate matters and how often the board should meet in full session.[3] In another phase, the inside and outside directors supplied in-depth perspectives on the appropriateness of bringing eight hypothetical, but factually-based, issues to the board's attention, concerning such diverse topics as mergers and acquisitions, selling high-technology to the Soviets, and sexual harassment charges against a male executive.[4] In still another phase, personal interviews and written correspondence with additional directors were used to augment and broaden our understanding of the more structured phases of the study.

The remainder of this article integrates and builds on this rather extensive body of data. Applicable procedures and concepts for more effective corporate communications with members of the board of directors are offered.

THE CEO's BALANCING ACT

Several considerations complicate the CEO's communication task as it pertains to his or her directors. In the typical large corporation, there is a veritable flood of information that conceivably might be relevant to board members. Judgment and delicate balancing are required to provide them with the "right" amount of information; i.e., not too much to create information overload but not so little that directors are uninformed or underinformed about items with which they need to be familiar.

Moreover, because of their fiduciary responsibilities to shareholders, and their concomitant economic and social obligations to a larger constituency, conscientious directors must do more than perfunctorily approve management's proposals and recommendations. For directors to make dutiful and defensible decisions, they must know and grasp the salient facts concerning the agenda topics (and request items for the agenda). Thus, they must have the right kinds of information as well as a manageable amount. In recent years, there have been a number of published reports of directors curtailing their board memberships precisely because of what they correctly perceive as increased legal liabilities and, consequently, growing demands on their time. Beyond the legal liability question, the increased scope and intricacy of business enterprise today further contribute to a growing workload for directors. The growth in the number of committees of the board in most major companies illustrates this increased workload.

Because of its importance, the dialogue between a company and its directors can be viewed as a special and vital case in corporate communications. The key questions are: what informational items do individual directors need and want to carry out legal duties to shareholders and societal obligations to other corporate constituencies; in what form; and with what timing (e.g., how often should the board meet)?

DESTROYING MYTHS

Two items of conventional wisdom about how boards of directors do or should function have long persisted, perpetuated by the popular and academic presses. We found these items to be more mythical than factual:

- that a board of directors ratifies overall corporate policy, whereas management proposes and implements it; and
- that nonemployee or outside directors are becoming increasingly activist and thus seek ever more involvement in corporate affairs.

Our findings clearly show that directors generally do not confine their interests and involvement in board matters to policy. In addition to the more traditional policy concerns, e.g., long-range plans, directors often want information pertaining to operational topics. These latter include annual plans and budgets at the strategic business unit level, labor relations strategies, and economic forecasts for industries/markets in which their respective companies operate.

Contrary to prevailing thought, however, it is not the outside directors who push for more information. It is the employee or inside directors who want to bring to board consideration a plethora of both policy and operational items. As we see it, this tack by the employee directors is an effort to share the burden of responsibility for decisions and, hence, the blame should the decisions later fail.

A third assumption about information needs of corporate directors has also prevailed in practice, albeit more implicitly:

- that for information purposes the board can be treated as a homogeneous group of people.

This assumption might have been true at one time. But the trend toward more nonemployee representation on corporate boards has weakened its validity. According to our respondents, it is now desirable for a large corporation to differentiate board information for employee and nonemployee directors. Inside directors have more knowledge of the corporate situation than their nonemployee director colleagues. Additionally, outside directors who are not from the business world—say, a university president or a clergy—normally do not have the financial sophistication and corporate acumen of directors who are active or retired business executives. Corroborated time and again by comments elicited from both inside and outside directors was this point—for comprehensibility and impact, it is useful to tailor information according to the degree of business expertise of the individual board member. And, according to whether a director is operationally involved with a company on a day-to-day basis.

MODELING THE INFORMATION FLOW

In order to better understand informational needs, we have developed a broad conceptual framework that depicts an efficient and effective information flow to and from directors. The use of such a prescriptive paradigm or model can simplify the arduous task for whoever compiles and selects information for the board's perusal and action. Such a frame of reference can also stimulate this individual's thinking about possible types of information the board needs, but is not now receiving, or, alternatively, about the types of information the board does not truly need, but is now receiving. Derived from our research among the *Fortune* 500 directors was the conceptual framework that we depict in Exhibit 1.

All information that a board can receive must emanate from one of two sources—from outside the corporation (society), or from inside the company (operations). Similarly, potential recipients of information pertaining to board deliberations and actions reside either in society—e.g., the general public, government, security analysts—or within the corporation itself.

There is a laborious and severely judgmental information screening and censoring process that goes on in this regard. Very

311

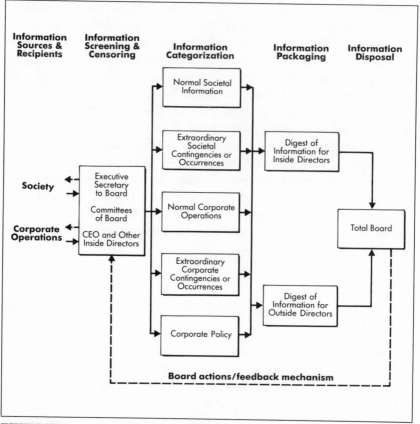

EXHIBIT 1.
Board of Directors Information Flow

little societal and operational information has relevance to directors as directors. In the same vein, some board actions are matters for societal and/or internal corporate consumption, but most are not. Screening and information dissemination are typically the responsibility of the CEO and other inside directors, the executive secretary to the board, and various functional committees of the board.

Based on factor analysis[5] of our data and on judgment, we feel that all information that could be presented to a board of directors can be orderly classified into one of five categories. Not only does this categorization process permit more directed thinking about what information directors "really" need, it simplifies the sorting of a huge amount of data into more manageable subgroupings. The five information classifications are:

(1) Normal Societal Information—Encompasses data concerning the usual and ongoing externalities that may impinge on the performance and well-being of the company. These externalities are mostly uncontrollable by management but often are predictable. Example: economic conditions; peaceful political and social change; and federal developments in antitrust or regulation/deregulation.

(2) Extraordinary Societal Contingencies or Occurrences—Entails data about events originating outside the company that are beyond management's control. An item falling into this category initially may later become so commonplace that it warrants reclassification as normal societal information. Examples: media and governmental focus on corporate bribery in international dealings; acceleration of terrorist acts against business; and revolutionary political and social change in overseas markets.

(3) Normal Corporate Operations—Includes the usual financial and operating data pertaining to corporate performance in the marketplace, in addition to other significant internally-generated information that might be useful to board members in carrying out their duties. Examples: quarterly financial statements; research and development breakthroughs; and intelligence reports on competitors.

(4) Extraordinary Corporate Contingencies or Occurrences—Concerned with possible or actual happenings within the company that under normal circumstances would not be matters for board consideration. These matters would normally be dealt with solely by management. However, because of potential ramifications, largely in embarrassing canards receiving widespread media attention, the item might well warrant board attention. Examples: a group of employees allege age discrimination; questions dealing with worker safety or hazardous waste disposal; charges of improprieties brought by a female employee against a division general manager.

(5) Corporate Policy—Pertains to those broad matters within and without the company that require board scrutiny and consideration in order to establish new policy or to affirm

313

that planned managerial action of a strategic nature is in accordance with existing policy. Examples: long-term plans for the company in the way of acquisitions and divestitures; plans to repurchase some of the company's stock; dividends

As the framework suggests, the information packaging and disposal phases of this communication flow require an intimate *understanding* of the heterogeneity of most boards today. Once the data have been categorized and the relevant items selected from each category for board attention, the job of packaging the data comes next. This tailoring process is essential if the information is to be comprehensible to *all* board members. We suggest at the minimum a package for inside directors and another for outside directors, with the latter requiring more elaboration. Moreover, if one or more nonemployee directors are nonbusiness-types, a third and even more detailed presentation is indicated.

Finally, as is recognized in Exhibit 1, the total board takes various formal actions that are relayed back to the information *recipients*. In addition, a feedback system is suggested that allows the board members to express their views on the "information package" they received prior to the board meeting. The executive secretary to the board and/or the CEO should determine the adequacy of the information provided to the board members, and do so on a regular and formalized basis. By this we do not simply mean that their "comments" should be solicited. Rather, we mean that a special survey form (questionnaire) should be developed and employed to assess the board members' reactions to the various materials.

CONCLUSIONS

In our view, packaging information for directors is analogous to packaging information for dissemination to the public or segments thereof via advertising and public relations. In both cases, the goal is lucid, concise, and germane communications tailored for comprehensibility by the intended recipient(s). Additionally, the quality of the information presentation at the formal board meeting itself is vital to director effectiveness. One CEO likened his role to that of a teacher, continually educating his directors about the relevant subject matter of the corporation.

Because of the importance and complexity of corporate communications with the board, we suggest the new position of corporate board communications executive. The CEO simply does not have the time to devote to the communications task that it needs. Yet, the job is too important and detailed to be delegated to someone not sensitive to the specialized task-at-hand. Whether this new position would require a full-time person depends, of course, on the size and complexity of a given board of directors. Even so, whether full-time or less, someone with "proper" communications expertise needs to assume the duties. Just as corporate advertising and public relations need the undivided attention and touch of communications specialists, so does corporate communications with the board of directors: an audience that deserves the same type of concern as (or better concern than) the firm's customer list.

Already, in fact, one of the authors has been contacted by a major consulting firm that is interested in the concept we have just suggested. As we told them, we believe that a corporate board communications officer should be responsible for the entire flow of information to and from the board as depicted in Exhibit 1. In this regard, the person would logically report directly to the CEO, who would provide guidance, or, if more independence were desired for the person by the board, to a designated committee of the board, most likely the executive committee.

NOTES

[1]Kenneth R. Andrews, "Interview Guide for Review of Board Effectiveness," *Harvard Business Review,* May–June 1979, pp. 52–56.

[2]William L. Shanklin and John K. Ryans, Jr., "Inside/Outside Director Information Needs: A Survey," *Directors & Boards,* Winter 1981, pp. 22–25.

[3]William L. Shanklin and John K. Ryans, Jr., "When Should a Fortune 500 Board Meet?" *Directors & Boards,* Summer 1981, p. 42.

[4]William L. Shanklin and John K. Ryans, Jr., "Should the Board Consider This Agenda Item?" *MSU Business Topics,* Winter 1981, pp. 35–42.

[5]Factor analysis is a statistical technique for determining the number and nature of the underlying variables among larger numbers of measures.

SELECTED
BIBLIOGRAPHY

Abell, D. F. "Strategic Windows." *Journal of Marketing,* July 1978, pp. 21–26.

Abell, D. F., and Hammond, J. S. *Strategic Market Planning* (Englewood Cliffs, N.J.: Prentice-Hall, 1979).

Abernathy, W. J., Clark, K. B., and Kantrow, A. M. "The New Industrial Competition." *Harvard Business Review,* September–October 1981, pp. 68–81.

Abernathy, W. J., and Wayne, K. "The Limits of the Learning Curve." *Harvard Business Review,* September–October 1974, pp. 109–119.

Anderson, C. R., and Paine, F. T. "PIMS: A Reexamination." *Academy of Management Review,* July 1978, pp. 602–612.

Ansoff, I. H., and Stewart, J. M. "Strategies for a Technology-based Business." *Harvard Business Review,* November–December 1967, pp. 71–83.

Armstrong, J. S. "How Expert Are the Experts?" *Inc.: The Magazine for Growing Companies,* December 1981, pp. 15–16.

Business Week. "For Executives of the 1980's, A Stress on Return." June 1, 1981, pp. 88–91.

———. "A U.S. Concept Revives Oki." March 1, 1982, pp. 112–113.

———. "Wanted: A Manager to Fit Each Strategy." February 25, 1980, pp. 166–173.

Buzzell, R. D., Gale, B. T., and Sultan, G. M. "Market Share—A Key to Profitability." *Harvard Business Review,* January–February 1975, pp. 97–106.

317

Cavanagh, R. E., and Clifford, D., Jr., "Lessons from America's Mid-sized Growth Companies." *McKinsey Quarterly*, Autumn 1983, pp. 2–23.

Cohen, K. J., and Cyert, R. M. "Strategy: Formulation, Implementation, and Monitoring." *Journal of Business*, July 1973, pp. 349–367.

Conley, P. *Experience Curves as a Planning Tool: A Special Commentary* (Boston: The Boston Consulting Group, Inc., 1970).

Cooper, A. C., and Schendel, D. "Strategic Responses to Technological Threats." *Business Horizons*, February 1976, pp. 61–69.

Day, G. S. "Diagnosing the Product Portfolio." *Journal of Marketing*, April 1977, pp. 29–38.

Doz, Y. L. "Strategic Management in Multinational Companies." *Sloan Management Review*, Winter 1980, pp. 27–46.

Doz, Y. L., and Prahalad, C. Z. "Headquarters Influence and Strategic Control in MNCs." *Sloan Management Review*, Fall 1981, pp. 15–29.

Drucker, P. F. *Management: Tasks, Responsibilities, Practices* (New York: Harper & Row, 1974).

———. *Managing in Turbulent Times* (New York: Harper & Row, 1980).

Ebeling, H. W., Jr., and Doorley, J. L., III. "A Strategic Approach to Acquisitions." *Journal of Business Strategy*, Winter 1983, pp. 44–54.

Ewing, R. P. "The Uses of Futurist Techniques in Issues Management." *Public Relations Quarterly*, Winter 1979, pp. 15–19.

Fahey, L., and King, W. R. "Environmental Scanning for Corporate Planning." *Business Horizons*, August 1977, pp. 61–71.

Fleming, J. E. "Linking Public Affairs with Corporate Planning." *California Management Review*, Vol. 23, No. 2, Winter 1980, pp. 35–43.

Foster, R. N. "Linkage Comes to United International." *Business Horizons*, December 1980, pp. 66–76.

Fox, H. W. "Quasi-Boards: Useful Small Business Confidants." *Harvard Business Review*, January–February 1982, pp. 158–165.

Gerstein, M., and Reisman, H. "Strategic Selection: Matching Executives to Business Conditions." *Sloan Management Review*, Winter 1983, pp. 33–49.

Gluck, F. W. "Global Competition in the 1980's." *Journal of Business Strategy*, Spring 1983, pp. 22–27.

———. "Vision and Leadership in Corporate Strategy." *McKinsey Quarterly*, Winter 1981, pp. 13–27.

Gottschalk, E. C., Jr. "Firms Hiring New Type of Manager to Study Issues, Emerging Troubles." *The Wall Street Journal*, June 10, 1982, p. 21.

Gregor, W. T., Kotler, P., and Pinto, S. K. "Taking Military Strategies to the Marketing Battlefield." *Industrial Marketing*, February 1982, pp. 70, 72, 74–77.

Hall, W. K. "SBU's: Hot, New Topic in the Management of Diversification." *Business Horizons*, February 1978, pp. 17–25.

———. "Survival Strategies in a Hostile Environment." *Harvard Business Review*, September–October 1980, pp. 75–85.

Hamermesh, R. G., Anderson, M. J., Jr., and Harris, J. E. "Strategies for Low Market Share Businesses." *Harvard Business Review*, May–June 1978, pp. 95–102.

Hamermesh, R. G., and White, R. E. "Manage Beyond Portfolio Analysis." *Harvard Business Review,* January–February 1984, pp. 103–109.

Harrell, G. D., and Kiefer, R. O. "Multinational Strategic Market Portfolios." *MSU Business Topics,* Winter 1981, pp. 6–10.

Haspeslagh, P. "Portfolio Planning: Uses and Limits." *Harvard Business Review,* January–February 1982, pp. 58–73.

Hedley, B. "A Fundamental Approach to Strategy Development." *Long Range Planning,* December 1976, pp. 2–11.

———. "Strategy and the 'Business Portfolio.'" *Long Range Planning,* February 1977, pp. 9–15.

Henderson, B. D. *Henderson on Corporate Strategy* (Cambridge, Mass.: Abt Books, 1979).

Hunsicker, J. Q. "The Malaise of Strategic Planning." *Management Review,* March 1980, pp. 8–14.

Keegan, W. J. "Multinational Marketing Management: Strategic Options." In *Multinational Marketing Management,* 2nd ed. (Englewood Cliffs, N.J.: Prentice-Hall, 1980), pp. 273–281.

———. "Strategic Market Planning: The Japanese Approach." *International Marketing Review,* Vol. 1, No. 1, Autumn 1983, pp. 5–15.

Kenichi, O. "The 'Strategic Triangle' and Business Unit Strategy." *McKinsey Quarterly,* Winter 1983, pp. 9–24.

Kiechel W., III. "Corporate Strategists Under Fire." *Fortune,* December 27, 1982, pp. 34–39.

———. "The Decline of the Experience Curve." *Fortune,* October 5, 1981, pp. 139–140, 144, 146.

———. "Oh Where, Oh Where Has My Little Dog Gone? Or My Cash Cow? Or My Star?" *Fortune,* November 2, 1981, pp. 148–154.

———. "Playing by the Rules of the Corporate Strategy Game." *Fortune,* September 24, 1979, p. 112.

——— "Three (or Four, or More) Ways to Win." *Fortune,* October 19, 1981, pp. 181–188.

Kotler, P., and Singh, R. "Marketing Warfare in the 1980s." *Journal of Business Strategy,* Winter 1981, pp. 30–41.

Kresch, S. D. "The Impact of Consumer Trends on Corporate Strategy." *Journal of Business Strategy,* Winter 1983, pp. 58–63.

Kristenson, L. "Strategic Planning in Retailing." *European Journal of Marketing.* Vol. 17, No. 2, 1983, pp. 43–59.

Lele, M. M., and Maher, P. "Getting It Together: Building a Strategic Analysis Model." *Business Marketing,* November 1983, pp. 59–72.

Levitt, T. "Exploit the Product Life Cycle." *Harvard Business Review,* November–December 1965, pp. 81–94.

———. "The Globalization of Markets." *Harvard Business Review,* May–June 1983, pp. 92–102.

Lubatkin, M., and Pitts, M. "PIMS: Fact or Folklore?" *Journal of Business Strategy,* Winter 1983, pp. 38–43.

Maher, P., and Lele, M. M. "Strategy: What Microcomputer Makers Are Missing." *Business Marketing,* November 1983, pp. 42–58.

McDonald, M. H. B. "International Marketing Planning: The Gap Between

Theory and Practice." *International Marketing Review*, Vol. 1, No. 1, Autumn 1983, pp. 42–58.

————. "International Marketing Planning: Some New Insights." *Journal of International Marketing,* Vol. 1, No. 2, 1982, pp. 90–103.

Morrison, J. R., and Lee, J. G. "The Anatomy of Strategic Thinking." *McKinsey Quarterly,* Autumn 1979, pp. 2–9.

Naylor, T. H. "Strategic Planning Models." *Managerial Planning,"* July–August 1981, pp. 3–11.

Odiorne, G. S. "Strategic Planning: Challenging New Role for Corporate Staff." *Business,* May–June, 1981, pp. 10–14.

Paul, R. N., Donavan, N. B., and Taylor, J. W. "The Reality Gap in Strategic Planning." *Harvard Business Review,* May–June 1978, pp. 124–130.

Polli, R., and Cook, V. "Validity of the Product Life Cycle." *Journal of Business,* October 1969, pp. 385–400.

Porter, M. E. *Competitive Strategy: Techniques for Analyzing Industries and Competitors* (New York: The Free Press, 1980).

————. "How Competitive Forces Shape Strategy." *Harvard Business Review,* March–April 1979, pp. 137–145.

Rapp, W. V. "Strategy Formulation and International Competition." *Columbia Journal of World Business,* Summer 1973, pp. 98–112.

Rappaport, A. "Strategic Analysis for More Profitable Acquisitions." *Harvard Business Review,* July–August 1979, pp. 99–110.

Robinson, S. J. Q., Hichens, R. E., and Wade, D. P. "The Directional Policy Matrix—Tool for Strategic Planning." *Long Range Planning Journal,* Vol. 2, No. 3, June 1978, pp. 8–15.

Rothschild, W. E. "How to Ensure the Continued Growth of Strategic Planning." *Journal of Business Strategy,* June 25, 1982, pp. 11–18.

Rutenberg, D. P. *Multinational Management* (Boston: Little, Brown, 1982).

Salter, M., and Weinhold, W. *Diversification Through Acquisition* (New York: The Free Press, 1979).

Schoeffler, S., Buzzell, R. D., and Heany, D. F. "Impact of Strategic Planning on Profit Performance." *Harvard Business Review,* March–April 1974, pp. 137–145.

Stata, R., and Maidique, M. A. "Bonus System for Balanced Strategy." *Harvard Business Review,* November–December 1980, pp. 156–163.

Steiner, G. A. *Strategic Planning* (New York: The Free Press, 1979).

Stevenson, H. H. "Defining Corporate Strengths and Weaknesses." *Sloan Management Review,* Spring 1976, pp. 51–68.

Tashakori, A., and Boulton, W. "A Look at the Board's Role in Planning." *Journal of Business Strategy,* Winter 1983, pp. 64–70.

Tichy, N. M., Fombrun, C. J., and DeVanna, M. A. "Strategic Human Resource Management." *Sloan Management Review,* Winter 1982, pp. 47–61.

Tregoe, B. B., and Zimmerman, J. W. "The New Strategic Manager." *Business,* May–June 1981, pp. 15–19.

Vancil, R. F. "Strategy Formulation in Complex Organizations." *Sloan Management Review,* Winter 1976, pp. 4–10.

Vernon, R. "Gone Are the Cash Cows of Yesteryear." *Harvard Business Review,* November–December 1980, pp. 150–155.

Wheelwright, S. C., and Makridakas, S. "Technological Forecasting." In *Forecasting Methods for Management,* 3rd ed. (New York: Wiley, 1980), pp. 267–288.

Wind, Y., and Douglas, S. "International Portfolio Analyses and Strategy: The Challenge of the 80s." *Journal of International Business Studies,* Fall 1981, pp. 69–82.

Wind, Y., and Mahajan, V. "Designing Product and Business Portfolios." *Harvard Business Review,* January–February 1981, pp. 155–165.

Zenter, R. D. "Scenarios in Forecasting." *Chemical & Engineering News,* October 6, 1975, pp. 22–24.

INDEX

330

331

ABOUT THE
AUTHORS

William L. Shanklin has been involved in consulting and executive development with organizations ranging from *Fortune* 500 companies to small businesses and was employed in industrial marketing by the Georgia-Pacific Corporation. His associations have included such corporations as Digital Equipment, General Electric, and Goodyear Tire and Rubber. He is a board member of Carrollton Graphics, Inc. Dr. Shanklin has published on a wide range of business and marketing topics; his articles have appeared in *Business Horizons, Directors and Boards, Harvard Business Review, Strategy and Executive Action,* and many other practitioner-oriented periodicals. He is the coauthor of several books, such as the recent *Marketing High Technology,* with John K. Ryans, Jr. Dr. Shanklin is a frequent speaker to business groups.

Dr. Shanklin is a professor of marketing in the Graduate School of Management at Kent State University in Ohio; his doctorate is in business administration from the University of Maryland.

John K. Ryans, Jr. is a prolific writer on a wide range of domestic and international business topics. Among his most recent books is *Management of International Advertising,* coauthored with Dean Peebles of Goodyear International. Professor Ryans has published articles in *Business: The Magazine of Managerial Thought and Action, Business Topics, California Management Review, Harvard Business Review,* and numerous other journals. He often speaks to business groups and is frequently a program leader at the World Trade Institute in New York. During his career, Dr. Ryans has been an active consultant, with such firms as Novi Industri, Xerox, and McCann-Erickson among his clients.

Dr. Ryans is a professor of marketing and international business in the Graduate School of Management at Kent State University. He has been a visiting professor at Columbia University, and holds a doctorate in business administration from Indiana University.